THE SPECTRE OF PRICE INFLATION

THE SPECTRE OF PRICE INFLATION

MAX GILLMAN

agenda
publishing

First published in 2023 by Agenda Publishing

Agenda Publishing Limited
The Core
Bath Lane
Newcastle Helix
Newcastle upon Tyne
NE4 5TF
www.agendapub.com

ISBN 978-1-78821-236-6 (hardcover)
ISBN 978-1-78821-237-3 (paperback)

British Library Cataloguing-in-Publication Data
A catalogue record for this book is available from the British Library

Typeset by Newgen Publishing UK
Printed and bound in the UK by 4edge

CONTENTS

Part III Purgatory: capital markets, interest and inflation

PREFACE

My namesake ancestor emigrated to New York to become a US citizen in 1900. His Austrian heritage stimulated my interest in the academic life of his birthplace, from where modern economics arose. He was born in Austria prior to the First World War a decade before Carl Menger became a professor of economics at the University of Vienna in 1873. Menger founded the Austrian School of Economics. His German-language *Principles of Economics* (1871) showed how people's utility went down for each additional good that they received. With this decreasing ("marginal utility") value per additional good, he laid the basis for why the price we would pay, per unit of the good, would be lower in markets as the quantity demanded of the good was higher. Menger thereby gave us a downward-sloping demand curve – revolutionary at the time.

This first foundation of the downward-sloping demand curve appeared in the same year in English with William Stanley Jevons's *Theory of Political Economy* (1871), and then again, in French, with Léon Walras's *Elements of Pure Economics* (1874). Suddenly, demand was conceived as opposing supply and providing an equilibrium that yielded the basis of value theory, or "price theory". This theory is still the foundation today of how markets determine equilibrium at the "market-clearing" price, which equates the quantity supplied to the quantity demanded. It laid the first microfoundations of macroeconomics. I learned about this evolution of macroeconomics through independent study of the history of economic thought with Professor Daniel Fusfeld at the University of Michigan, and with Professor George Stigler (Nobel laureate 1982) in graduate school, focusing on Adam Smith's work.

Austrian economics thereby began as an innovation in economics, which had focused till then on determining price only through the firm's cost of production – the "labour theory of value", in Marxian economics – to a balancing of price from firms and consumers alike. Austrian professors provided the concept of deriving market prices by considering scarcity as it affects both the cost of production by firms on the supply side and the demand for the good from the household "consumer" side. The latter was a technological innovation derived using an application of mathematical calculus theory, following up on Newton's use of calculus to provide the first principles of the laws of motion in physics. Einstein (born in 1879) later generalized the latter laws of motion using further dimensions of calculus at the same time (1905–15) that Austrian economics was evolving in Vienna after Menger.

As a student of Carl Menger at the University of Vienna, in 1880 Eugen von Böhm-Bawerk received the equivalent of a PhD. Böhm-Bawerk is sometimes known as the founder of capital theory – how investment requires a normal return on capital that can be expressed as a rate of return. By thinking of this return on capital as an equivalent interest rate on capital, Böhm-Bawerk pioneered the theory of interest.

Under Böhm-Bawerk at the University of Vienna, Ludwig von Mises focused on the money supply and how this can affect interest rates. Under von Mises, F. A. Hayek (Nobel laureate 1974) also studied at the University of Vienna. Born in Vienna, Hayek's discourses included how government money supply increases can temporarily drive down the interest rate.

Menger, Böhm-Bawerk, von Mises and Hayek formed a core of thought that became known as the Austrian school of economics, which continues to evolve today. Hayek left Vienna for the United Kingdom, taking these ideas to the London School of Economics. Hayek took his intellect to the United States, as a professor at the University of Chicago for more than a decade (1950–62). There he was a colleague of Milton Friedman (Nobel laureate 1976) during Friedman's formative years of what turned out to be a long career at Chicago (1946–77).

Friedman (1968) explained what the government money supply could do, such as leading to temporary changes in interest rates, while being ineffective in causing any permanent increase in the employment rate. Friedman emphasized that inflation is a tax that distorts efficiency, by showing the foundations for postulating the demand for money as a facilitator of exchange, while starting Chicago's Money and Banking workshop in 1954 with Gary S. Becker (Nobel laureate 1992) as co-director, and then organizing the macroeconomics course sequence at Chicago. Robert E. Lucas, Jr (Nobel laureate 1995), was a student of Friedman, along with fellow students Sherwin Rosen, Sam Peltzman and Eugene Fama (Nobel laureate 2013).

My studies involved classes with all four of these renowned economists while they were professors at the University of Chicago. This study included focusing on George Stigler's and Peltzman's economics of regulation, T. W. Schultz's (Nobel laureate 1979) and Becker's theory of human capital, and Lucas's monetary theory. Lucas organized the Money and Banking workshop and was already famous for showing rigorously in "general equilibrium" how a trade-off between inflation and unemployment disappears once people adjust their expectations of the inflation rate to the actual rate prevailing.

This Lucas article (1972) was later cited as the basis for his Nobel Prize. Lucas's *Critique* (1976) demolished the basis for building large models to conduct policy experiments, by showing how these models omitted changes in consumer behaviour in response to changes in policy. This was astonishing, since Lawrence Klein (Nobel laureate 1980), after starting as a professor at the University of Michigan, won his Nobel on the basis of developing these large models for policy evaluation.

My interest in studying at Chicago came from undergraduate work at the University of Michigan, including a stint as a teaching assistant to Professor Gardner Ackley. His macroeconomics textbook provided a concise explanation of Friedman's and Lucas's theories of inflation and unemployment. This occurred just after the end of the Vietnam War (which ran from 1955 to 1975), during which my older brother had to enter the draft, the money supply growth rate had taken off, the last vestiges of the Bretton Woods gold standard had broken down and the rate of inflation was still rapidly rising.

Paul Samuelson (Nobel laureate 1970) and Robert Solow (Nobel laureate 1987) had maintained in 1960 that high inflation was fine because it lowered unemployment. This became a basis of Keynesian economics, which I learned well at Michigan from Professor Saul Hyman, and which still provides the basis of new Keynesian economics today. In contrast, Friedman, Edmund Phelps (Nobel laureate 2006) and Lucas (1972) disagreed with this Keynesian foundation. Phelps (1967, 1969, 1970, 1972) also won the Nobel Prize for his work on the lack of a sustainable trade-off between inflation and unemployment. Together with Friedman (1968) and Lucas (1972), they strove to show that any such permanent trade-off was an illusion.

Consistent with many elements of Austrian economics but now with the rigorous mathematical precision that had previously been lacking, Lucas's work jolted us by showing how to understand inflation in rigorous ways. Edward C. Prescott (1987) and Thomas J. Sargent (Nobel laureate 2011) and Neil Wallace (1975) joined Lucas in this research agenda. Prescott with Fynn Kydland (joint Nobel laureates 2004) were cited in their Nobel awards for inflation theory and real business cycle theory.

Lucas served as chair of my PhD dissertation committee, with Becker and Yair Mundlak also on the committee. My dissertation built on Lucas's and Prescott's monetary modelling. It led me to correspond with Friedman. Altogether, Lucas and his colleagues stimulated a broad-based evolution of monetary theory. This has included new work on explaining interest rates as based on the role of the inflation tax, with a money supply increase and banking policy both able to affect interest rates. Much of this work is based on how money supply growth creates inflation.

Lucas pioneered several models of monetary economics that are used widely today, which Sargent (2015) reviews. Lucas (1980) laid the foundation for understanding inflation as a tax, which affects consumer behaviour just like any other statutory tax. Based on inflation acting as a tax, Lucas and Stokey (1983) built the rationale for a new monetary regime that could replace the gold standard lost during the Vietnam War.

The end of the gold standard was accelerated by the high US money supply growth to finance the fighting in Vietnam. The world transitioned to "fiat" currencies, which have since then been unbacked by any precious metal. Lucas and Stokey showed that controlling the inflation tax offered a basis for monetary stability like that under metallic standards.

Their policy on the inflation tax is now adopted across the world. Central banks target a certain low rate of inflation, known as "inflation rate targeting". An inflation rate target is in fact enshrined in current US law regulating the US Federal Reserve System, while all other tax laws must automatically, according to the US Constitution, originate in the US House of Representatives, with the Ways and Means Committee of the House responsible for initiating all US tax bills.

Taking leave from graduate school to be a legislative aide for Representative Bill Gradison, my responsibilities were the tax bills arising in Gradison's role as a member of the Ways and Means Committee. It was a time when the US inflation rate was peaking. While working on the various tax laws, Gradison taught me that taxpaying citizens do not like uncertain taxes. This includes the inflation tax, which, in short, can be defined as the level of the inflation rate.

Congress can at best direct the Federal Reserve ("Fed") on what the level of the inflation tax should be. They did this by specifying the US inflation rate target in a 1978 law. Only the Federal Reserve has the privilege of directly levying any inflation tax through its money supply policy. The low inflation rate targets enacted by Congress, and supported theoretically by Lucas and Stokey, brought the inflation tax steadily downwards to the first initial target stipulated in US law. The Fed never achieved its second, lower and final target, which was supposed to be in place indefinitely thereafter.

It might be surprising to find that the Fed has formally disregarded US law by establishing its own inflation target in 2012 that is higher than that in the federal law. After the 2001 terrorist attacks, the Fed instituted dramatic new increases in the money supply growth rate, while forcing down interest rates. Elements of this Fed policy led directly to the 2008 financial crisis. During that crisis, and ever since, the Fed has instituted a much more radical policy to allow an acceleration of the money supply growth rate, and unprecedented suppression of market interest rates. These Fed policies led to a build-up of money that was kept from entering circulation through a "sterilization" process, for all the years since 2008, with this policy intensifying when the Covid-19 pandemic occurred.

As might be unsurprising, we now see the inflation rate rising anew, beyond all legal and unofficial targets of both the US Congress and the Fed. This rising inflation rate is also occurring across the world, breaching the low inflation rate targets that were established internationally after the end of the Vietnam-War-era inflation. This inflation surge may be far from a temporary pandemic surge. It may be closer to that of the prolonged episode during the Vietnam War, also including rising oil prices – just as in my formative years.

ACKNOWLEDGEMENTS

After leaving Prague to join Central European University (CEU) in Budapest in the 1990s and visiting Vienna's Institute for Advanced Studies, which was founded as an economics centre in the 1960s, I benefited from teaching monetary economics and macroeconomics to students of CEU for many years. I continued this at CEU even as I taught it at Cardiff University in Wales and at the University of Missouri–St Louis (UMSL). To the latter, I appreciate their support through my Hayek Chair endowment, as well as for research assistance at UMSL from Michael Cassidy and Nora Jijane. As to CEU, the darkening cloud over capitalism and freedom forced it to relocate. Fortuitously, it reinstituted nearby in Vienna, just as it had moved from its founding in Prague to Budapest, while keeping its Budapest campus intact – the smile of a learned but vanished Cheshire cat.

I thank generations of my students and look forward to more of them. Some have become my co-authors, and special thanks go to them and my other collaborators. My Hungarian wife, who I met in Cardiff, has been supportive of my work (for which I am grateful), as have our children, one of whom is named after my Vienna ancestor mentioned in the Preface.

Enormous thanks go to Alison Howson of Agenda Publishing for approaching me some years ago to write about inflation, which at that time was dormant. Alison supplied many hours of work in ongoing revision suggestions. Thank you, Alison. I also thank Mike Richardson for the copy-editing. May the study of inflation innovate along with our forms of money and dispel the ghosts we fear.

Max Gillman
St Louis, Missouri

INTRODUCTION

The spectre at the feast manifests in Shakespeare's *Macbeth* as the ghost of Banquo. A former ally whose progeny is prophesized to become king, Banquo is murdered by Macbeth's men. Banquo's apparition then appears at the feast, seated in Macbeth's chair and seen only by the orchestrator of his murder, who goes mad, bringing the festivities to a premature end.

Modern events can mirror such tales when those obsessed with power do anything to hold onto it. The spectre of inflation has loomed historically as a threat to civilized economic exchange whenever wars or crises have induced high government spending deficits, with tax revenue falling well short of expenditure. Rising inflation is destructive and is caused by government agents clinging to their discretionary power by printing money at increasing rates. Such inflation threatens to fell any economy in which a government incurs high budget deficits. When inflation rears its head, it wipes out the gains in income and wealth that growing economies foster.

Once government deficits become too high, potential future inflation threatens money's value. Inflation had, until recently, been moderate and well contained by monetary authorities (namely central banks). This required the conditions of international peace and fiscal restraint by governments so that central banks were not pressured to finance wartime or crisis spending through the purchase of government Treasury debt and by giving fresh money to governments to spend. When fiscal restraint is broken, central banks typically help finance spending, with the result that inflation either rises or is suppressed – with even worse consequences.

Restraint on the part of central banks is designed to ensure money value through low or no inflation. When low inflation rate targeting became a widespread policy internationally, central banks had clear objectives that everyone could measure and consider in judging their policy success. But, ever since the terrorist attacks of 2001, the US government has run unending and rising deficits as a share of national output. The central bank of the United States, the

Federal Reserve System, in turn financed a large portion of this rising deficit by buying Treasury debt, which is how central banks "print money". In essence, the government borrows from itself, receives money from the central bank and spends it. When newly printed money enters circulation, the price level rises and inflation increases.

In fear of global capital market collapse, after 2001 the Fed chose to print enough new money by buying Treasury debt that it could drive down market interest rates for several years. This led to negative yields on government debt until inflation began rising three years later. Then the Fed quickly let interest rates rise, which led to massive defaults on the "safe" mortgage loans that had been widely sold.

The reason these mortgages suddenly took on significance is that investment banks began holding them across the global finance system as the seemingly "next best" safe asset, other than Treasury debt that was yielding a negative return. Hoping to get a higher yield on "safe" mortgage loans than on Treasury debt, this investment strategy failed once the Fed reversed its policy of pushing government debt interest rates below the inflation rate. Many of the mortgages were financed with variable interest rates, and households could not possibly afford the 4.5 percentage point rise in rates. The Fed policy led banks to seek the safe mortgage debt, which the Fed policy then turned into junk debt, worth little. This caused the 2008 financial crisis and "Great Recession", after which the Fed adopted an even more radical policy.

This post-2008 policy established increasingly negative returns on government debt. The Fed did so while inducing the banking sector to find a higher return on its market portfolio in ever more diverse ways. The Fed tried to preserve its throne-like power over major economic policy by keeping inflation near to its self-prescribed target. It artificially suppressed inflation by gathering excess reserves from private banks that would normally have been lent out. The Fed thereby met its inflation target while keeping on the good side of the US Treasury, as it was buying a large portion of the huge post-2008 Treasury debt. By scrambling to keep inflation suppressed, a measure by which central banks are easily judged, while printing vast amounts of new money, the Fed used new devices, unknown to the public, that inflicted far worse damage to value than an increase in inflation.

The Fed suppressed inflation by paying interest on reserves, which enabled much of the surge in money supply to remain out of circulation, as it was still held at the Fed as reserves. These reserves artificially induced a higher level of money demand, which kept the inflation rate near its target for many years after 2008. The Fed's mechanism for sterilizing the increase in the money supply was to fix interest rates in capital markets at levels well below their normal level, and below the inflation rate. This induced negative returns in capital markets across the global finance system.

The Fed's various officials then wrote about how they had saved the global finance system, even as their actions were distorting capital markets further by prohibiting, in effect, a positive return to capital. This post-2008 policy was part of the Fed taking over the job of insuring the private bank system against collapse, even though this was already *after* the collapse had occurred. The Fed then picked which banks survived and which ones failed.

Seen in the cold light of day, the Fed's post-2008 policy effectuates a protection of its growing power by trying to suppress inflation while killing capital markets. This is much like Macbeth protecting his rising power by suppressing dissent and killing off his future rival's father, Banquo. Similarly, Vladimir Putin is trying to protect his rising power by suppressing dissent in Russia while killing off his competition in Ukraine. The hunger for power, and its unintended consequences, repeat in many forms, but when the central banks are the key players the world's theatre is party to a different type of staging.

The competition in "money markets", as Walter Bagehot and John Maynard Keynes called them, is part of the broader capital markets for savings and investment, of which money markets are just a part. The Fed has been killing off capital market investment and saving while bottling up the new money created as "excess reserves", all the while supposedly protecting the private banking system against itself and keeping inflation within its self-proclaimed range of success – at least, until recently. The Fed has held onto its unwieldy power by financing Treasury borrowing, paying the private banking system not to make investments with its savings and keeping money sitting at the Fed as excess reserves.

The problem now is that the inflation rate has been surging anyway. Suppression of inflation is failing, and prohibition of a positive return to Treasury debt cannot continue, since US Treasury debt is the main source of liquidity in the international finance system. Costs mount from continual distortion to capital and labour markets through a policy that eliminates a positive real return on capital and leads to increasingly risky investment so as to make up for the lost Treasury debt yield. Eventually, even as the repression of inflation continues, money will escape from reserves into the economy and begin lowering the value of money at a faster rate.

It is better to allow inflation to rise with money supply growth, to suffer the inflation tax and to get capital markets back to normal functioning, than it is to continue to force worldwide returns to capital to be negative for a large segment of the capital markets. The Fed's failed efforts to provide efficient banking insurance have injured global capital markets by artificially inducing a greater quantity of money to be demanded by private banks through more excess reserves.

This policy has turned the economic feast of prosperity into an increasingly likely nightmare, including international war, which threatens to collapse the very global capitalism the Fed claims to have been protecting since 2001.

Current Fed hubris has amassed an army of spectres, all of which can descend with the onset of inflation – a position that will end only when the Fed stops acting beyond its statute without check. Only monetary restraint by the Fed, made easier through fiscal restraint by the Treasury, can decrease the rate of growth of the money supply and the future inflation rate. Only a well-conceived banking insurance policy can protect the global financial system without first taxing it to death through the negative returns on government debt that the Fed has propagated.

A high rate of either inflation or deflation can cause instability in money value, which in turn can kill off the private banking sector and economic growth. When the ghosts of private banks threaten the governors of central banks, and when these ghosts even sit prominently at the head of policy tables during monetary policy deliberation, the spectre of inflation's turmoil can torment central banks into taking unusual and even rash action.

Central banks can bring the feast quickly to an end, as is happening today. Central bank actions determine how inflation destroys money's value. But still the central banks have not provided an efficient bank insurance system for when banks do become distressed. Instead, since 2008 central bank policy has distorted private banking, repressed capital markets worldwide, curtailed global economic growth and threatened the capitalist ethic underlying democracy. This has led us to the dawn of nationalistic militarism, as recent events in Ukraine seem to prove. By making less attractive the most liquid asset of US Treasury short-term debt, the cure for capitalism has so far been to decrease liquidity.

The spectre of inflation is greeted with justified trepidation by ordinary people. Bad policy can cause our homes to be taken away, our families to be evicted and our society to be displaced. The government's central bank policy, decided by unelected officials, causes episodes of high inflation and can even cause bank panics.

Central bankers wield considerable power over our everyday welfare, without needing to answer to anyone except those appointing them, without passing their policy through the legislature and with the ability to act by simple declaration. They affect world welfare in ways that legislative government bodies could only dream about. The governors of the central banks have been described as the most powerful non-democratically elected officials in the world, or modern masters of the universe.

This book explains how central banks perform wizardry through inflation tax policy that determines which banks live or die, how income is redistributed from savers to borrowers and how capital markets are distorted. The book demonstrates how inflation has lurked as long as governments have needed revenue, with tradition guiding society to balance the perils of inflation and private bank collapse against the need for government finance through money creation. The traditions have been changed recently to achieve the central banks' internal goals while appeasing demands for government revenue and banking insurance, to create a mix that appears sharply askew.

This book presents how money and banking policy have historically progressed so that they can be untangled and a better set of policies proposed. The first part of the book deals with the age of innocence, when sound principles formed monetary policy and solving the mysteries of inflation came through straightforward investigation. The second part of the book describes how this innocence turned to ignominy, when the principles of constraint were lost in the chaos of war and crisis, and the Fed's fractured insurance policy began for private banks.

The third and last part describes the purgatory caused by disregarding principles and plaguing global capital markets. The book ends by showing how central bank money causes inflation today. It then presents a policy reform, based on historical principles, that would provide systematic global bank insurance against both insolvency and illiquidity. This would dispel the ghosts of money and capital market participants killed off by central bank policy and stay the murder of money's value.

PART I

INNOCENCE: WHEN PRINCIPLES GUIDED POLICY

1

DRS FISHER AND FRIEDMAN
AND NO INFLATION

Defining inflation was not always easy. Irving Fisher began this task in earnest in the early twentieth century. He organized the first meeting of the Econometric Society in 1930, was elected its first president and oversaw the first issue of the society's renowned *Econometrica* journal, which published the proceedings of its first meeting. The society's constitution was also published there, declaring that it was "for the advancement of economic theory in its relation to statistics and mathematics".

Fisher had long been interested in price stability. He devised a statistical index that could be used to measure changes in the aggregate price level, called Fisher's (1921) "ideal" index. The next year he published a treatise on price indices, *The Making of Index Numbers* (1922), that included implementing the index to provide a historical sequence of data on the US price level during the high-inflation war years of 1914–18.

The rate of change in the aggregate price level is the definition of the inflation rate. Fisher and others since him have applied this measure, or similar ones, to the US economy and shown how the index changes over time. This is typically presented as the rate of change at an annual rate.

This annual rate of inflation measures the change in the price index relative to a year ago. It is measured relative to the average price level over the current month compared to that average in the same month a year ago. Alternatively, the comparison can be to the average price level over the current quarter of a year relative to the average over the same quarter a year before. Equally, it simply can measure the percentage change in the index over a calendar year. This allows the calculation of an annual percentage change in the price level, as given from one month to the same month a year later, from one quarter to the same quarter a year later or on a calendar year basis.

Fisher showed how money changes in value in terms of the actual goods and services that people can buy with money. If you hold a dollar bill, then you can purchase one dollar's worth of goods. What if that dollar somehow becomes worth less during the period that you hold it? Then all you can buy with it is less. This happens if the aggregate price index rises.

Your dollar's value falls when the aggregate price level rises. This means that, when the inflation rate is positive, the amount of goods that you can buy with your dollar is less than before the price level rise. If you can purchase only fewer goods per dollar, then the real value of your dollar has declined during the period. What you can buy with a dollar is also sometimes called the "purchasing power" of the dollar, which falls as the inflation rate rises, and is measured as one divided by the price index.

In contrast, during periods of deflation the aggregate price level declines, the inflation rate is negative, each dollar buys more goods and your dollar purchasing power rises. Both falling purchasing power from a rising inflation rate and rising purchasing power from a falling inflation rate have detrimental effects on the ease of exchanging goods for money. Changes in the price level are hard to predict and understand once they are under way.

As an example of how the price level can affect a household, consider that you might keep some dollars somewhere on a table. You might try to add dollars to your collection so that, when you need some money, you can use the bills you have collected. What may be surprising is that the amount of goods, say a certain brand of candy, shoes or bread, that $1 buys can go down while it has been sitting on the table.

This happens if during that time the aggregate price level of the economy's goods rises. This rising price level means that a set amount of dollars can buy only a smaller amount of goods relative to the beginning of the time when you accumulated the dollars. The decrease in the value of the dollar's ability to buy goods is a result of inflation.

The loss of your real resources, or goods that you can buy with your money, is often called the inflation tax. This tax lowers the value of your money. It yields revenue to the government, which levies the inflation tax through its new money creation that it uses to buy additional goods for itself, while taking away your money's ability to buy as many goods as possible.

When the aggregate price level changes, the prices of some goods may fall, while the prices of other goods rise. This means that there will be a change in prices relative to each other, which is called a relative price change. But, if the average price level rises across all the goods purchased in the economy, as weighted by the quantity of goods purchased, then this is said to be an increase in the aggregate price level.

During rising inflation, relative prices of goods can be jockeyed around. The general price level still rises at an accelerating rate. The sustained acceleration of the price level causes a sustained higher rate of aggregate price change, which is the definition of a higher inflation rate.

The acceleration of the price level itself almost inevitably induces some goods, labour and capital prices to rise at different rates, while averaging near to the average rate of price increase. Such leads and lags in the prices of output and the prices of the inputs to production can cause higher or lower costs of production, which disrupt the supply of goods. Bottlenecks can arise and shortages appear because of accelerating inflation (and accelerating deflation).

Shortages of goods such as food and baby formula during a crisis, "supply chain problems" during a pandemic or limited oil and gas supplies when these prices are surging can be symptomatic rather than causal of an inflation epi-sode in which the money supply is being rapidly increased. Individual prices of goods may rise because of a fad or some isolated event. A store's prices may fall, for example, because of a build-up of unsold inventory that a store wants to reduce by lowering the price. But widespread changes in relative prices during accelerating inflation constitute a different type of relative price realignment, often blamed for causing inflation when the causality tends to be the reverse.

Relative price changes unrelated to rising inflation are attributable to factors unique to the item being bought and caused by the underlying supply and demand for the particular good. It is the fundamental supply and demand changes that cause relative price differences between goods. And such relative price change can also occur regularly over the business cycle, as the economy has accelerated growth of output in an expansionary phase and then decelerated output growth during a recession.

The aggregate price level tends to be affected by supply and demand factors of broad economic expansions and contractions. During expansion, the demand for many goods rises, and supply must hasten to catch up with demand. Scarcity arises, which increases profits, and the price of goods rises relative to the cost of production.

The reverse tends to happen in an economic contraction. As demand falls while supply is still high, prices are reduced, profit is decreased and the aggregate price level tends to either fall or rise at a lower rate of growth. On average over the entire business cycle of the expansion and contraction, the aggregate price level change will balance around its trend rate, which may be a zero-inflation rate or a higher one.

Although the changes in the aggregate price level are identifiable and can indi-cate relative price change, it is the prolonged changes in the trend of inflation or deflation that we focus on as being unrelated to relative price changes. The infla-tion rate trends become clear when we measure this over long periods of time, even centuries. The inflation and deflation episodes can be clearly identified, and likewise be seen to be clearly unrelated to short-term changes in the supply and demand of goods that cause relative price change. Looking over historical periods, inflation and deflation episodes mark distinct parts of history that can be both identified and explained.

As we embark on such historical study ahead, it helps to first set out exactly how the price index is computed. Measuring the change in the average cost over time for the entire economy's set of goods provides a way to measure the change in the aggregate price level. To do this requires keeping constant the quantities of goods being bought, or letting them change slightly in accordance with consumer patterns, and then seeing then how the cost of this basket of the economy's goods changes over time.

The change in the cost level, given the same amount of goods, tells us about the change in the average price level for the whole economy. By dividing the change in the cost of the goods over time by the total cost of the goods in the initial period, we derive the "percentage change in the aggregate price level over the period". This is the definition of the inflation rate for that period.

Typically, prices of brands stay the same for a certain period. Consider that each month you may tend to go shopping (online or in store) and buy a similar basket of goods. The basket represents your typical expenditure across all the goods that you buy. We measure the aggregate price level through the cost of the economy's whole basket of goods.

To devise a measure of the cost of the basket for the national economy, we can take the quantity of each good in that basket and multiply it by its price for that month. Adding together all the costs for all the goods purchased in the national basket of goods (the "final goods and services", as found in government national income and output accounts), the total cost will equal the value of our national output. Then we measure the inflation rate as the percentage change each period in the total cost, keeping constant the quantities purchased.

Adding together all the costs in an economy is called "aggregation". By aggregating the costs, and holding the quantities constant, we see how the aggregate price level changes. Inflation is defined by the percentage change in the aggregate price level over a certain period of time.

Each period, be it a month, a quarter or a year, we use the new prices that appear along with the same quantities as in the initial cost valuation. We then compute the new cost of the basket with the new prices and initial quantities. The change in this cost gives us the change in the aggregate price level. For example, if the total cost of the basket was 100, and after 12 months the same quantities cost 105, then we have a measure for how all the prices in the national economy have risen over the past year: by 5 per cent. This will be the inflation rate for that period.

A feature about any aggregate price index is that its current level, say 100, tells us nothing by itself about inflation. It is only the percentage change in the aggregate price level, or price index as we measure it, that tells us about the rate at which prices overall are going up or down in the economy. In modern economies, the aggregate price level as measured by a price index tends to continually rise. It might rise by 5 per cent in one year, and 1 per cent the next year, and by 3 per cent in the following year, or even go down on occasion. We call the 5 per cent, 1 per cent and 3 per cent the economy's "inflation rate".

As stated above, and supplemented with the method of defining how the price index is formed to measure inflation, the problem of inflation is that it decreases the amount of goods that you can buy with money. Being able to buy fewer goods because of inflation causes the demand for goods in the economy to decrease by the amount of the effective "inflation tax". If people use cash to buy some fraction of goods each year, and there is a 5 per cent inflation rate, then people have to reduce by 5 per cent the quantity of goods that they buy with their average cash holdings over that year.

The inflation tax paid by households is the 5 per cent reduction in goods for each dollar of money that they hold. This makes their total tax equal to 5 per cent factored by the total amount of money stock that they hold over the period. This inflation tax reduces the amount of the economy's output that is sold to private citizens.

The government, however, can spend more, since it collects the inflation tax through the act of printing the money that causes the inflation. The government uses the new money to cover its insufficient funding through normal tax revenue and buy additional goods that are financed by having new money to spend.

The mechanism whereby the government gets new money from the central bank to cover its budget deficit works in the following way. The federal government Treasury first borrows the funds needed to cover its budget deficit when expenditure is less than revenue. The Treasury uses this new money to buy goods and services as stipulated by the expenditures of the government budget plan.

Suppose then that the central bank uses new money to buy some fraction of this Treasury debt that has been issued by the government to cover its budget deficit. Even if the central bank buys the Treasury debt from private banks that have bought the debt from the Treasury, it is as if the central bank is directly giving fresh money to the Treasury for its debt, albeit going through the middlemen of the private banks. When the government Treasury spends money, it is acquiring output from the economy or providing income to people through transfer payments.

By the Treasury spending this new money that the central bank has used to buy the Treasury's debt, the Treasury collects the "tax" in an amount equal to the goods it buys or income it supplies. These expenditures are how the Treasury collects the inflation tax in the form of goods and income provided with new money to cover its budget deficit. All budget deficits are financed by tax revenue; either direct taxes, such as income taxes, or indirect taxes, such as the inflation tax.

The definition of the inflation tax, as in Bailey (1956) and Lucas (1981), can be given by the level of the inflation rate under certain assumptions. More generally, it equals the level of the nominal market interest rate, which moves closely with the inflation rate in normal unregulated capital markets. The tax arises only when the central bank buys the Treasury's debt.

First, the government borrows money from the public to finance budget deficits, which occur when government taxes raised are less than government expenditures made. This borrowing by the government occurs when its Treasury sells debt to people who lend their savings to the government in return for the debt that promises to pay interest on the loan, and then repay the loan principal amount. Private banks act as intermediaries between the households and the government by buying the debt from the government and selling it in turn to the households.

If the central bank were not to intervene in this process of the government borrowing by issuing new debt that it sells in markets to cover its budget deficit, then no inflation would occur and, instead, real interest rates would rise because of the government's increased demand for funding in capital markets. But what usually happens is that new money is printed and enters circulation. This occurs when the government borrows through an increase in Treasury debt and the central bank of the nation buys a fraction of the Treasury debt being issued.

The central bank buys the Treasury debt in a secondary market from the private bankers, who first bought the Treasury debt directly from the Treasury in the primary market. The bankers are the middlemen between the central bank and the Treasury. For a fee, the bankers allow the US Treasury to get and spend the freshly printed money provided by the US Federal Reserve System when it buys Treasury debt, which Friedman (1994: 206–7) characterizes as a smokescreen to shield the act of the Fed printing money for the Treasury to spend: "Legally, the Treasury is limited in the volume of bonds it can sell directly to the Fed. But the limit is easily evaded: the Treasury sells the bonds to the public; the Fed buys bonds from the public. The effect is the same as that of a direct sale, except for the commission collected by the intermediaries – their payment for providing the smoke screen."

When the central bank buys the Treasury debt from private bank in the secondary market, the bankers are credited with reserves at the central bank equal to the value of the Treasury debt purchased. Once the private banks spend the reserves held at the central bank, say the US Fed, by using the reserves to make investments in the form of new loans to households and firms, then the money enters circulation. Thus, going through the middlemen of the private banks to buy Treasury debt, the Fed prints new money that enters circulation.

The increased reserves of private banks are a part of the base money stock, or monetary base (MB). After the increase in private bank reserves, when these banks lend out the reserves, they create new customer bank deposits by crediting them with the amount of the new loans. When households and firms spend their deposits at the bank, this base money enters circulation.

This is how the money supply is increased by the central bank buying its government's Treasury debt. If the Fed increases the rate at which it buys US Treasury debt from private banks, then the rate of growth of the reserves held by private banks at the central bank also increases. If this increased rate of growth of reserves is fully lent out, except for the fraction of reserves required to remain at the Fed (a small fraction, which has gone down steadily over time), then the rate of growth of the money supply increases, the rate of growth of the price level increases and the inflation rate rises.

Another dimension to the inflation tax mechanism is that it can alternatively be calculated in terms of the interest that the central bank earns on government debt that it buys as it finances its Treasury's deficit spending. The average interest rate earned by the central bank on its holdings of Treasury debt, as factored by the central bank's total holdings of Treasury debt, is equal to the inflation tax earned by the central bank. Since this Treasury debt is bought with fresh cash, the Treasury debt held by the central bank tends to equal the amount of currency in circulation. This is shown historically for the Fed in the next chapter. And, since the Fed's Treasury debt earns interest, this means that the amount of the inflation tax also equals the interest rate factored by the real base money stock.

This gives a set of nearly equivalent measures to gauge the amount of the inflation tax: how much the households pay in lost purchasing power; how much the Treasury collects in goods and income expenditure with new money from the central bank; and how much the central bank earns in interest on the Treasury debt it buys with new money. Further, central banks return the interest earned on the debt to the Treasury, after subtracting the central bank's cost of operation. This means that the amount of the inflation tax revenue that the Treasury receives and spends is equal to the interest on its debt that is owned by the central bank and that the central bank returns to the Treasury after subtracting its cost of supplying the money. This cost would be near to zero if it were only printing the money, which the government's mint usually supplies, but it is greater than zero because of the cost of the people and buildings providing research on how to conduct monetary policy.

Viewed differently, the Treasury pays interest on all its debt, including to the central bank according to the amount of Treasury debt that it holds after buying the Treasury debt in secondary markets. The central bank then gives back this interest each year that is paid to it from the Treasury, after deducting its middleman costs. This leaves the Treasury with the goods purchased with the fresh money as the amount of the inflation tax earned by the government.

This amount of real goods purchased can be shown to be approximately equal to the interest that the central bank earns on its holdings of Treasury debt, so that the goods purchased with new money and the interest earned by the central bank on the Treasury debt that it bought with new money are both ways to measure the amount of the inflation tax collected by the government.

Note the large difference between a one-time increase in the money supply and a continual increase in the money supply. When the Treasury spends the fresh money and it enters circulation, it causes an increase in the money supply. If it were a one-time increase in the money supply, it would cause a one-time increase in the price level. This in turn would cause a temporary increase in the inflation rate as the price level rises. After that temporary increase in the inflation rate, it would go back to its original rate, say of zero.

A one-time increase in the money supply is never the problem in economies on a fiat standard unbacked by gold or silver. The problem is that the government continually uses central bank money to buy goods and services. This causes the money supply to increase at a certain rate of growth that results in a certain rate of increase in the price level, and a particular inflation rate.

The effect of the inflation tax is felt by those holding money when the money devalues by the rate of inflation. If the government budget deficit increases, and the central bank continues to buy a constant or larger share of the Treasury debt that is issued to cover the deficit, then the rate of growth of the money supply increases. If this money enters circulation, then it causes a higher inflation rate and a faster rate of devaluation of the money being held by households.

The government buys some output of the economy using this new money, while private demand for goods falls because of the effects of the inflation tax in reducing purchasing power. This redistributes the economy's output from the private sector to the government, just as with every other tax. Because government expenditure tends to stimulate the economy less than private citizen expenditure, the inflation tax causes output to fall.

The strongest evidence for how inflation ends up causing lower output is, again, not in terms of the level of output or the level of a one-time money supply increase. Rather, it is in terms of the rate of growth of the economy's output being decreased by the rate of growth of the money supply. Evidence shows that, for higher rates of growth in the money supply and in the inflation rate, there results a lower rate of growth of the economy's output. Sustained inflation causes lower economic growth. The decrease in economic growth from the inflation tax causes a decreased standard of living.

A nation using money printing to finance government expenditure, while also promoting a policy of increasing its economic growth, faces the dilemma that inflation weakens the economic growth that the government is trying to increase. Therefore, nations closely watch both the inflation rate and the rate of growth of the real value of its aggregate output, which is how we measure economic growth.

Note that, to measure the growth rate in the real value of output, we subtract the increase in the cost of output attributable to aggregate price inflation. One way to do this is to construct an aggregate output index. Output growth in current dollar terms, or "nominal" terms, can be measured simply using the change in the total cost of the economy's basket of goods each year. If we measure output growth in this way, we are including the new prices that come about each year. When there is inflation, this current dollar measure of output growth includes both the inflation from the price level increase and the actual increase in the real value of output. To isolate the change in real output, the inflation component needs to be taken out.

To do this, we do the opposite of what we used when constructing the price index. Rather than keeping quantities of goods constant and letting prices change, instead we keep the prices constant of all the goods in the basket being bought, while allowing the quantities to change as computed for the economy. With prices held constant, we can see how the value of the total economy's quantity of goods changes over time.

This constant price measure of the value of an economy's output is also an index measured on either a monthly, quarterly or annual basis. With "constant prices", it is an index of the real value of the quantity of goods being bought in the economy, with its change over time measuring the real economic growth rate. Alternatively, instead of constructing a real output index, we can simply take the rate of growth of the "current dollar" output and subtract the rate of growth in the price index, which is the inflation rate.

The most important index when accounting for inflation is the aggregate price index itself. Internationally, the most commonly used price index is the consumer price index (CPI). It uses a basket of goods exactly as described in the example above. If the price index remains stable, fluctuating only slightly, then that is consistent with zero inflation over time.

Positive levels of the inflation rate cause many problems, not only for purchasing power and the economy's economic growth rate, but also uncertainty in how both purchasing power and economic growth will change in the future. This uncertainty creates another large set of problems, which the economy tries to solve by anticipating future inflation. People have to form "expectations" of what the inflation rate is likely to be so that they can act efficiently. For example, the effect of expected inflation on unemployment is an area of much interest, as well as its effect on prices such as oil and gas.

The mechanism of how inflation is created and what inflation's consequences for the economy are have long been of interest to households, government policy-makers and academics. Irving Fisher, like David Hume before him and Milton Friedman after him, considered inflation to be caused directly by increases in the government's money supply. The concept is that, when an increase in the growth rate of the money enters circulation, it causes an increase in the growth rate of the price level that translates into an increase in the inflation rate.

Keynes, Fisher and Friedman all emphasized how inflation might affect employment and growth. All three of these famous economists argued that the government's policy should be to maintain a stable price level, without government significantly raising finance through the printing of money. Using a price index, this goal could be monitored and achieved, and could result in a rate of inflation that was zero.

Fisher's book *Stabilizing the Dollar* (1920) makes the case for price stability. It is based on his earlier work *The Purchasing Power of Money* (1911), which shows how the price level is determined by the amount of money circulating in an economy. Fisher's theory is known as the "quantity theory of money". Fisher used this theory to advocate for sufficiently controlling the government money supply to achieve a stable aggregate price level. As Nobel laureate Robert E. Hall (1997) puts it: "Irving Fisher believed passionately in the social benefits of a stable price level."

Keynes's book *A Tract on Monetary Reform* (1923) was based on Fisher's quantity theory of money and on Fisher's advocacy for stable prices. Keynes argues that the government monetary policy can anticipate money demand since it depends on the cost of holding money. Keynes's "reform" was that the money supply need only follow money demand to achieve price stability and zero inflation.

Friedman followed up this line of reasoning in *A Program for Monetary Stability* (1960). Friedman (1994: 227) summarizes these 1960 proposed reforms: "My own suggestions have centered on means of assuring that the quantity of money will grow at a relatively stable rate." Like Keynes, he advocates a constant low or zero inflation rate by letting money supply grow in accordance with the growth in money demand. Friedman (1994: 193) emphasizes that money demand grows with the economy's rate of output growth, and any higher rate of money supply growth causes inflation: "Inflation occurs when the quantity of money rises appreciably more rapidly than output, and the more rapid the rise in the quantity of money per unit of output, the greater the rate of inflation. There is probably no other proposition in economics that is as well established as this one."

Others have followed suit in advocating for zero inflation, such as William T. Gavin and Alan C. Stockman (1988) in "The case for zero inflation". The famous quantity theory of money that Fisher (1911, 1920), Keynes (1923) and Friedman (1960) promulgated argues that the price level is determined mainly by the amount of money circulating in an economy, along with the rate of growth of the economy. When the money supply growth rate is high, this dominates the effect of output growth, such that the simple statement is that the money supply growth rate can be said to determine the inflation rate.

As the Great Depression began, and strong deflation ensued, economists began to rethink what causes changes in the price level. Keynes championed this revision of monetary theory first in his *Treatise on Money* (1930), in which he declares the quantity theory of money to be invalid.

Instead, he argues that the cost of production determines the aggregate price level. Rather than causality being from money supply increases to price level increases and then to cost of production increases, Keynes eliminated money from the sequence, determining the price level as a fully developed repudiation of the quantity theory of money. Instead, he argues that the price level is determined solely by the cost of production, with money having no role.

In putting forth this relative price theory of inflation, Keynes drew upon his former professor's work, that of Alfred Marshall (1920). Marshall's eight editions of *Principles of Economics*, from 1890 to 1920, provided the neoclassical advance of combining demand for goods, based on the marginal utility theory of Menger, Jevons and Walras, with the supply of goods in order to determine the equilibrium price in markets. Marshall showed how, in this theory, a firm would set its price equal to its average cost of production plus a profit per unit of output that depended upon demand.

This Marshallian profit is often called the firm's "mark-up". Keynes used this Marshallian theory of the representative firm to provide a relative price theory of the aggregate price level. He argues that the aggregate price level equals the economy's aggregate cost of production per unit of goods plus the economy's aggregate profit per unit of goods. Keynes (1930) defines the aggregate profit as being equal to aggregate investment minus savings. Many economists disputed Keynes's definition of profit, arguing that it was incorrect.

Using the definition of profit as investment minus savings, Keynes (1930) extends his relative price theory of the aggregate price level to a theory of business cycles in which negative profit leads to economic contraction and positive profit leads to economic expansion. In his next book, *The General Theory of Employment, Interest and Money* (1936), he alters his theory of business cycles by eliminating the profit definition, which is incorrect, and defends the 1930 definition of profit only in footnotes. Instead, he describes the competitive equilibrium market for capital as given by the demand for capital as investment and the supply of capital as savings, with government expenditure having the ability to increase investment demand (Gillman 2002).

Keynes's 1930 and 1936 books gave rise to a school of economic thought called Keynesian economics, which in modern mathematical form is known as new Keynesian economics. Both old and new Keynesian schools define inflation as being a relative price increase in the average cost of the aggregate good plus the aggregate mark-up profit, just as in Keynes (1930). But modern new Keynesians assume "monopolistic competition" as a new definition of the profit mark-up, one that has also been disputed as being consistent with an optimizing equilibrium (Stigler 1949; Mincer 1983; Rosen 1993). Like Keynes (1930), this modern Keynesian school deletes the role of money in determining the inflation rate. All inflation is caused by relative price change, resulting from a monopoly mark-up that spreads slowly upwards as a result of an additional assumption of price rigidity.

The quantity theory of money and the relative price theory of monopoly mark-ups give two strikingly different views of what causes inflation. These views have led to a division in how people view inflation – a division that continues today. In the monetary approach of the quantity theory, inflation is attributable to the rate of growth of the money supply. In the Keynesian relative price view, all inflation results from monopolies increasing their prices relative to the cost of production.

Yet both quantity theory adherents, going back to Fisher (1920) and Keynes (1923), and modern Keynesians, with a relative price theory of inflation going back to Keynes (1930), have advocated the monetary policy of a zero-inflation rate. Would this policy be feasible today? Establishing such a zero-inflation rate would require official policy with the intent of implementing such a policy. Is there a case for zero inflation today?

We live in an age when inflation has been variable, usually well above zero and, at times, alarmingly high. It might be that no one would consider zero inflation as a reasonable, plausible or achievable target. The introduction of fiat money has led to a trend upwards in its supply relative to the previous gold standard. The average trend inflation rate during the gold standard was zero, while under the fiat standard the average trend inflation rate is positive. A zero-inflation target in a fiat money regime could enable a similar trend inflation rate to that achieved under the gold standard. As Friedman (1994: 222) puts it: "Zero inflation is a politically feasible objective; a 10 percent inflation is not. That is the verdict of experience."

The gold standard transitioned in the 1970s to fiat money – that is, money unbacked by metal and easy to create by having the government buy its own debt using its central bank. Growing inflation caused by the Fed buying Treasury debt to finance the Vietnam War led to the gold standard breaking down. Following its demise, high inflation rates emerged around the world. With an end of the gold standard, the countries that had been a part of it no longer needed to "sterilize" their growing hoard of US dollars by keeping them as reserves to maintain the US dollar as an anchor for the gold standard.

After the Vietnam War and the gold standard both came to an end, and as the US inflation rate continued to rise, the United States passed into law a zero-inflation-rate target that is still the current law for the Federal Reserve System. This statutory, legal inflation rate target in the United States is currently equal to zero. This zero-inflation target was set to begin in 1988 and remain in place indefinitely, unless it was changed by the US Congress or the president. To date, this law has never been changed.

The law was enacted after the high US inflation rates in the 1970s. The US inflation rate rose from zero in 1955 to 6 per cent in 1970. After a modest drop after the 1971 recession, it rose again to 11 per cent in 1974. In January 1975 James Earl Carter left the Georgia Governor's Office to run for US president in 1976, assumed the office of the president of the United States in January 1977 and faced an inflation rate of 6.5 per cent in his first year in office.

The Vietnam War had recently ended, and was apparently on the mind of the ex-governor of Georgia. On Carter's first day in office he followed in the footsteps of his predecessor, Gerald Ford, by making permanent a pardon for Vietnam draft evaders. Concern for people evading the human tax levied by forced military conscription to conduct the war coincided with concern for people avoiding the high inflation tax that devalued their money to pay for the war.

The high inflation of the Vietnam War era was to the fore in economics, politics and dinner table discussions. There is no mention in Wikipedia under "Jimmy Carter" for his establishing the first and only US statutory inflation rate law. Yet H.R. 50 of the 95th US Congress, which began on 3 January 1977, was introduced by Representative Augustus F. Hawkins of California on 4 January 1977, with the title of the Full Employment and Balanced Growth Act. This was passed in Congress and signed by Carter into law on 27 October 1978 as Public Law 95-523.

The 1978 Act amends the US Employment Act of 1946. This 1946 Act is often cited, without reference to the 1978 Act, as the law that currently governs the Federal Reserve System of the United States. Since the 1978 Act fully amends and refines the 1946 Act, however, it is in fact this Act that governs the Fed more than the 1946 Act.

But continual reference to the 1946 Act without acknowledging the inflation targets imposed on the Fed is either disingenuous, lacking in knowledge or dismissive of the congressional law binding the Federal Reserve. The 1978 Act established a series of aims to reduce the inflation rate and bring it down to zero. There were two steps to the law: a target of 3 per cent inflation was to be achieved by 1983, and a zero-inflation rate was to be achieved from 1988 onwards.

The Act clearly demarcates the law and prohibits any other body, such as the Fed, from changing the target. By explicit wording of the Act, in section 4.d, this target can be changed only by the US Congress or the president:

> [I]f the President finds it necessary, the President may recommend modification of the timetable or timetables for the achievement of the goals provided for in subsection (b) and the annual numerical goals to make them consistent with the modified timetable or timetables, and the Congress may take such action as it deems appropriate consistent with title III of the Full Employment and Balanced Growth Act of 1978.

The US government's reaction to the passage of the 1978 Act was equally historic. Arthur Frank Burns had been appointed by President Nixon as governor of the Fed in 1970, and in 1978 Carter replaced Burns with William Miller as governor, just as the Full Employment and Balanced Growth Act was about to be passed in Congress. Eight days before the full US House passed its version of the 1978 Act, Miller took office as governor, on 8 March 1978.

As seen in Figure 1.1, in March 1978 the United States' annual inflation rate was 6 per cent. By August 1979 the US inflation rate had risen to 12 per cent. Given that these inflation rate increases occurred after the 1973 breakdown of the Bretton Woods gold standard, President Carter was swift to change course over who governed the Fed. After little more than a year as governor, Carter reacted

Figure 1.1 US monthly year-on-year CPI inflation rate, January 1948–November 2021
Source: Federal Reserve Economic Data (FRED) database, produced by the Federal Reserve Bank of St Louis, available at: https://fred.stlouisfed.org.

to the accelerating inflation rate by firing Miller and nominating Paul Volcker, who assumed office in August 1979. It is widespread folklore that Paul Volcker tamed US inflation on his own initiative. But Volcker simply implemented the 1978 Congressional law on inflation rate targeting. Volcker reduced the inflation rate by using what has always been known by the quantity theory of money economists. He lowered the US money supply growth rate by reducing the rate of Fed purchases of Treasury debt.

After peaking at 14 per cent in May 1980, US inflation dropped abruptly to 2.5 per cent in July 1983. On an annual basis, the US inflation rate in 1983 was 3.16 per cent, almost exactly as called for under the 1978 Act. Although Volcker was indeed successful as governor of the Fed, almost no one mentions the 1978 Act and how President Carter magnificently executed this law and ushered in the era of inflation rate targeting, which has reigned ever since 1983.

During the dramatic reduction in inflation, the gross domestic product (GDP) output growth rate fell from 6.5 per cent in the first quarter of 1979 to a trough of −1.6 per cent in the third quarter of 1980, after which it rose again, but then fell back to −2.5 per cent in the third quarter of 1982. This 1981 recession experienced higher-than-normal interest rates in capital markets, lower output growth and higher unemployment. Ronald Reagan had been elected president during the downturn of 1980, and he led an economic revival by passing far-reaching tax reduction acts in 1981 and 1986.

Since Volcker's two terms as governor of the Fed, the zero-inflation-rate target has been ignored, as well as the idea of price stability, going back to Fisher and his development of a price index to measure inflation. In partial justification, the 1978 Act also sets an unemployment target of 4 per cent. This allows some leeway in achieving the inflation target: if the Fed claims that the unemployment rate is too high to achieve the zero-inflation-rate target, the 1978 law allows it to ease back on achieving the inflation target. Volcker ignored the unemployment target, however, and achieved the 3 per cent inflation rate right on schedule by 1983.

Even when the US unemployment rate recently fell below 4 per cent, the zero-inflation-rate target continued to be ignored. The unemployment target of 4 per cent was reached in January 2019, and the rate was in the 3 per cent range until February 2020. This gave no room for the Fed to skirt the zero-inflation-rate target. Yet, unlike Volcker, the subsequent Fed governors have continued to ignore the law.

Nonetheless, the achievement of the 1983 target is tangible. Economists characterize a break in monetary policy by the Fed as occurring in 1983, after which time the "Great Moderation" followed. This was a period with little economic volatility that lasted right up until the financial crisis and the "Great Recession" of 2008–09.

In an ongoing academic debate, Keynesians, who maintain that inflation is caused by relative price increases, attribute the Great Moderation to "good luck" rather than good policy. Monetary economists explain the Great Moderation as a result of decreases in the money supply growth rate, which then ushered in an era of low inflation that decreased economic volatility. In this view it is seen as good policy rather than good luck.

Since the Great Recession of 2008–09, also referred to as the "Great Financial Crisis", the Fed has been in crisis mode. It even went so far as to openly violate the 1978 statutory law through its January 2012 Federal Open Market Committee (FOMC) statement. In this the Fed declared that its inflation target would henceforth be 2 per cent (Board of governors of the Federal Reserve System 2012), even though the 1978 Act prohibited the Fed from establishing any inflation rate target except zero (Gillman 2020).

The Fed further contradicted the 1978 Act in the 2012 statement by adding that it would refuse to establish an unemployment rate target. The 1978 Act amendments to the 1946 Act dictate a statutory unemployment target of 4 per cent for the Fed. Nonetheless, the 2012 FOMC statement includes words to the effect that it is unable to target the unemployment rate, so it refuses to do so: "The maximum level of employment is largely determined by nonmonetary factors that affect the structure and dynamics of the labor market. These factors may change over time and may not be directly measurable. Consequently, it would not be appropriate to specify a fixed goal for employment" (Board of governors of the Federal Reserve System 2012).

The Fed's 2012 official 2 per cent inflation rate target was thus established. Although the US Congress has left unchallenged the Fed's constitutionally illegal change in the official inflation rate target from zero to 2 per cent, there was a lone voice that was quite taken aback by the Fed's action. Paul Volcker, then aged 91, published a book that includes discussion of the Fed's 2012 establishment of this 2 per cent inflation target.

In his book, *Keeping At It: The Quest for Sound Money and Good Government* (2018), he writes: "I puzzle at the rationale … a 2 percent target, or limit, was not in my textbook years ago. I know of no theoretical justification." Although Volcker carried out the 1978 law that set a 3 per cent target by 1983, he states that he was politically unable to attain the last part of the target, namely zero per cent by 1988, since his new boss, President Reagan, did not want to risk another recession. Volcker had significantly decreased the rate of growth of the money supply to achieve 3 per cent inflation in 1983, but only at the cost of a recession in 1981 to 1982. After falling as low as 1.2 per cent in December 1986, inflation then rose back up to over 4 per cent in Volcker's last year in office, in 1987.

Volcker was governor for eight years, having been reappointed by Reagan, until August 1987. The zero-inflation rate for 1988 onwards never materialized. The unemployment rate in 1988 was still above 5 per cent.

The problem with reducing the inflation rate suddenly is that it requires a large decrease in the money supply growth rate. If this occurs while government deficits remain high, then the central bank's rate of purchasing Treasury debt has to decrease. This lower rate of "monetizing the debt" causes a higher "real" interest rate in capital markets. Put simply, as first stated in Irving Fisher's *The Rate of Interest* (1907), the real rate of interest is defined by the market rate of interest minus the inflation rate.

In capital "money markets", the real interest rate indeed does equal the market interest rate minus the inflation rate. The United States experienced a significantly higher real interest rates in the early 1980s when Volcker's Fed bought a smaller share of Treasury debt. A sudden government-caused increase in the real interest rate acts as an unexpected tax on new investment that makes the cost of private investment higher, although it rewards savers with a higher real interest rate.

Governments with high deficits have to decide whether to finance them by printing more money and using the inflation tax, or by borrowing more heavily in capital markets and raising the real interest rate. A look at government money supply policy since money's origin in metal shows how wars, banking crises and government finance have affected money supply, inflation, real interest rates and capital markets. The balance of the government's implicit taxes, including the indirect inflation tax and capital market taxes, along with the amount of government spending, affects the growth rate of real output, the accumulation of wealth and the strength of financial markets worldwide.

To start the historical journey towards understanding the current inflation and money and banking policy, the next chapter discusses how the gold standard and its zero-inflation trend came to an end, and fiat money unbacked by metal began. It includes historical developments under the gold standard to illustrate how metallic regimes work.

2

THE RISE OF INFLATION

After having an inflation rate averaging near to zero during the gold standard, and dating back to the inception of the United States, the march towards a statutory zero-inflation-rate target in the country began with the march into Vietnam. This war arose from the tensions stemming from the First and Second World Wars. In the Korean War the United States had continued its long rivalry by fighting directly against China, and then it confronted the Soviet Union in the decades-long Cold War. The Vietnam War perpetuated these conflicts, with the United States fighting both Chinese and Soviet military assets across southeast Asia.

Inflation was high during both the First and Second World Wars. It rose again during the Korean War. It comes as no surprise that the subsequent Vietnam War once more involved high inflation for the United States. How do wars cause inflation?

The answer is short and simple: the government finances the war by printing money. To understand how the printing of money covers government budget deficits during wartime, we need to investigate the "monetary regime" that exists at the time of war. US history provides ample opportunity to demonstrate the effect of war on inflation, and the effect of the US involvement in the Vietnam War precipitated an inflection point in the world's monetary regime history.

The first US war-induced inflation took place even before the Constitution was enacted. The American Revolutionary War and the Articles of Confederation led to money printing to finance that war, because the US federal government had no power to raise taxes. The Continental currency became worthless, the monetary regime collapsed and the United States was forced to default on its debt. As Peter Bernholz (2016: 55) writes: "During the American War of Independence against Britain the war efforts of the emerging United States were to a large degree financed by issuing a new paper money, the Continental Currency."

Bernholz attributes this to the inability of the confederated states to raise taxes or offer such financial help. Bernholz plots (2016: 56, fig. 4.4) a price index that has been computed for that period, along with the stock of Continental currency and the currency price of gold. They all rise together five- to ten-fold from their original level, or by between 500 and 1,000 per cent. Rockoff (2015: 10, 13) also describes this:

> During the Revolution Benjamin Franklin, perhaps in an over-zealous effort to defend American financial practices, recognized that inflation was a tax … The Continental Congress therefore took to the printing press. Ease of access, low administrative costs, and the difficulty of evading the inflation tax carried the day. Overall, Farley Grubb … estimated that 77 per cent of the expenditures of the Continental Congress were financed by issuing continental dollars. By year: 100 per cent in 1775 and 99 per cent in 1776, when no alternatives were feasible, then 59 per cent in 1777, 75 per cent in 1778, and 77 per cent in 1779.

The co-movement of the price index and the supply of money exemplifies a form of the "quantity theory of money". As the supply of the Continentals increased, the US Continental Congress bought military supplies with the paper money, and the same quantity of goods were being sold for higher and higher prices. Consider that an artillery gun was originally being sold for metal such as silver and gold. Then the government tells the producer of such guns that it has to accept the new paper money. The producer charges a price for the artillery in terms of paper money that is sufficient to buy an amount of gold that the artillery gun producer usually receives for the sale of the equipment.

Over time, as the government prints more money to buy goods, people selling gold demand increasingly more paper money to buy an ounce of gold. This means that the artillery producer needs to begin selling the equipment for more Continentals in order to buy the equivalent amount of gold. Next month the government buys the artillery guns with even more paper Continentals, which it is printing at an increasing rate each month, since the prices for goods in terms of Continentals is rising. For example, if the government has doubled the supply of paper money in circulation, then the same amount of the basket of goods in the aggregate economy will sell for twice the price that it sold for beforehand. Gold would also double in price in terms of Continentals.

The rising price level as measured by the price index indicates that inflation is occurring. Bernholz (2016) states that the inflation rate peaked at near 50 per cent for a single month, in November 1779. If it did that for 12 months in a row, the annual rate of inflation would be 600 per cent. This resulted in a loss of confidence in the value of the Continental, which Bernholz (2016: 58) describes through a letter written by Josiah Quincy to George Washington: "I am firmly of the opinion … that there never was a paper pound, a paper dollar, or a paper promise of any kind, that ever yet obtained a general currency but by force or fraud, generally by both."

Inflation at this sort of rate is called "hyperinflation", and it occurred in the American Revolutionary War against European powers (mainly Britain). It was a type of world war of the major powers, in that France shipped military equipment and made loans to the Continental Congress for the war. The Continental Congress also had loans from Spain and from private Dutch bankers.

Trying to pay off the loans without a means of taxation under the Articles of Confederation added to the amount of money printing and the collapse of the value of the Continental dollar (hence the expression "not worth a Continental"). The United States defaulted on the Continental debt. After this episode of war-induced hyperinflation, the country was keen to establish a stable currency and a stable government that could participate in international capital markets.

The collapse of the Continental monetary regime led to calls for a federal government that had the ability to raise taxes, to the Constitutional Convention in Philadelphia and to the subsequent implementation of the US Constitution. Under that framework, Congress could raise revenue through taxation by following a specific legislative process, and money could be coined in metal.

The US government came into being on 4 March 1789 after nine of the 13 states ratified the Constitution. Article I provided that the US Congress could levy taxes, pay debts and provide defence, as well as having coinage, whereas the states could not. This began the US metallic standard for money. And, since the Constitution specifies that either gold or silver could be used for coinage for legal tender, it was a bimetallic standard based on gold *and* silver.

The use of metal for currency goes back thousands of years to antiquity. For example, ancient Egypt used silver, along with gold *shats*, and a 12-*shat* equivalent was called a *deben*, shaped in rings. Ancient Greece, Rome and Renaissance Europe used metal coins, as did Britain at the time that America was first settled and in the American colonies under British rule.

A practice that grew in antiquity was to balance the gold and silver within the coins so that they were of the same value as prevailed in the markets for silver and gold. The Coinage Act of 1792 specified that US dollars be made with both gold and a mix of gold and silver in a balance that reflected current market values. A mint was established to make the coins.

The Coinage Act specified gold Eagles worth $10, Half Eagles worth $5 and Quarter Eagles worth $2.5. Gold and silver were to be used in combination for dollars, half dollars, quarter dollars, dismes worth one-tenth of a dollar, and half dismes. Cents, worth one-hundredth of a dollar, were to be made of copper. These denominations are similar to today's US currency; the $2.5 coin did not survive, but the United States did begin in 1976 the reissue of a $2 paper note, which still circulates.

The US government could not "print" money in any conventional sense. The tricky part was what would happen when there was a war while on a metallic standard, and the government could not borrow enough to finance military expenditure. At first, during war, the government borrows as much as it can, which is invariably a limited amount because the government can be viewed as being at risk of failing because of the war. Facing a natural limit on borrowing while under a metallic standard, governments typically suspend their metallic regime in favour of printing money in the form of promissory notes. These cannot be redeemed into metal at the mint but include the promise of later redemption.

During the American Civil War, from 1861 to 1865, the United States was intent on not defaulting on either its currency or its debt. The government borrowed directly from the public. When that source ran out, the United States sold its bonds to banks, which in turn would sell them to the US public. Once that route soon also became saturated, the government issued new paper money called "greenbacks", which were dictated to be "legal tender".

The new greenback money was the predecessor of the current green US dollars. During the Civil War, however, a large increase in greenback printing led to a doubling of the price level. In 1864, as the North began to assert dominance, people believed the greenbacks would be converted back to their stated gold equivalent. Bernholz (2016: 60) shows that this led to the price level beginning to drop.

As the United States was committed to restoring redemption of the greenback into metal at the pre-war level, the price of the metal in terms of greenbacks had to continue to fall. This could be achieved only by reducing the growth rate of the greenbacks in circulation. Then the amount of these dollars required for an ounce of gold would fall as fewer dollars circulated. After a continued decrease in the money supply growth rate and the aggregate price level, the price of dollars per gold reached its pre-war parity level by around 1872.

The US Coinage Act of 1873 resumed redemption of greenbacks into both silver and gold. The coinage redemption process was revised in 1879 to allow redemption only in gold, thereby dropping silver from coinage. Thereafter the United States remained on this gold standard, following the standard established concurrently in Britain, until the end of the Second World War. There were times, however, when the United States suspended the gold standard, during the First World War, the Great Depression and the Second World War (Crabbe 1989).

In the Second World War the United States experienced high inflation while remaining on the gold standard for most of this period. Friedman and Schwartz (1963) put this down to the inflow of gold from Britain to buy US military equipment. Financing First World War military expenditure with money backed by gold increased the money supply in the United States and led to high US inflation. They show that the money stock rose by 300 per cent from 1939 to 1947. Friedman and Schwartz's (1963) work was highly influential because they had pieced together data across nearly a century, before money supply figures were readily available.

Much of the current US information found on the FRED database begins in 1947, when the price level began to stabilize after the Second World War. This reflects the convention that the "modern era" of economics in the United States began in 1947, after the war. This practice facilitates exclusion of the episodes of very high inflation rates during the First and Second World Wars when using data, however, thereby eliminating the "outliers" of high-inflation years when doing analysis.

The tendency to use only "postwar" data de-emphasizes how wars and inflation coincide throughout history. This can bring a dissociation that encourages inflation episodes to be viewed as being unrelated to war and crisis. The serious caveat here is that this practice hides this facet of economic reality from the analysis of inflation. It even leads to consideration of the high inflation episode during the Vietnam War as being unrelated to money supply finance of government spending, which in turn has given rise to a host of alternative explanations for inflation unrelated to the money supply.

An alternate common starting point for modern data is after the Korean War, which also involved high inflation, just as in previous wars. In particular, the Fed begins its current monetary data series in 1959. This was made uniform across a set of different groupings of public money (currency, for example) and private money (such as private bank demand deposits by customers). These alternative monetary "aggregates" that the Fed collects in its FRED database include the monetary base (reserves plus currency) and M1 (currency plus demand deposits), traditionally the most used aggregates for measuring the US money supply, along with M2, which, essentially, adds money market accounts to M1. In 2020 the Fed added money market accounts to M1, making it virtually the same as M2.

By beginning the monetary data series in 1959, however, another major war – the Korean War – is dropped from data. Post-1959 data leaves out all the major US wars of the twentieth century except for the Vietnam War. Omitting monetary data during the First and Second World Wars and the Korean War, along with the wartime money to inflation linkage, has often enabled the Vietnam War inflation of the 1960s and 1970s to be misconstrued as an inflation episode without money printing to finance war.

In fact, the twentieth-century wars in Europe, with China in Korea, and with both China and the Soviet Union in Vietnam all played a large role in US money supply and in inflation rate history. During the 1960s and 1970s war finance by money printing caused inflation. The Vietnam War also led the international monetary regime to evolve from its previous incarnation as a gold standard into a fiat standard.

The evolution away from the traditional gold standard began during the Second World War. A January 1942 declaration to fight as an alliance was formally drawn up through the Anglo-US Atlantic Charter, as a "Declaration of United Nations". Britain and the United States then met in 1943 in Quebec, Canada, and agreed to draft a charter for an international organization that maintained the sovereignty of nations.

Next came a conference in Moscow with a further cooperative declaration, followed by an agreement reached in Tehran between President Franklin D. Roosevelt and Joseph Stalin that the new order would be enforced through the joint effort of the United States, Soviet Union, China and Britain. From this, the United Nations was established in October 1945, by 29 nations, with a Security Council having the initial four enforcing nations as permanent members.

With the experience of high inflation internationally during the war, an international conference was held in the United States in 1944 with 730 delegates from 44 nations, sponsored by the early form of the United Nations. The "Monetary and Financial Conference" in Bretton Woods, New Hampshire, considered creating a world central bank and a central means to make loans for postwar reconstruction.

Influential British economist John Maynard Keynes argued for a global central bank to serve the international economy by issuing a single currency backed by metal. The conference reached an agreement that included lesser steps than he suggested, by establishing the International Monetary Fund (IMF) and the International Bank for Reconstruction and Development (IBRD). The IMF could maintain and lend reserves to countries (called "special drawing rights", or SDRs), whereas the IBRD could make loans to help postwar reconstruction and later became part of the World Bank, which focuses on making loans for development.

The IMF began operations in December 1945 after the 29 countries signed its Articles of Agreement as founding members. A new monetary gold regime was set up as well. It was based on fixing the price of gold in terms of a set number of US dollars, with the United States as the anchor of the new international monetary regime. This became known as the Bretton Woods agreement, and it ushered in the era of the Bretton Woods monetary regime.

The US dollar was an obvious choice for the reserve currency as the United States had accumulated most of the world's stock of gold during the war. In 1945 the US dollar price of gold of $35 per ounce became the fixed price of gold. It remained at that level every year thereafter, except for 1949, up until 1967. Under Bretton Woods, only US dollars were convertible to gold (besides jewellery and other non-monetary uses of gold) and only central banks could redeem the US dollars for gold at the fixed price of $35 per ounce.

This central bank redemption was allowed in the marketplace up until 1968, and later only through the US Treasury. To fix the prices of other international currencies to the gold price, other countries had to fix the exchange rate of their currency with the US dollar at an agreed rate. This stabilized the prices of all other Bretton Woods member countries through a system of fixed exchange rates, with each country's currency converted into a set number of US dollars, which, in turn, could be converted to gold through redemption between central banks.

Exchange controls had been established after the war in many countries, however, so that their currencies were not freely convertible into other currencies. In 1958, once these controls had been fully lifted, the Bretton Woods system entered full operation. But in 1968, when the US market's dollar price of gold rose above $35, central banks agreed to cease trading for gold in the marketplace and, instead, central banks acquired gold for US dollars at the official, undervalued dollar price of $35 only through exchange with the US Treasury.

Since the market price for gold in dollars exceeded the official price, central banks could trade dollars in for gold at the US Treasury and make a profit. But this would draw down the US gold reserve and end the Bretton Woods system. Bretton Woods countries preserved the monetary regime with the $35 dollar price of gold by buying up US dollars with their own currencies, holding the dollars as reserves, rather than redeeming them for gold at the US Treasury, and thereby sterilizing some of the US dollar increase by keeping them out of circulation.

Robert Hetzel (2013), on the Federal Reserve's "History" website, describes this change in the monetary system as going from a gold standard to a "dollar standard": "In 1968 central banks stopped buying or selling gold in the open market. Only foreign central banks could then ask the US Treasury for gold. This changed the Bretton Woods system from a de facto gold standard anchored by a fixed dollar price of gold into a dollar standard" (Hetzel 2013).

When the Bretton Woods monetary system came into force, it was a far cry from traditional gold standards, in which anyone could convert a currency into gold, such as the US resumption of its redemption of "greenbacks" into gold at the US Mint by anyone after 1879. The Bretton Woods system showed that gold could stay in a single place (in the US Mint), not circulate, and still be a foundation for an international monetary regime tied to the value of gold. It was still a gold standard through which all currencies could be converted to gold, albeit by exchanging for the US dollar and with conversion to gold enabled only by central banks redeeming US dollars for gold at the US Mint.

Bretton Woods was innovative in establishing a metallic currency system that was more efficient, since gold did not need to be carried around. The burden on the United States loomed large, however, as the cost of such efficiency. Given the large US role in both world wars, and its accumulation of the world's gold, the US-centric gold system was viewed as a reasonable risk in establishing an efficient form of international monetary stability.

Had war really ended in 1945, Bretton Woods may have survived indefinitely. But then came the Berlin airlift in 1948–49, directed against the Soviet Union, followed by the United States' war with the new Chinese communist regime following the invasion of South Korea by North Korea in 1950. This war has never officially ended, with the Korean Armistice Agreement being signed on 27 July 1953 without South Korea as a signatory and without a peace agreement.

The Korean War immediately spilled over into Vietnam. The postwar Potsdam Declaration partitioned Indochina between China in the north and the United Kingdom in the south, which was a former French colony. The UK and French forces were already fighting the Viet Minh in 1945, resulting in the French taking back control of Saigon late that year. After the Chinese Revolution of 1949, communist China in 1950 began an alliance to fight alongside the North Vietnamese forces against the French. The French ended their role in Vietnam by signing the Geneva Accords in July 1954, after which the United States stepped in to support the South Vietnamese. In October 1954 President Eisenhower pledged military support for South Vietnam, in return for certain reforms by the pro-Western prime minister, General Ngo Dinh Diem. US involvement ratcheted up until January 1968. During the January lunar new year Tet festival, the North Vietnamese attacked the US and the South Vietnamese forces, inflicting such large losses that the United States began to de-escalate and gradually withdraw from the war.

The Vietnam War was, essentially, the Third World War or Fourth World War, depending on how you count the Korean War. The French followed the British in ruling Vietnam. The United States followed the British and French. As the war was against the Chinese and Russians, it involved all four of the major powers of the UN Security Council.

The US inflation rate and money supply steadily rose from Eisenhower's presidency right through to Nixon's. Yet economics textbooks have long described the sustained inflation of the 1960s and 1970s as the largest US peacetime inflation (see also De Long 1997). In fact, the Fed bought US Treasury debt at an even faster rate than the US Treasury increased its debt during the Vietnam War. This amounted, as is always the case, to printing money at an accelerating rate. So much money was printed to finance US expenditure during the Vietnam War that in 1971 the gold standard collapsed, never to be seen in the world economy again. As the United States ramped up its wartime spending, the inflation rate increased from 1959 through the "end" of the war in 1973. US inflation then rose again after floating exchange rates commenced in 1973, and countries could unload their unwanted dollars accumulated during the high US wartime expenditure before Bretton Woods collapsed. Inflation continued to rise so much that it led to the US Balanced Growth and Employment Act of 1978, the US zero inflation rate statutory target and Paul Volcker's tenure as Fed governor.

How did the Federal Reserve print money under the Bretton Woods gold standard? The Fed's money printing started in earnest during the gold standard period after the First World War, even before the Bretton Woods meeting. Governments and their central banks that were concerned about hyperinflation disallowed central bank purchases of Treasury debt above a minimal level. This would avoid one hand of government giving freshly printed money to the other hand to finance a deficit.

The Fed could not buy unlimited US Treasury debt directly from the US Treasury. After a period of serious deflation from 1920 to 1922, Benjamin Strong, then governor of the Federal Reserve Bank of New York, decided that the Fed would buy US Treasury interest-bearing debt from private banks, earn interest income and increase the supply of money. The Fed's purchase and sale of US Treasury debt became known as "open market operations". The US Treasury sells debt to private banks and the Fed in turn buys the US Treasury debt from private banks, which is the practice of monetary policy to this day.

Besides explicit government taxes, Friedman (1994: 205–6) tells us how the government raises revenue by printing money:

> The only other way to finance higher government spending is by increasing the quantity of money. The US government can do that by having the US Treasury, one branch of government, sell bonds to the Federal Reserve System, another branch of the government. The Federal Reserve pays for the bonds either with freshly printed Federal Reserve notes or by entering on its books a deposit to the credit of the US Treasury. The Treasury can then pay the government's bill either with the cash or with checks drawn on the Treasury's account at the Fed. When this additional high-powered money is deposited in commercial banks by its initial recipients, the money serves as reserves for the banks and as the basis for a much larger addition to the quantity of money.

US presidents could finance the Vietnam War by having the US Treasury borrow money at an increasing rate. Then the Fed could buy the debt. Money was printed as a result, and the amount of currency in circulation rose. Figure 2.1 illustrates how this worked from January 1953 to September 1980. Stated in billions of dollars, the amount of Treasury debt (the solid line, normalized by dividing by four) rose steadily from 1953 to 1974, after which it accelerated. The Treasury debt held by the Fed (the dotted black line) rose at an even faster rate than overall Treasury debt.

In 1969 the Fed's Treasury holdings rose above one-quarter of total Treasury debt, as seen by the intersection of the two lines, and continued to rise more rapidly than total Treasury debt until after the Bretton Woods breakdown in 1973. The currency in circulation (the grey line) rose in tandem with the Fed's holdings of Treasury debt. The CPI price index (the grey dashed line, normalized to fit the diagram) rose at a similar but slower rate than currency, since economic growth increased the demand for money as the economy expanded.

Figure 2.1 shows not only rising Treasury debt but the accelerating rate of it being purchased by the Fed. The Fed was buying Treasury debt at a faster rate than the Treasury was borrowing, raising the share of the Fed's holdings of debt as a percentage of GDP (a measure of national output). The Fed was allowing the Treasury to rely ever more on the Fed giving it money for deficits during the Vietnam War. The rate of US currency in circulation and the CPI price index both accelerated, meaning that the money supply growth rate and the price level growth rate – namely the inflation rate – also accelerated.

The "smoke and mirrors" that Friedman describes reveal that the man behind the curtain performing the finance magic is the Federal Reserve governor. "Printing money" means that the Fed gives freshly printed money to the US

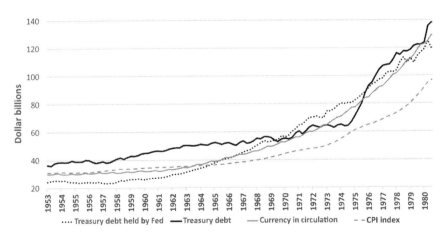

Figure 2.1 US Treasury debt held by the Fed, currency in circulation, the CPI and US Treasury debt overall, 1947–81
Source: FRED.

Treasury to cover deficit spending. But the Fed must go through the middleman via open market operations with the private banking sector (for which the private banks get a share of the transaction).

Under the Bretton Woods system, this money printing caused havoc, with US dollars flooding overseas into international capital markets. The only way that the price of gold could remain at $35 an ounce was if the excess supply of dollars was soaked up by other countries. This forced the other signatory countries to the gold system to buy the excess supply of US dollars using their own currencies.

To buy the excess dollars, these countries had to print more of their own currency. This raised their own domestic inflation rates. Effectively, the other countries had to import the US inflation into their own economies. Alternatively, the countries could use their sparse international reserves on hand to buy the dollars, but, with most international reserves being held in US dollars, they could not soak up US dollars using US dollars.

France's central bank finally said "*Assez!*" ("Enough!") and began to redeem its holdings of US dollars into gold. As Friedman (1994) describes it, this meant marking a drawer at the US Mint as "French gold" instead of US gold. Rather than removing gold from the US Mint, the gold could just move within the US Mint, or simply be relabelled.

Re-marking drawers nevertheless led the US to "lose gold reserves" through an "outflow of gold". President Nixon responded by closing "the gold window" on 15 August 1971, when the amount of US currency in circulation, the CPI and the Fed's holdings of US Treasury debt were all accelerating. The Bretton Woods gold standard ended on that day.

The problem that Nixon faced with a fixed price of dollars for gold was that the free market price of dollars for gold had risen above the official price, and France had decided to stop importing US inflation and, instead, to start redeeming US dollars for gold. Any nation within a fixed exchange rate system is subject to losing reserves once its currency becomes less valued in markets than the official exchange rate. With the fixed official exchange rate, in this case of $35 per ounce of gold, set below the respective market rate, then once reserves began to flow out there would soon be no more reserves left.

With no reserves at all, the dollar could not be converted into gold and the gold standard would necessarily fail. Given the amount of money printing taking place, Nixon could see this scenario unfolding until the US ran out of gold, so he suspended indefinitely the exchange of dollars for gold. This pulled up the golden anchor of the Bretton Woods system in the storm of the Vietnam War, sank the gold standard-bearer of the US dollar redemption and blew in the fiat era of currency without explicit backing by gold.

From 1961 to 2021, as Figure 2.2 shows, rising US inflation spread internationally throughout Bretton Woods countries. Using quarterly data, the annual CPI inflation rate is given for Germany, the United Kingdom, France, Switzerland, Japan and the United States. The inflation rates began rising in the 1960s and accelerated between 1971 and 1973, when the market price of gold began rising while the fixed exchange rates of Bretton Woods were still in place.

As with the US inflation, the signatories of the Bretton Woods agreement suffered similar increases in inflation as the Vietnam War progressed. They valiantly attempted to keep in place the benefits of the stability of the $35 anchor, despite the cost of importing the US inflation under the fixed exchange rate system. Shortly after the fixed exchange rates were ended in 1973, the inflation rates of the non-US signatories peaked and then began to trend downwards.

The United States also reached a peak inflation rate around the same time, but it then experienced an even bigger increase in inflation several years later. After accumulating high quantities of US dollars to protect the $35 price, and importing inflation, the non-US signatories could finally let loose their increased dollar reserves that they no longer needed. This wash of US dollars flooded back into the United States, with the result that the United States experienced even higher inflation than after fixed exchange rates ended.

The IMF describes in its online report "The end of the Bretton Woods system (1972–81)" that "[a]n attempt to revive the fixed exchange rates failed, and by March 1973 the major currencies began to float against each other". The German central bank, the Bundesbank, writes online about the Deutsche Mark (D-Mark,

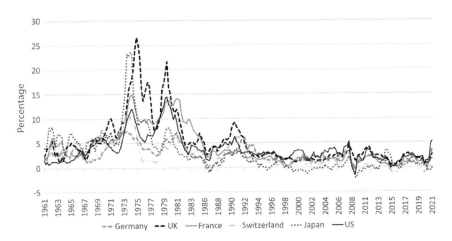

Figure 2.2 CPI inflation: Germany, the United Kingdom, France, Switzerland, Japan and the United States, 1961Q1–2021Q3
Source: FRED.

or DM) exchanges at the time that were required to stabilize the US dollar gold price:

> In 1971, the greenback came under pressure and frequently landed at the lower intervention limit against the D-Mark. That was the point at which the Bundesbank had to intervene to support the dollar. In April and early May 1971, the Bundesbank had to buy USD 6 billion, for which it paid DM 22 billion. The higher money supply stoked inflation.

In the first quarter of 1974 the German inflation rate peaked at 7.5 per cent. In the third quarter of 1974 the Japanese inflation rate peaked at 23.5 per cent, followed in the fourth quarter of the year by the Swiss inflation rate peaking at 11 per cent, the French peaking at 15 per cent and the US reaching a peak of 12 per cent. In the third quarter of 1975 the UK inflation rate peaked at 26.5 per cent. Then, in the second quarter of 1980, US inflation reached its highest rate since the Second World War, of 14 per cent.

In January 1973 the United States signed a peace treaty with North Vietnam, but the fighting continued until April 1975, when Saigon was captured by North Vietnam. With the gold window closed in August 1971, a new set of fixed exchange rates was established in December 1971, with the US dollar devalued within these rates, until a final breakdown of the second set of fixed exchange rates occurred in March 1973. During the breakdown of Bretton Woods, from 1971 to 1973, the world moved onto a "fiat monetary standard".

Just as Roman dictators made laws by "fiat", or by declaration, the US Federal Reserve Note is a legal means of exchange as declared by fiat. Since 1971 the currency has been without the promise of redemption into metal. The US currency has never yet returned to the metallic standard stipulated by the US Constitution. And yet, gold still sits in the central banks' vaults. The next chapter describes this gold, the ages when the gold standard was in place and how it worked, and the relation of money to the metal. It outlines the modern history of the gold standard, how the ratio of money to gold value changed and what gold central banks hold today.

3

THE END OF METAL FOR MONEY

The Bank of England is located around the corner from Lombard Street in central London. When visitors walk in through the door, very few ever view the vault's gold, the value of which is second only to that of the Federal Reserve Bank of New York.

The United States also holds gold, in its US Mint depository at Fort Knox, made famous by the movie *Goldfinger*. Movies about gold made in the 1960s were filmed when the Bretton Woods system bound together the Western alliance in a US-based metallic gold monetary standard. The US gold backed the US dollar, just as the Bank of England's gold backed sterling after the Bank Charter Act of 1844, passed by the government headed by Sir Robert Peel, as described in Bagehot's *Lombard Street* (1873).

Once the Bretton Woods system had broken down, we might expect that the gold would be dispersed, and be used to finance normal spending by governments. In the United States, the Gold Reserve Act of 1934 required the Fed to transfer ownership of its gold to the US Treasury. The Treasury owns the gold in Fort Knox, issues US debt in order to borrow to cover deficits when its spending exceeds tax revenue and could sell the gold assets to cover some of the government deficits.

In the event, however, the main repositories of gold during the gold standard period retain much of the same gold today as they did when currency was redeemable in gold. Central bank gold stocks have not been sold off. They languish indefinitely in vaults at the cost of security and storage space, despite the paper-based fiat world in which we live.

The US Federal Reserve Bank of New York has the largest depository of gold in the world. The New York Fed holds only about 5 per cent of US Treasury gold, however, which in total is worth about $11 billion in 2018 prices. The rest of the gold is held for other countries.

The US Mint stores the remaining 95 per cent of US Treasury gold, weighing in at 8,133 metric tonnes. Founded in 1792, the US Mint acts as custodian for the US Treasury gold. Most of this gold still resides in the US Mint's Fort Knox depository, built after President Roosevelt issued an executive order in 1933 outlawing the private ownership of gold coinage.

Recent data show that the Mint depository at Fort Knox is home to 4,580 tonnes, or 56 per cent of the gold holdings. Other major storage facilities are in West Point, New York (21 per cent of the holdings), and in Denver, Colorado (17 per cent). In 2021 the total amount of US-owned gold ranked first in the world, followed by Germany (3,359 tonnes), Italy (2,452 tonnes), France (2,436 tonnes), Russia (2,292 tonnes), China (1,948 tonnes), Switzerland (1,040 tonnes) and Japan (846 tonnes).

The value of gold is measured in terms of "fine troy ounces". Internationally, quantities of precious metals are measured in weight using this standard of troy ounces. Ancient Rome divided bronze bars into a dozen pieces, each called an "ounce", and weighing 31.1 grams. In medieval times this weight system was adopted in Troyes, France, giving rise to the "troy ounce".

The United States officially values its gold at a fixed price of $42.22 per troy ounce. This is quite different from the current market value of gold, although close to its market value when the gold standard ended. For September 1971 the price was $42.40. The United States values its gold stock using the price that existed shortly after President Nixon closed the gold exchange "window" at the Fed in August 1971.

The dollar price of gold remained approximately at its official price of $35 throughout the years from the founding of Bretton Woods in 1946 until 1967. When the Bretton Woods regime began to weaken because of the acceleration in the money supply, the market price of gold began rising above $35, starting in 1968. US dollars flooded the market while the Vietnam War raged, causing the dollar price per ounce to rise.

This can be seen in Figure 3.1. Starting in 1968, it shows the gold price of the London bullion market in US dollars. It also illustrates, for comparison, the US dollar oil price, as normalized by multiplying it by 15, from the first quarter of 1946 to the third quarter of 2021. After closing the gold exchange window in 1971, the remnants of Bretton Woods continued with fixed exchange rates among signatory nations for about two years. As the complete end of the regime approached, the market price of gold rose dramatically, to $115 by July 1973.

The $115 price occurred three months before the Middle East "oil embargo", announced on 19 October 1973. At the end of September 2021 the gold price stood at $1,788. The normalized oil price level moved rather closely with the US dollar price of gold. This is because both gold and oil prices build in the expected future US dollar inflation rate.

Without the Bretton Woods gold standard, the dollar price of gold was no longer "fixed". Oil and gold prices moved together once Bretton Woods ended.

Figure 3.1 US dollar gold (London fixing) and oil (West Texas Intermediate [WTI]) prices, 1946–2021
Source: FRED.

But when it operated, so that oil price contracts were certain of a set value of the US dollar, how did the gold price remain fixed at $35 per troy ounce while the Bretton Woods system reigned?

In essence, the United States had to stabilize the price of gold in terms of US dollars by buying and selling gold with US dollars (and other international reserves) so that the $35 target price was achieved in the open marketplace, by sufficiently regulating the amount of dollars in circulation relative to the amount of gold in the marketplace for gold. For example, the United States could have printed only enough money during the Bretton Woods regime to supply the growing demand for money resulting from the ongoing economic growth as the US economy gradually expanded. As an economy's total value of output expands, it tends to demand more money for transactions. If the Fed had supplied enough money only to meet the naturally rising money demand, then keeping the gold price a constant $35 would have remained feasible.

The US dollar price per ounce of gold had varied over time, however, because of the Fed printing more US dollars than were strictly needed to meet the private economy's naturally growing demand, by financing the Treasury deficits incurred during wartime spending. In Figure 3.2, looking at the difference between the total Treasury debt and the Treasury debt held by the Fed shows the increasing rate of Fed purchases of such debt. For the first quarter of 1954 to the third quarter of 1974, the growth rate in the amount of the US Treasury debt held by the Fed largely exceeds the growth rate in the amount of the total

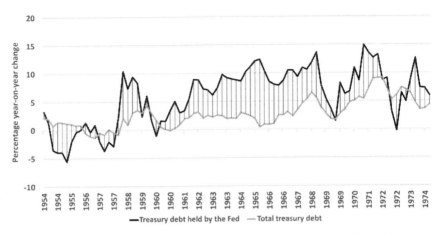

Figure 3.2 US Treasury debt held by the Fed and total US Treasury debt, 1954Q1–1974Q3
Source: FRED.

outstanding US Treasury debt. The vertical shading lines show the difference in the growth rates.

Starting after 1957, the Fed increased its holdings of Treasury debt at a faster rate than the Treasury increased the debt. After a 10 per cent surge in the Fed's holdings in 1957–58, the Fed steadily accelerated its Treasury debt holdings from 1959 up to a 13.6 per cent rate of accumulation at the peak of the United States' Vietnam War troop presence, in 1968. This rose to a 15 per cent growth rate in Fed holdings of the debt in 1970, and was rising at a 13 per cent rate when Nixon closed the gold window in the third quarter of 1971.

The Fed's acceleration of its buying of Treasury debt, to a rate that was even faster than the debt was being issued, is equivalent to the Fed printing money at an accelerating rate from 1959 to 1968, with another surge after 1969 until Bretton Woods abruptly ended in 1971.

A stable gold price had a long historical precedent through a stable exchange rate between a currency and its purchase of a set amount of gold. Although many countries were on the gold standard from 1880 to 1914, we will consider two major ones, those of the United Kingdom and the United States, in more detail. This history begins with a famous physicist.

After the founding of the Bank of England in 1694, Sir Isaac Newton, as master of the Royal Mint, in 1717 set the price of gold at £4.25 per troy ounce. It stayed at that price until 1914, except during the war years of 1797 to 1821, when Britain suspended the gold standard while fighting France. After Britain again suspended the gold standard in 1914, it marked the end of what is known as the "classic gold standard" according to monetary historians (such as Bordo 1981).

The United States started out on a bimetallic standard in 1792, with its first Coinage Act denoting the weights in gold and silver that $1 could buy, namely 24.75 grains of pure gold. Here one troy ounce of gold equals 480 grains of gold, or 31 grams. The dollar equally could buy 371.25 grains of pure silver. This implied an exchange rate of silver for gold of 371.25/24.75 = 15.0.

With the 1792 Act, the official US price of gold was $19.75 per troy ounce, which it raised somewhat to $20.67 in 1834 when the country was still on a bimetallic money standard using both gold and silver. The US price of one troy ounce of gold remained at $20.67 even after the United States had gone onto a gold-only standard in 1879, when silver was no longer redeemable for coinage. This price held up, with occasional departures, until the Fed was founded in 1914. For other countries also on the gold standard, from 1879 to 1914, this ensured fixed exchange rates between one country and another's currency.

The same $20.67 price in British pounds ("sterling") was £4.25. Therefore, when going onto a gold-only standard in 1879, the United States did so with parity to the UK pound sterling. One dollar could buy 1/(20.67) = 0.0484 ounces of gold, and one pound sterling could buy 1/(4.25) = 0.235 ounces of gold. The ratio of 0.235/0.0484 = 4.86, which gives how many dollars were needed to buy £1.

The international exchange rate was thereby established between the Bank of England's pound notes and US dollars, based on the amount of gold that could be bought with each currency. £1 cost $4.86 in US currency. Dividing the US price of $20.67 per ounce of gold by the UK price of £4.25 per ounce gives exactly 4.86 dollars per pound sterling, which is the exchange rate between the currencies.

The end of this classic gold standard in 1914 marks an inflection point in monetary history. Given Figure 3.1, one can imagine that there is always a market price for a metal, or a commodity such as oil, which in turn is determined by the supply and demand for that metal or commodity. With the Fed's establishment in 1914 came the stresses of the First World War, which led to the printing of money to cover wartime deficits, increasing currency relative to the gold supply and making the $20.67 price untenable, and the suspension of gold conversion during the war.

The First World War thereby began a further evolution in international monetary regimes. After starting under a bimetallic standard of both gold and silver coinage redemption, the US regime went to a gold-only coinage redemption, and then to a regime with gold changing hands within the US Mint at a higher fixed dollar price of gold. After 1971 came the fiat regime, with gold remaining in vaults and with the dollar price of gold rising exorbitantly as the price index rose at an accelerated rate.

To see the evolution, it helps to understand how a bimetallic standard works, as Friedman (1994) details. A bimetallic standard allowed the stabilization of the dollar price of gold, as well as that of the dollar price of silver, by using a pre-specified mix of silver and gold in making coins for legal tender. The idea was that, by specifying an exchange rate between silver and gold that approximately matched the relative world supply of silver to gold, a stable dollar price in terms of both silver and gold could be maintained for a long period of time.

In 1792 Treasury Secretary Alexander Hamilton recommended that the US Congress establish coinage with a 15 to 1 ratio of silver to gold. Friedman (1994) tells us that the current price of silver in terms of gold was precisely at that ratio. Soon after 1792, however, the world price of gold in terms of silver rose above 15 to 1, so that the official price of gold was below the market price.

The 1792 Act required that the US Mint freely provide dollar coinage (which included some alloys) given in either silver or gold. And the coins could be converted back to silver or gold. In coinage, one ounce of gold was worth fifteen ounces of silver. In the marketplace, one ounce of gold bought more than fifteen ounces of silver.

With gold being more valuable in the market than in the US Mint, people chose to use silver for conversion into coins. They kept hold of their gold and, if needed, they could convert it into more silver on the free market than at the US Mint. With the US Mint taking in silver for coinage rather than gold, the United States became, in effect, a silver regime monetary system, with silver used for getting coinage as money.

An 1834 Act reversed people's choice instead to using gold for coinage. It did this by setting a price of gold above its then prevailing market price rather than below it, as previously. According to Friedman (1994), by 1834 the market price of gold in terms of silver was 15.625 to 1. The Coinage Act of 1834 reset the official US Mint exchange rate of gold in terms of silver at 16 to 1.

With an official price of gold higher than the market price, gold was now exchanged for coins rather than silver. People thus kept their silver and sent gold to the US Mint in exchange for dollar coins. They could sell the silver on the market for more gold than they could get from the US Mint for their silver.

With the US Mint now collecting gold for coins instead of silver, the 1834 change in the official exchange rate induced the United States to switch to a gold-based monetary standard. The Specie Payment Resumption Act of 1875, which took effect at the beginning of 1879, allowed coinage only for gold. It ended the exchange of silver for coins. The United States went from an unofficial silver standard from 1792 to 1834 to an unofficial gold standard from 1834 to 1879 to an official gold-only standard from 1879 to 1914.

In 1914, as we have seen, the United States suspended the gold standard during the war, as did other nations. In his study of the interwar period, Crabbe (1989) describes the wartime inflationary finance motive for the gold standard suspension: "During the First World War, the United States and other belligerents fully or partly suspended the gold standard, de jure or de facto, to prevent it from hampering the war effort."

In 1920 the United States returned to a $20.67 redemption of gold for dollars, inducing a deep recession, as the money supply had to contract to regain the pre-war gold "parity" price of $20.67. Crabbe describes how the United States also helped the United Kingdom to restore the gold standard at this original parity, culminating in Winston Churchill, as Chancellor of the Exchequer, ending limits on the export of gold. The UK Parliament then passed the Gold Standard Act of 1925, and officially returned the United Kingdom to the gold standard at pre-war parity. By the end of 1925 this had led 39 countries to re-establish parity with the US dollar through similar actions (Wandschneider 2008).

For 1879 to 1924, Figure 3.3 shows the market value of the US gold reserve holdings versus the currency in circulation. During this gold standard period the estimated average is drawn in a line (with a slope of 1.23) that shows almost a one-to-one relation between gold value and the currency value up until the First World War. Money currency increased as the gold stock increased, the currency

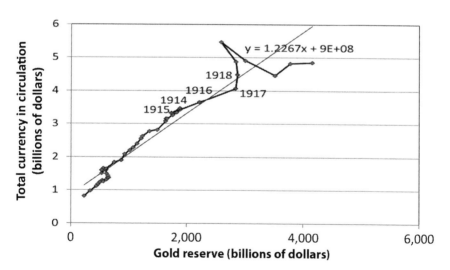

Figure 3.3 Total currency in circulation versus gold reserves, United States, 1879–1924. Data corresponding to the First World War
Sources: FRED; and Macrohistory database, produced by the National Bureau of Economic Research (NBER), section XIV, "Money and banking", available at: www.nber.org/research/data/nber-macrohistory-xiv-money-and-banking.

price of gold remained fixed and the ratio of the amount of the currency to the value of the gold remained stable.

In July 1914 Austria-Hungary declared war on Serbia, with Russia, Belgium, France, Great Britain and Serbia drawn into war with Austria-Hungary and Germany, so that by August the First World War had begun. The US Federal Reserve System began operating in November 1914, when its 12 regional banks opened. The Fed's job was to print new currency as Federal Reserve Notes that were backed by gold, to keep sufficient gold reserves so that the money could be converted back to gold and to convert the paper money back into gold upon demand.

Initially, the war caused a large outflow of US gold reserves. This happened after London exchanges shut down in July, panic ensued and pounds sterling became scarce and could buy more gold in the marketplace than at the official price. The market price of US dollars per British pound rose to $6.75, above the official price of $4.86. This made it worthwhile to buy pounds with US dollars, causing an international redemption of dollars for gold and an outflow of US gold (Crabbe 1989).

After the Fed opened, other nations abandoned the gold standard, whereas the United States did not. Gold began flowing back into the country from abroad. The value of the US gold stock rose 82 per cent, from $1.57 billion to $2.85 billion, between August 1914 and April 1917. The gold inflow caused increases in the US money stock and price level, with high inflation ensuing.

US CPI inflation rose from 1 per cent in October 1915 to 20 per cent in May 1917, while currency and bank deposits rose by 70 per cent from November 1914 to November 1918 (when the armistice was signed) and wholesale prices doubled. When the United States entered the war, in 1917, it effectively suspended gold conversion by requiring special permission for conversion, which lasted until June 1919. From January 1917 until August 1920 the US year-on-year inflation rate was between 13 per cent and 20 per cent every month. Then, from February 1921 to October 1922, a deflationary period followed with negative inflation rates, ranging between −5 per cent and −16 per cent.

In Germany, a different scenario unfolded when the government attempted to pay war reparations to the Allies without having a sufficient tax base for raising revenue. This led it to printing money for government expenditure. The value of its paper money in circulation fell steadily after 1918, until hyperinflation ensued during 1922 and 1923 so that, by November 1923, one US dollar was worth more than 4 trillion German Marks. Meanwhile, France and Belgium militarily attacked parts of Germany in January 1923, because of insufficient war reparation payments from the country, helping lay the ground for the Second World War.

With Britain's temporary return to the gold standard in 1925, there was a short-lived gold regime called the "gold exchange standard", which lasted from 1925 to

1931. The US and UK gold acted as reserves for a set of countries attempting to return to a gold standard. This ended after the United Kingdom abandoned the gold standard in 1929. For 1925 to 1931, Figure 3.4 shows how the US currency in circulation circled around relative to the value of gold reserves, ending in 1931 at the point in the upper right of the graph.

The United States officially remained on the traditional gold standard until President Roosevelt suspended it in April 1933, set a fixed price of gold at $35 an ounce in January 1934 and effected a 59 per cent depreciation of the dollar relative to the $20.67 value of 1834. The US Gold Reserve Act vested the US Treasury with all gold ownership, prohibited redemption in gold domestically and allowed only international transactions to be settled in gold. This created a narrower ability to convert dollars to gold compared to the original bimetallic standard of 1792 and the gold standard of 1879, since Americans making transactions in the United States could not convert their own currency into gold.

After the US stock market crash of 1929 and subsequent bank panic, despite the latter gold inflow, the decline in bank deposits caused a major deflation. In the words of Leland Crabbe (1989): "From October 1929 to March 1933, wholesale prices in the United States fell 37 per cent, and farm prices plummeted 65 per cent."

Through the creation of the Federal Deposit Insurance Corporation (FDIC), with the Emergency Banking Act of March 1933, Roosevelt renewed confidence

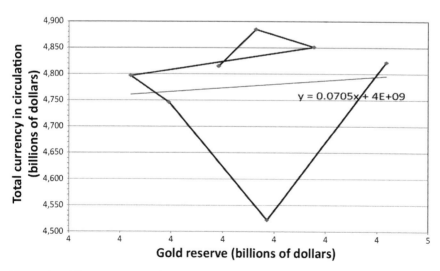

Figure 3.4 US currency in circulation versus gold reserves, gold exchange standard, 1925–31
Sources: FRED; and Macrohistory.

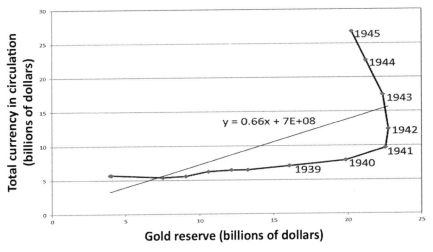

Figure 3.5 US currency in circulation versus gold reserves, weakened gold standard, 1932–46. Data corresponding to the Second World War
Sources: FRED; and Macrohistory.

in the private banking system, ended the run on the banks and caused currency to be redeposited back into them and then lent out for investment. There was an immediate resurgence of private bank demand deposits, an end to deflation and the end of the Great Depression (dated as March 1933). Despite a rapid recovery in the level of real GDP by 1937, however, malaise continued in the US economy. The unemployment rate, 25 per cent as of March 1933, steadily fell to 11 per cent by 1937, but during a short recession rose to 20 per cent in June 1938, before falling back to 16 per cent at the beginning of 1940.

After Germany annexed western Poland in 1939, starting the Second World War, Roosevelt in 1941 began the "Lend-Lease" programme of supplying military supplies to the United Kingdom. By June 1942 the US unemployment rate was zero – as it had been in August 1929. The US–UK agreement between Roosevelt and Churchill, the British prime minister, agreed that repayment would take place through "joint action directed towards the creation of a liberalized international economic order in the postwar world" (US State Department website).

For the period from 1932 to 1946, Figure 3.5 shows the amount of the US currency relative to the value of gold, starting at the bottom left in 1932, with each year linked together sequentially. With the gold inflow being met by a small increase in currency from 1932 to 1940, the line in the graph curves upwards and backwards after 1940. This reflects the rapid increase in the amount of currency in circulation during the US military build-up for war. Through the Fed buying

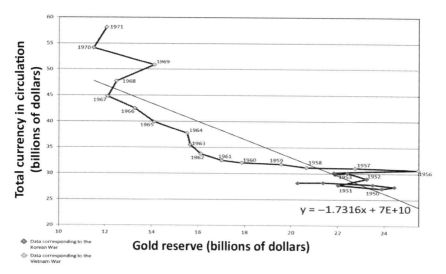

Figure 3.6 US currency in circulation versus gold reserves, Bretton Woods system, 1946–71

Sources: FRED; and Macrohistory.

Treasury debt more rapidly than it accumulated gold, it financed government expenditure during the war and led to periods of high inflation. From October 1941 to December 1942 the inflation rate ranged between 9 per cent and 13 per cent, and from July 1946 to August 1947 it ranged between 9 per cent and 20 per cent.

High US inflation during the conflict, the Allied victory and the US–UK Lend-Lease provisions for establishing a liberal economic setting led to calls for the resumption of an international gold regime for Western countries. In considering how to establish a new gold regime, the 1944 Bretton Woods conference called for a gold standard even more narrowly defined than that of Roosevelt. As emphasized above, the new Bretton Woods gold regime, which began in 1946, allowed only international central banks to convert US dollars to gold.

For the years 1946 to 1971, Figure 3.6 presents the data from the Bretton Woods era for the value of currency versus the value of the US gold reserve. Now the negative slope of the graph is the reverse of the positive slope during the 1879–1914 classic gold standard era. Starting in the bottom right corner in Figure 3.6, for 1946, the line moves to the right as the US gold value initially rose relative to currency. The line becomes jagged, however, during the Korean War years, 1950 to 1953, which saw US inflation of 9 per cent in the first half of 1951.

From 1956 to 1967 the line in Figure 3.6 moves to the left (with a negative slope), as the money supply rises and the US gold reserves are exported, mainly

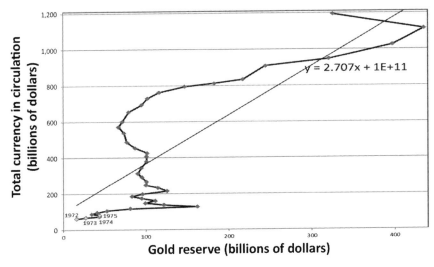

Figure 3.7 US currency in circulation versus gold reserves, 1972–2013. Data corresponding to the Vietnam War
Sources: FRED; and Macrohistory.

to Europe. This occurred during the era of US involvement in the Vietnam War, which began in November 1955 when the United States established the US Military Assistance Advisory Group, Vietnam. With a jagged movement upwards from 1967 to 1971, as the Bretton Woods system attempted to maintain the $35 price of gold, the system finally collapsed when the United States prohibited further dollar conversion to gold.

After the Bretton Woods system was abandoned in 1971, for the fiat years 1972 to 2013, Figure 3.7 presents data for currency versus the value of gold that was based on a free market price. With the Vietnam War continuing into 1975, and with the freely floating price of gold as seen in Figure 3.1, the value of the gold reserve initially increased relative to currency holdings as the gold price built in expected future inflation. This continued until 1980, at which point the Volcker decrease in the inflation rate occurred.

After 1983, Figure 3.7 shows a vertical movement upwards in the graph, as the Fed continued printing money and currency rose relative to the value of gold. The 2001 terrorist attacks marked when this march up in currency relative to gold value took a turn to the right, which in the figure is shown to last up until 2012. As occurred after 1971, the post-2001 US money supply acceleration caused the gold price to rise more rapidly than currency, as the price of gold also included an increase in the expected inflation rate. The value of US gold rose right through the 2008–09 financial crisis. Gold prices fell sharply

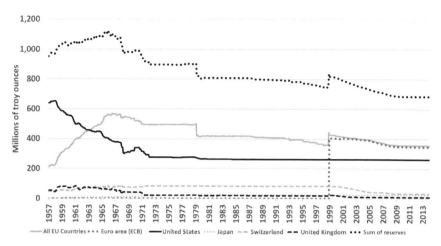

Figure 3.8 Gold holdings in major areas, 1957–2013
Sources: FRED; Macrohistory; and IMF.

for nearly a year after September 2012, and the gold value relative to currency fell in 2013.

The fiat era years here indicate currency rising relative to gold value, with an average relation of 2.7 to one (as seen in the regression line), as opposed to a one-to-one relation under the traditional gold standard. The gold standard illustrated in Figure 3.3 has a similar relation to the fiat era, the difference being that the fiat period had about two to three times the ratio of currency to gold value relative to the classic gold standard. This resulted in a positive trend inflation rate during the fiat era, as opposed to a zero-trend inflation rate during the traditional gold standard. The strong caveat, as illustrated in the next chapter, is that the metallic regime entailed much greater volatility in the inflation rate, which is harmful to the economy.

Gold reserves were needed under a gold standard to redeem currency for the stipulated metal indicated by the currency. If the dollar market price of the gold exceeded the official price, reserves would flow out until none were left. Bimetallism offered a way to help keep sufficient metals on hand to meet the official exchange rate of metal for currency, perhaps in a more stable but complex fashion than was possible with just a gold standard.

When the Bretton Woods standard ended, the ratio of US currency to the free market value of the gold stock had doubled. But there was still a lot of gold being held across the world. From 1957 to 2013, Figure 3.8 shows gold in millions of ounces held by the United States, the United Kingdom, the European Union, the European Central Bank (ECB), Switzerland and Japan, and the sum of these.

Starting in 1957, the total gold for these nations (omitting the ECB, to avoid double-counting) rose above 1,000 million ounces in the 1960s, fell to 900 million ounces between 1971 and 1978, stepped down to 800 million ounces until about 1998 and then fell to 700 million ounces up to the end of the sample. The total world gold reserve has been stable since the Bretton Woods regime ended, with world gold reserves standing at 1,085 million ounces in January 1957 and 1,025 million ounces in December 2013, and little fluctuation as the world transitioned from a gold standard to fiat. Ten countries in 2021 altogether held 765 million ounces: the United States, Germany, Italy, France, Russia, China, Switzerland, Japan, India and the Netherlands.

The Vietnam War took its toll on US gold. After starting in January 1957 with 639 million ounces, this fell to 308 million ounces in February 1969, to 291 million ounces by August 1971 (when Nixon closed the Fed gold exchange window), to 276 million ounces from 1972 to 1978, and to between 263 and 265 million ounces from 1979 to 1985. From 1986 until today the holding has been a constant 262 million ounces.

The United Kingdom's gold reserve started at 53 million ounces in August 1957 and fell to 22 million ounces in August 1971. From this level at the start of the fiat era, the UK gold holding dropped to 10 million ounces by 2002, where it has remained up until 2021. The United Kingdom divested itself of half its gold during the fiat era and then held tight.

The EU nations started at 212 million ounces in 1957, increased their reserves to 562 million ounces in 1967 under Bretton Woods and settled at near to 355 million ounces in 2013. The ECB gold is close in amount to that of the European Union. Switzerland had 83 million ounces of gold from 1971 to 2000, and then dropped to 33 million ounces. Japan's gold stock since 1973 has varied between 21 and 27 million ounces.

Currency now has no intrinsic value, but almost 80 per cent of the gold stock held at the end of Bretton Woods remains in reserves for these countries. It seems that central banks implicitly back up their new post-1971 fiat currencies by still holding gold reserves. As Sargent (1986) and Bernholz (2016) describe the history of central banking, central banks have to recapitalize after a currency breaks down, such as during a period of hyperinflation, to regain confidence in the new currency.

Even though the paper money that circulates can no longer be converted into gold by the central banks, central banks still love gold, as its price rises with inflation. Holding about 20 per cent less gold since the end of the gold standard, the fiat world could be viewed as one step further along in the evolution of narrowing the degree by which currency is backed by gold. Now gold can remain in vaults, without changing hands or drawers, and instil confidence in currency even during moderate inflation.

Friedman (1994: 16) notes the difference between the market price of gold and the official price, with the latter coming from the end of Bretton Woods: "Central banks, including the US Federal Reserve System, still carry an entry on their balance sheets for gold, valued a fixed nominal price, but that is simply the smile of a vanished Cheshire cat."

The real value of gold reserves may still have value to people holding currency. We print money to finance government expenditure, target the inflation rate and keep the gold vaults almost full – just in case. The next chapter provides examples of how changes in gold or silver supplies can affect the price level. Then it lays out a fuller historical record of how the price level changed during the metallic regime, and after its ending with fiat money – with gold still shimmering in our vaults.

4

WAR, PEACE, DEFLATION AND RECESSION

In the *Goldfinger* movie of 1964, as based on Ian Fleming's 1959 book, the eponymous Goldfinger accumulates as much gold as possible for "50 years" and then attempts to render the US Fort Knox gold stock radioactive. With the Fort Knox gold reserve unable to circulate, the idea is that the value of the remaining gold stock should increase dramatically. This would be the result of an act of terrorism ("economic chaos in the West") to enhance Goldfinger's personal wealth.

Although this might bring to mind the real and equally fiendish efforts by Russia's president, Vladimir Putin, to monopolize oil and gas wealth, consider the question of whether the act of making radioactive the gold in Fort Knox would devalue that gold at all. If everyone respected that the United States had the same amount of gold before and after Fort Knox became radioactive, then the price of gold would be unaffected. The gold would still be in Fort Knox, and it would still be valued at the international price of gold.

Friedman (1994) tells the story of Yap, an island in Micronesia that during the twentieth century used stone wheels ("fei") for money hewn from limestone rock on an island 400 miles away. One large wheel had been made for an islander and was being delivered by boat; the boat capsized, and the wheel sank to the bottom. The islanders acknowledged that the islander owned the wheel in the sea and gave monetary credit against the value of that wheel even though it could not be retrieved.

The stone wheel story illustrates how an asset's value holds, even if it is not in circulation. The world may be less trusting than the people of Yap, however. It might not respect the US ownership of the Fort Knox gold if it was radioactive, which, like the Yap stone, could no longer circulate. If not, then this would effectively decrease the quantity of the gold from the rest of the world stock of gold. The decrease in the gold supply would make the remaining gold more valuable, as Goldfinger envisaged.

A decrease in gold, as in Goldfinger's scheme and Friedman's sinking of a stone near Yap, actually occurred in the United States when the SS *Central America*, or "the Ship of Gold", sank in September 1857 with thousands of pounds of gold that New York bankers were awaiting. After the August 1857 failure of the Ohio Life Insurance and Trust Company, which had a branch in New York, a bank panic ensued in September that spread across the United States and to Britain, being one of the first international financial crises. In the United States, deflation occurred, railroad companies failed and the northern states financing risky railroad and westward expansion suffered. The agricultural southern states became emboldened, and tension built up that spilled over into the American Civil War.

During historical metallic standards based on gold and silver, the price of goods in terms of the metal varies as the supply of the metal changes. Schwartz (1973: 245) documents ancient inflation because of war, by Alexander the Great. After conquering the Persian Empire and importing gold back through the Hellenistic economy, that economy effectively went from being on a silver standard to a gold standard. Gold became cheaper than silver. Gold coinage became dominant, and prices rose as the amount of gold increased. As Schwartz (1973: 245) relates:

> The one case of a documented price level change in the annals of ancient Greece occurred because of Alexander the Great's conquest of the Persian kingdom (330 BC). Immense hoards of Persian gold were introduced by him into the Greek economy, transforming a silver into a predominantly gold standard. Prices and wages increased not only in Greece but also throughout the Hellenistic empire, as gold coinage was diffused through trade in markets from India and Egypt to Western Mediterranean lands.

Five hundred years ago the Aztecs expanded by military conquest throughout Central America. Hernán Cortés landed in North America and in 1520 fought the Aztec emperor Moctezuma, who subsequently died. In 1531 Francisco Pizarro attacked the Inca in Peru, as did Diego de Almagro. These military expeditions and the subsequent conquests resulted in the arrival of gold and silver into bimetallic Europe (Machemer 2020). Schwartz (1973: 250) also documents this influx of metal into Europe: "By 1660, the close of the period of Spanish imports, the European stock of gold had nearly doubled, and the stock of silver had increased three and two-fifths."

She finds that the inflation rate for a century, from about 1500 to 1600, averaged between 1 and 2 per cent a year in England, France and Spain. The large metallic stock increase in Europe occurred over a sustained period, leading to what today we view as a very modest inflation rate. Bernholz (2016: 29) tells us this moderate inflation was known as the "Great Price Revolution of the 16th century", which it may have seemed relative to the stable prices during the centuries of the Renaissance.

During a freely floating price for gold in terms of dollars, when the gold stock increases, the price of goods in terms of gold must also increase. There is more gold (and silver) to buy some amount of goods so the price of goods in a given weight of gold (or silver) coin rises. Conversely, the value of each ounce of gold must go down in terms of how many goods it can buy. If the value of gold in terms of goods is lower, and the price of goods in terms of gold is higher, then more gold has to be given up for each good purchased, and the aggregate price level for goods in terms of a set gold coinage also rises.

Inflation like this can be more intuitive than deflation from less of the metal used as a monetary standard. The Goldfinger scenario is the opposite case, in that here the quantity of gold would be decreased. Nevertheless, this takes place during a fixed price regime for the amount of dollars per gold. The gold decrease would take place only in the reserve vault of the US Mint, rather than in the amount of gold circulating other than in central banks.

Different scenarios are possible if the Fort Knox gold became radioactive and people feared that this gold essentially went out of existence. If the United States could simply borrow from the rest of the central banks the same amount of gold reserves as had become radioactive, it could shore up its reserves in that way. Then the public might resume having confidence in the gold standard as it was, with the dollar price of gold remaining stable.

At the time, however, the United States held most of the world's central bank gold reserves. Another possibility is that other central banks would or could not lend gold to the United States. If people viewed the gold stock as being decreased once news of the radioactivity of Fort Knox became public, then the market value of gold might indeed rise, meaning that every ounce of gold could buy more goods.

During historic increases in the gold stock, each ounce of gold could buy fewer goods and the price level went up and caused inflation. With an ounce of gold instead being able to buy more goods, the opposite would happen. The market value of gold in dollars would fall below $35 and the price level would fall, as in a deflationary episode. If spread internationally to the Bretton Woods countries, this could cause a worldwide deflation as a result of terrorism by detonation of a neutron bomb in the US Mint, as had happened by the sinking of a ship of gold at sea.

Severe deflation can lead to bank panic and depression, as also occurred in the Great Depression. As the price level drops, businesses receive fewer dollars on sales of goods but must pay back loans in the quantity of dollars that was specified during price stability. Loans go into default and companies and banks become insolvent.

If the United States could not borrow gold reserves, the United States could still avoid deflation. It could buy up gold on the open market, increase the quantity of dollars and US gold reserves and possibly stabilize the price of gold in dollars at $35. If a deal was reached with Goldfinger to buy his gold, the United States might stabilize the international economy at the cost of enriching the terrorist through negotiation with him.

Negotiation with Goldfinger could induce others to act similarly. This would constitute the "moral hazard" of ensuring international banking stability, in that it might increase the likelihood of the threat emerging again in the future. This insurance of the international monetary and banking regime, after the Goldfinger crisis had already occurred, would be less efficient because of moral hazard than ensuring beforehand that such a crisis could not occur in the first place. For example, the gold reserve might have been dispersed across different locations, at higher cost, but with less risk of moral hazard from acting only after the crisis.

Under the traditional gold standard, countries faced similar threats of deflation, typically after war. During the American Civil War, after the US Treasury borrowed as much gold and silver from private banks as was possible, the United States began printing the "greenback" dollar to finance the war expenditure. The increase in these notes was not immediately redeemable in gold, although they promised future redemption. This led to a higher price of gold in terms of dollars and wartime inflation as the price of goods in greenbacks increased.

At the end of the civil war the United States could have devalued its currency, and its international debt denominated in that currency, or returned to parity at pre-war levels. Parity meant returning to the UK price of gold, and the pre-war US price of gold at $20.67 dollars per gold ounce. To achieve parity, the United States had various options.

It could have increased its Treasury gold stock by borrowing and using the gold to buy up US greenback dollars until the dollar price fell back to parity. The United States was already heavily indebted, however, and interest rates on loans were high. This was because central banks were then limited in number, such as in Sweden (1668), England (1694) and France (1800), and international private banks would be the only source. If the United States could not increase the Treasury gold stock by borrowing, then the country would need to decrease the rate of growth of the greenback dollars until parity was achieved.

The United States chose to decrease the money supply growth rate, and deflation occurred for over a decade until the pre-war parity of dollars for gold could be re-established. After silver redemption in dollars was ended in 1873, so that only gold could be redeemed, the Specie Payment Resumption Act of 1875 re-established gold redemption of the greenback dollars at pre-war parity. This redemption became effective in 1879.

Deflation continued after 1879, when gold became relatively scarce in supply as the economy grew. Friedman (1994) argues that the deflation could have been avoided by maintaining redemption in both silver and gold. He calculates that the supply ratio of the metals would have remained sufficiently stable to keep the price level more stable.

Large deflationary episodes historically have been disruptive to economic activity, like episodes of high inflation. Countries want to avoid these. By being on a bimetallic standard of gold and silver, rather than a gold-only standard, France was able to keep a stable price level for longer through an increase in its gold supply.

France's bimetallic standard lasted from 1803 to 1870, about which both Irving Fisher and Milton Friedman have written. It illustrates how a stable price level can be achieved under a metallic standard, even during the Napoleonic Wars (1803–15). As gold became increasingly scarce, from 1803 to 1850, it seemed that France would have to transition to a single metallic standard of silver. But then the 1849 gold rush in the United States supplied gold to markets and lowered its price against silver.

In 1850 France began importing gold while holding its quantity of silver nearly constant. Its bimetallic standard allowed its currency to be redeemed in the increasingly less scarce gold as well as in silver, so that it maintained a stable aggregate price level until 1870. The average market price of silver to gold remained near to its government-set rate of 15.5 to 1 throughout the period from 1803 to 1870.

Then, as Friedman (1994) and Wiegand (2019) describe, France lost the 1870–71 Franco-Prussian War and paid war reparations to Germany in gold-convertible currency. This flow of gold into Germany induced France to sell off its silver and move onto a gold standard in 1871–73. France ended its silver coinage in 1873, at the same time as the United States, after completing its war reparations and went onto a gold standard, as did the United States.

Britain started on the gold standard in 1821, after suspending it in 1797 during the Napoleonic War era (Newby 2012). That gold standard spread internationally, starting in 1874. Dating from a treaty signed in 1865, the Latin Monetary Union, based on the French franc and consisting of France, Belgium, Italy and Switzerland, transitioned to a gold standard in January 1874 (Bae & Bailey 2011). India moved to gold in 1893.

Wars often bring an end to monetary regimes, as with bimetallism in France after 1870. Although the US Civil War involved a high rate of money printing, and high inflation, its later achievement of parity with the UK gold price enabled it to keep a gold regime. It did this without devaluing its debt, while losing the bimetallic standard and incurring a prolonged deflation.

When Franklin D. Roosevelt ("FDR") became US president in March 1933, he could have resumed the gold standard at its parity of $20.67, but only by inducing a severe deflation, since the price of gold in dollars had almost doubled. He would have had to contract the currency in circulation and face further deflation just after the United States had experienced a negative 10 per cent inflation rate in 1932–33. This made the option of resuming the redemption of gold at parity level unpalatable. FDR instead devalued the dollar by allowing redemption at its then current market price of gold at $35.

As Britain, India and Japan left the gold standard in 1931, China remained on a silver standard. FDR also signed the Agricultural Adjustment Act of 1933, which included the "Thomas amendment", allowing the United States to buy silver again and hold it in reserve. When the United States did purchase silver, it did so at a price above the market price, so as to subsidize US silver producers. These purchases drove up the world price of silver (Friedman 1994).

When the price of silver in US dollars doubled in 1933, China at first maintained its currency at the silver parity. This forced down the Chinese price level, causing severe deflation. The Chinese economy contracted, and political upheaval increased. The Communist Party of China (CPC) was strengthening, Japan had invaded and taken control of Manchuria, and China was building up its military strength. During the deflation, China left the silver standard in October 1934, went to an unbacked paper currency, increased its currency notes by 100 per cent on average every year from 1937 to 1945, then entered a period of extreme hyperinflation from 1946 to 1949. In 1949 Chiang Kai-shek, leader of the Nationalists defeated in the Chinese Civil War, took the remaining Chinese gold reserves to Taiwan (Friedman 1994; see also Huang 1948).

Friedman (1994) presents the case that the United States caused, or at least accelerated, Chinese deflation and the rise of the CPC. He argues that the US silver purchases were made to subsidize US silver miners. But then, inadvertently, despite warnings about the consequences of this domestic policy, it led to the deflation that destabilized the Chinese economy and political system.

In the United States, periods of disruptive deflation occurred across its metallic regime history. From 1774 to 2020, Figure 4.1 shows the level of the US aggregate price level using the CPI index. The inflection upwards after the fiat money standard began after 1971 dominates the graph and shows how the rate of growth of the aggregate price level fluctuates around zero during the pre-1971 metallic money period, and constantly rises after 1971, during which period the inflation rate has almost always been positive. This illustrates through the price level how the fiat standard changed the trend inflation rate from near to zero to a significantly positive rate.

During the metallic standard time, however, Figure 4.1 shows four major US deflationary episodes, starting in 1778, 1814, 1865 and 1920. These are hard to discern using the level of the aggregate price index because of its strong trend upwards after 1971. To sharpen the focus on the deflations, Figure 4.2 shows

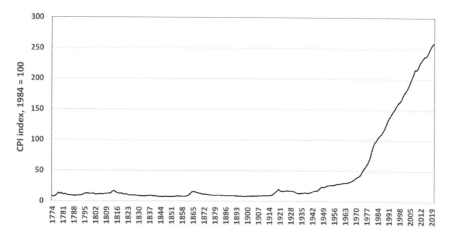

Figure 4.1 US aggregate price level, 1774–2020
Source: Measuring Worth website, available at: www.measuringworth.com/datasets/uscpi/result.php.

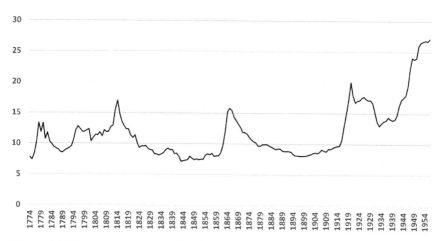

Figure 4.2 US aggregate price level under metallic money regimes, 1774–1956
Source: Measuring Worth.

the price index only for the period from 1774 to 1956, making the four major deflations more apparent.

Sharp declines in the CPI occurred after the US treaty with France in 1778 to jointly fight Britain, marking the beginning of the end of the American Revolutionary War. A long period of deflation occurred after the War of 1812, from 1814 to 1833, after which the Coinage Act of 1834 reset the bimetallic weights to make gold the effective standard. The third deflation occurred after the civil war, from 1865 to 1897, and the fourth deflation came after the First World War, from 1920 to 1934.

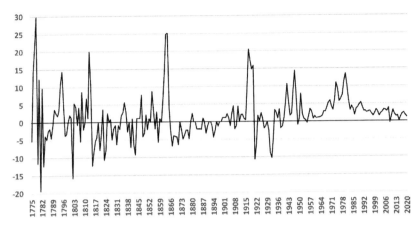

Figure 4.3 US CPI inflation rate during metallic and fiat eras, 1774–2020
Source: Measuring Worth.

Each of the four major deflations followed, or began towards the end of, a major war and a large wartime inflation. Writ large, these deflations occurred as the United States brought its currencies back in line with the metallic standard parity prices that were established internationally. War brought inflation and war's end brought deflation.

Figure 4.3 presents the percentage change in the US CPI price index from 1774 to 2020, thereby giving the history of the US inflation rate rather than the price level itself. The inflection point in the price level that occurs after 1971 in Figure 4.1 cannot readily be seen here. Instead, it shows a vastly more volatile rate of inflation with an average rate of inflation near zero, for the metallic standard era up until the 1950s. After that time, the average inflation rate rises until inflation rate targeting takes hold at a low but positive inflation rate in 1983.

A fiat standard, especially with inflation rate targeting after 1978, provides less inflation rate volatility than the gold standard. Referring to Fisher's plan to stabilize the price level along with inflation targeting, Bordo, Dittmar and Gavin (2003) draw similar conclusions: "We find that strict inflation targeting … provides more short-run stability than the gold standard and as much long-term price stability as does the gold standard for horizons shorter than 30 years. We find that Fisher's compensated dollar reduces price level and inflation uncertainty by an order of magnitude at all horizons."

Judging the metallic versus fiat standard requires weighing deflation versus inflation, including the "thickness" of the periods of high inflation during the Vietnam War era, and the volatility of each regime. The decreased volatility of fiat might mark the advent of a technological revolution in monetary regimes. The dramatic rises and falls of the aggregate price level during the metallic standard compare to fiat effectively ending the threat of deflation. Now the concern turns towards too much inflation.

The metallic standard has involved large volatility in the price level, at great cost to the economy. The fiat standard has avoided a significant amount of this volatility, at the cost of a higher average inflation tax, as part of the evolution of monetary regimes. The next chapter examines how stable monetary regimes were established and how they came to an end. With a set of historical examples, it illustrates that money has two lives before it fades out for good.

5

SEIGNIORAGE VERSUS HYPERINFLATION

As either coinage or paper, the history of metallic-based monetary regimes shows that such money remains convertible to its respective metal until it is debased too far. The issuance of paper money can herald the beginning of debasement. Money lives on as a means of exchange when its value is stable or declining at an acceptable rate. Its second life occurs when people begin to stop using the money and seek alternative means of exchange at a rapid rate. Substituting a nation's unstable currency for another nation's more stable currency can lead to increasingly high inflation, or even hyperinflation. This second phase bodes the end of the life of the currency, when its practical use for exchange diminishes.

Once people anticipate that a monetary regime is nearing collapse, its money becomes increasingly worthless. This hastens the end of the regime and increases the speed at which the system collapses. The only positive action becomes ending the monetary regime and establishing a new one that citizens respect and accept as a means of exchange.

During this life cycle of money, monetary regimes continue to evolve. The common thread is that, whenever the government supplies a stable form of money, it yields revenue for the government Treasury as long as the economy grows. A stable money with a growing economy in turn means a growing demand for the stable money, and an economy grows more readily when the price level is stable. To achieve a stable price level with a growing demand for the money, a government debases the money at the rate of growth of the economy and reaps the revenue from the debasement. This is the original meaning of natural seigniorage.

When a government begins to debase the money at a faster rate than the economy is growing, the price level in terms of the money begins rising, causing inflation. People tolerate moderate inflation, albeit with a decreased demand for the money in real terms. Deflating the money by dividing the stock of money by the price level gives the real money stock. This real money falls as the price of holding money rises. The inflation rate, plus the real return on capital, constitute the price of holding money instead of investing it. When inflation rises and the real money stock declines, the government has to increase the money growth at a faster rate to get the same revenue, causing higher inflation. This can create an upward spiral of inflation, leading to hyperinflation.

A key concept, however, is that inflation tax revenue is yielded even at a zero-inflation rate as long as the economy is growing. The growth rate in the economy is closely linked to the real return on capital, or the real interest rate. This is also a cost of holding money: by carrying it around and not investing it you lose the real rate of interest on capital. Money is a form of capital, kept in a "liquid" form by not investing it in any project and thereby inducing the opportunity cost of forgone interest. Therefore, at a zero rate of inflation, the only cost of holding money is the real interest rate. This is also the basis of the yield to the government that supplies a stable currency with a zero inflation rate.

Once the inflation rate rises above zero, the opportunity cost of money is still the market interest rate. But, as Fisher's (1907) theory of market interest rates tells us, this means that the cost of holding money is now the real interest rate plus the positive inflation rate, while with a zero inflation rate it is just the real interest rate. Both the real rate of interest and the inflation rate are additional elements comprising the nominal return on capital investment. This return builds in the need to account for the inflation of the price level that occurs over the period of the investment, while also including the real return. When the inflation rate is stable, such as a zero rate, it is easy for investment to build in the expected change in the price level, since there is none. This becomes more difficult once the inflation rate is positive.

Governments that run an increasingly large budget deficit tend to rely increasingly on the inflation tax. They debase the money ever more. This leads people to continually decrease their real demand for the money. They avoid the inflation tax through the use of private-bank-supplied exchange credit and they may begin substituting other government money for their own government money, through currency substitution. As the nation's government begins losing inflation tax revenue thanks to currency substitution, the other government that is issuing the currency now used in the original country instead begins receiving inflation tax revenue from citizens of the other country as they use its money.

Currency substitution typically marks the beginning of the end for the monetary regime of the government, especially as it resorts to trying to levy an ever higher inflation tax. These regimes end once hyperinflation takes place. Then the first life of money is when it begins as a stable money, in terms of having a zero inflation rate that yields natural seigniorage as the economy grows. In this life it can survive with a moderate rate of inflation, and possible episodes of moderately high inflation, and an increased level of the inflation tax. Its second life kicks in when this moderate inflation turns into a high and accelerating rate of inflation that eventually ends the life cycle of that money.

Along the way of history, this life cycle of money evolves through the selection of traits that are most helpful for its survival. From shells used in a local island economy to metals that are found across a civilization in limited supply to mere paper that is used across nations while forming institutions that limit its supply, monetary regimes evolve into more efficient forms that involve a lower cost of transacting exchange with the money. This is the natural evolution of the life cycle of money, with two forms of life within each cycle, and with subsequent generations of the monetary form being more efficient than those that went before them.

Metal and paper have been the two predominant types of monetary regimes in regional or international civilizations since antiquity. According to Bernholz (2016: 3), money "evolved as an unplanned social institution by a number of inventions and innovations during a period of perhaps 2500 years", with inflation itself being no older than money. Metallic standards allow for inflation through debasement of the coinage.

Debasement can occur without causing inflation, however. The exchange rate between the metal in use as money and the goods being bought with the metal is determined as a free market price. If the government issues just enough coins, in gold, silver or copper so that the stated value of the coin stays in line with the market exchange rate of the metal embodied in the coin, then that coin can be used for a sustained period without any inflation emerging.

If a city state or kingdom supplies a coin of stable value, such as in ancient Athens, ancient China and Renaissance Venice and Florence, and trade continues to grow around that city state, then the demand for that coin in use for trade will grow. The city state finds a growing demand for the metals contained in the coin that is in line with the growing trade. This provides the opportunity for the city state to reap revenue for its government while having a constant aggregate price level.

Consider how this works. The value of the metal rises if its supply is relatively constant and the demand for the coins using that metal grows. The value of the metal in the coins then also rises. This means that each coin can buy more goods. If the supply of the coins is not increased, so that the coins become relatively scarce compared to the amount of the goods being produced and sold in the growing economy, then there can be only one result: the price of goods must fall so that the limited stock of money can be allocated to buy all the goods. This means that the aggregate price level for goods falls. This result is deflation of the price level, or a negative inflation rate. Falling prices make trade more difficult, compared to a stable price level.

Deflation and inflation both eliminate price stability, and people instead have to anticipate the change in aggregate prices, which is costly and can result in errors in anticipating how much to produce and how much to buy. With a stable price level, the need to calculate what the prices are expected to be is eliminated from the cost of any transaction with the money. Without such uncertainty, the demand for the coinage is higher.

A city state in historical times reaps a natural government reward for supplying a public good in the form of a stable money that coincides with a stable price level. Price stability in terms of a widespread money coinage engenders growth in the economy. During growth, the city state can slightly decrease the amount of the metal content in the coin, say a drachma, as the demand for the coin grows. Then the value of the stamped coin can remain constant in terms of the amount of goods that it buys. It holds a slightly smaller amount of metal, as it retains the stamp of being one drachma, and prices for goods in services in drachmas stay constant.

The government is rewarded for supplying the stable price level through decreasing the metal content of the coins, collecting the metal and forming new coins with it which its Treasury can spend on goods for the government that help it expand its public institutions. This government expansion is reaped without levying any explicit taxes on its citizenry.

Traditionally, this type of revenue to the government is called natural seigniorage, perhaps deriving from the Renaissance France seignior who was the head of a village or manor. Even modern economies can choose to collect only natural seigniorage by keeping the price level stable or having an average inflation rate of zero. With positive inflation rates in modern times, seigniorage is often used as just another name for inflation tax revenue, which denigrates the ancient tradition of keeping inflation tax revenue limited to a natural reward for providing a stable price level.

Elliott (2020) states that "coined money was first invented in the Greco-Roman world". Certainly, it proved an advantage for ancient city states to invent ways to create coinage and then make its use widespread. At the end of the seventh century BC Athens was largely an impoverished, "backward", undeveloped city state (Milne 1945: 231). The name "drachma" came from the verb "to grasp", *drakh*. The drachma at first was a "handful" in weight equivalent to six iron spits that were used for cooking over a fire. This circulated as a "token" equal to the commodity value of the iron that it contained.

Economic growth and coinage circulation became evident around the Aegean Sea. The more ancient Minoan kingdom on Crete exported silver to Egypt for corn. So did the nearby city states of Corinth and Aegina similarly trade silver for corn using a silver–gold alloy coin ("*stater*") of irregular weights.

An Argos ruler subsequently standardized these weights (around 670 BC) by supplying coins made from Aegina silver. This became a state-controlled currency that was used in exchange across the trading region, based on the weight of the metals within each coin. In Egypt silver was scarce, whereas in Aegina it was plentiful. Aegina could trade silver alloy coinage from their mines to buy more corn in Egypt than the same coins could buy in Greece, where the metal was in greater supply.

Aegina then sold the excess corn from this trade in Greek markets. Although Aegina benefited from these sales, they drove down the corn price in Greece, made production of corn in Greece less profitable and decreased Greek agricultural production. The Aeginian arbitrage between Egypt's high demand for silver and Greece's high supply of silver led to reduced output by the Greek economy even as Aegina itself prospered.

With the use of coinage established, a further significant innovation took place that existed until the end of metallic standards. Solon came to an Athens that was agricultural, had legalized slavery and was unable or unwilling to take part in the commercial prosperity in the sea trade that flourished in the Aegean Sea. Its government was in debt. After being chosen as the chief magistrate in Athens, or archon, Solon began reforms that included innovations for the monetary regime.

Seeing the depressing effect on Greek agriculture, Solon as the Athenian archon changed the nature of the agricultural economy to enable it to prosper. He banned agricultural exports except for olive oil, established property rights that disallowed the taking of persons or property for debts and honoured the Athens government debt, but only by paying it in debased drachmas. These drachmas were stamped with the same nominal value but contained less metal content, so that the government debt was manageable in the new drachmas. For this new coinage, Solon joined the Euboea trade group, adopted its weight standards and issued an Athenian drachma in terms of weight that for the first time had a nominal value approximately equal to the coin's metallic value. This marked a technological innovation in coinage. It avoided weighing each coin separately to determine its metallic value, since the new drachma's stated value was standardized to equal approximately its metallic market value.

Solon's standardization of the coinage included the fact that its value in metal (silver), while approximately equal to its worth in metal, was actually worth slightly less than its stated nominal value. This is how he provided a debasement that earned the Athenian treasury government revenue while providing for a stable price level in drachmas in the growing regional economy. Solon earned for Athens approximately 5 per cent in coinage, minting 105 drachmas for 100 in metal weight value.

As this method of coinage production was systematic and well known, and since it eliminated the need to weigh coinage with every trade that was made, the standardized coins circulated widely in trade. Solon's metallic weighted drachma dates from 566 BC, after which the drachma depreciated slowly over the centuries, with intermittent periods of war compromising the coin. This included debasement during the Peloponnesian War with an implicit promise to repay token coins for silver ones at the war's end, similar to the greenbacks issued in the American Civil War. Giovannini (1975: 189–90) documents this:

> In order to finance their final war effort, the Athenians began in 406 to mint gold and bronze coins ... The gold was struck for meeting such external obligations as pay for mercenaries or the purchase of ships from Macedonia; it probably was not used in Athens at all. The bronze coins, on the contrary, were struck only for domestic use, since only Athenian citizens and residents would have been inclined to accept mere token coins ... [W]hen the war was over, the Athenians resumed the production of silver and progressively recalled the token coinage by exchanging it against coins of silver.

Despite war, Solon's drachma maintained its use in trade for about 400 years, up until Roman conquest in 146 BC. Solon's reforms included cancelling part of the debt by devaluing the drachmas in which the debt was paid, coining drachmas using Attica silver, providing seigniorage until the first century BC, stabilizing agriculture for basic foodstuffs and establishing an agriculturally based means of growth through trade in olive oil. Starting in the fifth century BC, Solon's reforms are considered to have enabled the creation of a high form of civilized society in Athens, which set the foundations of Western civilization.

It could be said, therefore, that the emergence of Western civilization as we know it all started with money. Solon's technological innovation of metal coinage into a standardized form allowed for a steady source of revenue, which was considered a fair return to the government for the service that the money provided. Simultaneously he devalued the debt in real terms so that the Athens government could begin to borrow anew. He regulated the economy in consideration of the metal supply for coinage so that it could prosper for centuries through agriculture exports.

As the Greek civilization faded, the Athenian drachma was replaced by the Roman denarius coin, also at first made of silver. Although the drachma did not burn out through high inflation, its use was diminished through the conquest by Rome, which provided its own coin and means of obtaining seigniorage. In contrast to Greece, the imperial coinage of Rome was stamped with the head of state, first by Julius Caesar in his last year of life, and then by Augustus with additional laurels as conquests took place (Sutherland 1940).

Compared to Athens, ancient Roman emperors over time used a greater degree of debasement of the coinage, which came to be based in both silver and gold. Bernholz (2016) supplies Roman evidence of moderately high and volatile price inflation of 4 per cent annually from 250 to 293 AD, 22 per cent annually for the next 18 years, and an annual average inflation rate of 14 per cent for 305 to 380. The Roman emperor Diocletian abdicated in 305 after instituting price controls that failed despite penalties including death.

Taxes under Diocletian had to be paid with goods rather than money and led to the establishment of a hereditary caste system that distorted the economy's production and undermined its civilization (Bernholz 2016). As inflation became moderately high, Roman civilization declined until the demise of the Western Empire and end of the Roman coinage regime. The Roman coinage ended with moderately high inflation but not hyperinflation.

In the East, a technological evolution in the form of money occurred as Western civilization was coming out of the "dark ages" after the collapse of the Roman Empire. China is said to have created the first government paper money in 1024 in the Northern Sung dynasty, called the *chiao-tzu*, which was convertible to metal. Nonetheless, a subsequent, and sustained, period of paper money inflation started in 1072, according to Bernholz (2016). He finds that the subsequent Mongol dynasty in China, starting around 1276, as well as the Ming dynasty (1368–1643) experienced sufficiently high paper money inflation to have their currencies replaced by a new metallic coinage.

As Western civilization arose again in Renaissance Venice and Florence, these city states supplied coins that served for centuries, like the experience of Athens. In 1192 Venice issued a silver coin; in 1252 Florence introduced the gold florin. With a nominal value that accorded to its value in metallic weight, as with Solon's drachma, the florin supplied a stable currency that was used for some three centuries for international trade.

Both city states benefited from the seigniorage earned in minting coins with slightly less valuable metal over time, as the demand for the coinage rose. With this slight debasement, they supplied coinage that yielded both stable price levels and natural seigniorage. Bernholz (2016) provides evidence that little inflation in florins occurred over these centuries. Competing coins were created by other western European kingdoms also trying to receive steady seigniorage for their Treasuries.

Widespread stable banking arose on the basis of a stable currency, making the latter all the more important for commerce. The stable coinage of the Renaissance coincides with the time when modern private banking began. The advance in banking, relative to Ancient Greece and Rome, then led over the centuries to certain private banks becoming central banks. Goodhart (1988) credits the 1668 founding of the Swedish central bank as the first central bank.

Central banks began taking the role of imperial Rome in stamping money by dictum for a large economy. With the further technological innovation of issuing paper money at times that was unbacked by metal, however, central banks could more readily induce episodes of inflation that rose beyond moderately high rates into hyperinflation. When hyperinflation ends, so does that form of money, and also often the government itself. Both ancient and modern currencies have lived on as long as there are stable prices or moderate inflation, in line with flourishing civilizations.

Hyperinflation creates a completely new phase in the life of a currency. Real money demand declines in a continual fashion. This leads to complete substitution to another country's currency until the hyperinflated currency becomes worthless. That marks the end of the life cycle of the monetary regime.

Hyperinflation results when the central bank finances too large a share of government revenue with freshly printed money. Bernholz (2016) finds that, once more than 40 per cent of the government budget is financed by printing new money, hyperinflation ensues. The money printing is from the central bank buying Treasury debt directly from the government, or, alternatively, from banks as middlemen in the process. The middleman role can easily break down during hyperinflation, with direct purchase of Treasury debt by the central bank.

Modern hyperinflation experience has been described in a large body of research. A landmark study is Cagan's (1956) account of the hyperinflations occurring across Europe after the First and Second World Wars. He shows how the demand for money, in real terms, falls as the level of the inflation tax rises, even during the exorbitant levels that characterize hyperinflation. That a stable money demand could be found during the unstable economic chaos that hyperinflation brings was a remarkable accomplishment that enshrined the Cagan study. His form of the money demand function was specified to capture hyperinflation but has since been found valid for many moderate inflation periods as well.

Besides these world war examples, hyperinflations subsequently also followed the end of the Cold War. Åslund (2012) counts 22 hyperinflations across eastern Europe after the demise of the Soviet Union in 1991. The new governments received little tax revenue from a citizenry that had never voluntarily paid taxes under the Soviet Union. Lacking government tax revenue, as did the postwar governments that went into hyperinflation, they resorted to printing money to finance government expenditure.

With central banks that can print money, monetary regimes continue to come to an end. The root cause is financing a large government budget deficit by printing money. But the deficit may result from internal civil war or, more broadly, from political reach by parties far beyond the government's means of finance. Recent hyperinflations have occurred in this fashion without world war in South America and Africa.

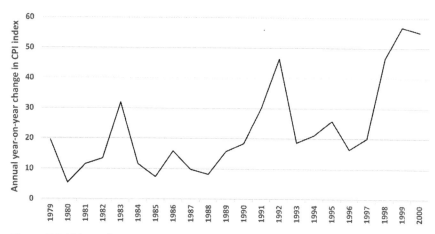

Figure 5.1 Rising inflation in Zimbabwe, 1979–2000
Source: FRED.

One recent example is Zimbabwe. From 1979 to 2000 the Zimbabwean currency remained in use, even as its inflation rate went from moderately high to increasingly higher peaks. As Figure 5.1 shows, its inflation rate went above 30 per cent in the early 1980s, above 45 per cent a decade later and then close to 60 per cent before the year 2000. After 2000 the high inflation rate rose further, until hyperinflation emerged and the monetary regime ended.

Figure 5.2 shows that inflation reached 200 per cent at an annual rate in 2002, up to 600 per cent in 2003 and stood at almost 1,300 per cent in 2006. This is already hyperinflation territory. Cagan (1956) uses a definition of 50 per cent monthly inflation rate as being indicative of hyperinflation. For 12 months, a simple sum gives a 600 per cent annual inflation rate, which Zimbabwe had in both 2003 and 2005. By 2007 the (ungraphed) annual rate of inflation was over 66,000 per cent.

Once hyperinflation accelerates to unfathomable rates, the currency ceases to be used and a new stable monetary regime needs to be put in place of the old. Bernholz (2016) details when such reforms tend to be successful and documents examples when the reforms fail and when a new monetary regime has been instituted. The main requirement is that the government budget deficit is decreased or financed sufficiently, including through loans from international organizations or other governments.

Typically, the end of hyperinflation may see the creation of a new central bank that has independence from the government Treasury demands. Alternatively, there may be different means of limiting the money supply, such as through fixed exchange rates, or even currency boards. These boards limit the money

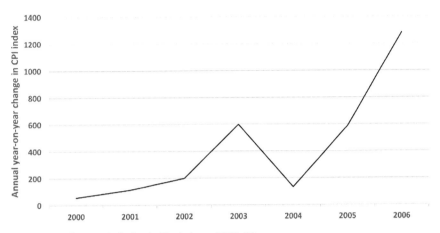

Figure 5.2 Extreme inflation in Zimbabwe, 2000–06
Source: FRED.

supply to the stock of a different country's currency that are held as reserves by the government. This backs up their new currency with another nation's stable currency, with examples of Hong Kong and Argentina having used the US dollar, and Estonia and Bulgaria the German Deutsche mark.

A return to the metallic standard has not occurred even after hyperinflation. The evolution of the monetary regimes has seen the need to limit the stock of money for stable or low inflation. It has also seen the ability to increasingly reduce the transaction cost of exchange by adopting a money that can be easily carried and used in international banking.

A return to a metallic standard is highly unlikely unless world civilization breaks down in war. Control of the paper fiat money standard remains fundamental for controlling the rate of inflation and providing the foundation for banking, however. The technological evolution of money has gone from being metallic coinage that lives with stable or moderate inflation to a fiat currency that can likewise survive but then dies in hyperinflation. The lesson is that modern monetary regimes can continue only if the paper currency finances a distinctly limited share of government budget deficits.

Financing increasing shares of the budget deficit by printing ever more money, as was the case with Zimbabwe, can result in galloping inflation. Suppressing such inflation through government regulation, as Diocletian tried, can be far worse that allowing the inflation to occur and the currency to live or die. Inflation suppression can cause a weakening of the foundations of civilization, including modern banking.

The next chapter shows consequences from inflation that seem distant from any money supply increases to finance budget deficits, yet in fact the opposite is true. Confusing the causality can result in judgements that blame the victim rather than the perpetrator. The cure for the problem can seem to be anything but limiting growth in the money supply, especially after war and crises.

6

BLAMING THE VICTIM

Like gold, diamonds last forever, and often experience similar price fluctuations to gold. These price changes are, in turn, like those of oil, which is also drawn from limited ground-based reserves. The ups and downs of the dollar prices of diamonds, gold and oil tend to follow each other rather closely during periods of accelerated US money supply growth. These co-movements help give insight into an ongoing puzzle about the relationship between oil prices and inflation.

One theory posits that oil prices are relative price changes that cause inflation. Another says the causality is the opposite: that inflation and the expectation of inflation cause oil price increases, and that both are, in turn, caused by the growth rate of the money supply.

In the 1960s and 1970s a popular theory circulated that inflation was not caused by money at all, and that theory has reared its head again, as oil prices and inflation have both risen during the ongoing Covid-19 pandemic and, now, with Putin's war on Ukraine as the pandemic subsides. The oil price theory of inflation is that oil prices are increased by monopolistic "price-gouging" behaviour on the part of the suppliers of oil. The origin of the idea was that oil suppliers are able to form a monopoly, so that they become the only suppliers of oil and therefore are able to dictate a monopolist world price of oil that maximizes their profit.

The monopoly was said to be the Organization of the Petroleum Exporting Countries (OPEC). In September 1960 OPEC began as a group of five nations trying to coordinate new oil production. Prices for a barrel of oil were denominated in US dollars, while the Bretton Woods monetary regime locked the US dollar price for an ounce of gold at $35.

The choice of using US dollars per barrel enabled the price of oil to remain stable as long as the gold standard lasted. The dollar oil price from the start of OPEC until the breakdown of the Bretton Woods system fluctuated very little, keeping at a near-constant $3 dollars a barrel from June 1953 to November 1970. During this time there were many other oil producers, such as the United States, in which oil production nearly doubled from over 5 million barrels of oil a day in 1950 to over 9 million barrels a day in 1971.

After US inflation reached 6 per cent in 1970, the world price of oil rose slightly to $4 per barrel in 1972 and 1973. In October 1973 US inflation reached 8 per cent. Then, from 6 to 23 October 1973, a Middle East war took place between a coalition of OPEC oil-producing nations and Israel (the war is known variously as the Yom Kippur War or the Ramadan War). On 17 October OPEC embargoed the export of oil to the United States and other allies of Israel. The price of oil then rose to $10 per barrel in January 1974.

In December 1975, by the US Energy Policy and Conservation Act of 1975, the United States in turn banned the export of US oil, even though US exports of oil were close to zero. US imports had risen steadily from about 1 million barrels a day in 1970 to 4 million barrels a day in 1975. After the OPEC oil embargo there were temporary shortages of gasoline in the United States, while at the same time the world oil price had doubled.

A new Keynesian theory arose, saying that the slow growth in US real output (GDP) and high inflation at this time was caused by the OPEC monopoly increasing oil prices. The combination was called stagflation. US inflation was described as "cost-push" inflation, driven by the increased cost of production for output because of higher oil prices. Stagflation theory was derived from the Keynesian theory that relative price changes cause inflation. Here a stagnating economy was caused by high "cost-push" inflation from oil prices. Mankiw (2015: 450–1) describes the Keynesian view of stagflation, which is still current today: "Some of the largest economic fluctuations in the US economy since 1970 have originated in the oil fields of the Middle East ... Firms in the United States ... experience rising costs, and they find it less profitable to supply their output of goods and services at any given price level. The result is a leftward shift in the aggregate-supply curve, which in turn leads to stagflation." Money supply plays no role in the explanation. This theory lives on even though the world oil supply has been considerably diversified since then. It becomes topical whenever oil prices and inflation rise, and when low economic growth occurs, such as during crises such as the Covid-19 pandemic and then with Putin's war on Ukraine.

Of course, there can be some feedback from rising oil prices to the inflation rate, and especially if supplies are suddenly cut off, as in 1973 by OPEC and in 2022 by the US prohibition on importing Russian oil. The question becomes whether temporary supply disruptions can cause prolonged inflationary episodes, unrelated to money supply growth and budget deficits. Had it not been for the rising oil prices during the Covid-19 pandemic, one might have presumed that such language, and even the Keynesian theory of stagflation, had become ancient history.

The oil crisis of 1973 occurred the same year the United States withdrew from Vietnam. Perhaps emboldened by the US southeast Asian withdrawal, a war against Israel broke out and oil supplies were disrupted – much like the US retreat from Afghanistan in 2021, Putin's subsequent invasion of Ukraine and the cut-off of Russian oil by the United States. And, as is common after a war, the United States entered a recession after withdrawing from Vietnam, while the inflation rate had been rising in tandem with growth in the money supply used to finance the Vietnam War.

Yet consider how history has written up the oil crisis, with the blame on OPEC. Focusing on the part to hit consumer pockets, National Public Radio entitled an article on 16 October 2013 "The 1973 Arab oil embargo: the old rules no longer apply", and included a photo of American motorists waiting in gasoline lines on 13 December 1973. Focus on the oil disruption continued, with the Center for Strategic and International Studies producing a 13 October 2013 article titled "The Arab oil embargo – 40 years later" (Verrastro & Caruso 2013).

Wired magazine headlined an article on 16 October 2008 "Oct. 17, 1973: angry Arabs turn off the oil spigot" (Long 2008), concluding: "It also awakened the West to just how dependent it was on Middle Eastern oil, and how fragile that lifeline really was." During the pandemic *The Washington Post*, on 14 August 2020, posted an article by Ryan Williams with the standard Keynesian "cost-push" theory that oil prices caused the inflation of the 1970s (Williams 2020): "Then in 1973, Arab members of OPEC placed an oil embargo on nations they blamed for supporting Israel in the Yom Kippur War. In the US, the embargo led to skyrocketing oil prices. Businesses passed along that cost but also retrenched, as what economists call a supply shock made goods scarcer, adding to a rise in inflation."

Counter-arguments to the Keynesian stagflation theory have been around for an equally long time, even in official US government documents. On 30 January 1975, in connection with the Energy Policy and Conservation Act of 1975, at hearings before the Senate Committee on Finance, testimony was given by H. A. Merklein, director of the International Institute of the University of Dallas, that includes the following (Committee on Finance 1975: 32):

Unless the United States is prepared to break the dogmatic stranglehold Keynesian economics has held for too long, a major stagflation is inevitable … It is easy to blame OPEC for our current economic troubles, too easy, and terribly superficial. As a nation, we were driven in a corner long before November 1973. After all, wage and price controls were instituted here, I am tempted to say "in desperation," a good two years before the embargo.

Nixon had imposed wage and price controls (like Diocletian) to decrease inflation on the same day, 15 August 1971, that he closed the gold window and ended the gold standard. *The Wall Street Journal* wrote in 2021 about how "Nixon taught us how not to fight inflation" (Walker 2021). As inflation began to gallop, and exchange rates began to float, Nixon resigned in 1974. Diocletian imposed price controls in 301, then abdicated in 305 (Bernholz 2016), a similar lag in time to Nixon's between imposing misguided inflation controls and leaving government office.

A commentary by the Cato Institute on 17 October 2003 (Taylor & Van Doren 2003) argues against the oil price Keynesian theory of inflation under the heading "Time to lay the 1973 oil embargo to rest". The authors conclude: "In short, the oil weapon is a myth. It's high time that we stop believing in ghosts." Were they premature, given the oil price increases and inflation after the Covid-19 pandemic had begun, or correct that the spectre of inflation is based in money and only reflected by oil prices in the capital market mirror?

The academic debate continues onwards on the cause and effects of oil prices, both in the 1970s and ever since then. Since the 1970s Keynesian economics has argued that OPEC used its monopoly power, in the sense that OPEC controlled the entire market for oil and its price per barrel. The Keynesian theory posits that OPEC suddenly, on 13 October 1973, stopped exporting oil in order to exercise monopoly power and raise the real price of oil.

Yet a lot more was going on at the time, relating to money. The Bundesbank's first-hand account explains what else was happening in 1973 before the oil embargo, namely the breakdown of the Bretton Woods gold standard of fixed exchange rates (Bundesbank 2013):

> After the Bundesbank had to buy USD 1.7 billion on the morning of 1 March 1973, because the US currency had again fallen below the intervention limit, there was a showdown at the Central Bank Council meeting of 1 March 1973. Vice-President Otmar Emminger left the meeting to attend a hastily arranged meeting of the West German government under Willy Brandt in Bonn. Shortly beforehand, Emminger had called on the government to release the bank from its obligation to buy US dollars. A day later, on 2 March 1973, the government finally conceded. The Bundesbank was permitted to stop buying US dollars. Germany's exit from the system of fixed exchange rates sealed the fate of Bretton Woods. It was officially abandoned shortly afterwards.

The gold standard's remaining system of fixed exchange rates, put in place to ensure price stability based on the US conversion to gold at a fixed $35 price per ounce, broke down rather suddenly, and for good, in March 1973. What if all oil prices had been put in contract up until 1973 in terms of a US dollar price as based on the US dollar being of fixed worth, namely the $35 per ounce of gold guaranteed under Bretton Woods? What if the actual dollar oil price had been almost constant right up to October 1973? And what if nearly all oil barrel contracts had been long-term and that a "spot" oil price with competitive daily market prices had not existed in 1973?

On the latter question, Mabro (1984: 6–7) describes early oil contracts with fixed prices in the 1960s and 1970s, and how a spot market in trading oil did not exist: "In the old concession system, which prevailed in the OPEC region until the early 1970s, posted prices were initially used to indicate a company's selling price ... At that time spot transactions were few and far between."

In fact, all the above hypothetical questions were true. The breakdown of the gold standard left OPEC selling oil through previously established long-term contracts at a price that, after March 1973, became worth increasingly less, as the US dollar depreciated in open market exchange rates. The rate for the German Deutsche mark to one US dollar was 3.63 on 1 January 1971; it fell steadily to 3.00 on 1 February 1973 and to 2.41 on 1 October 1973. This is a 34 per cent drop in the value of the US dollar relative to the Deutsche mark as the United States financed the Vietnam War by printing money, with Nixon trying to stop inflation through "wage and price controls" that were soon to be abandoned.

OPEC oil was always traded in US dollars, as it is today, and its historical fluctuations have matched those of the gold price, as shown earlier in Figure 3.1. With the value of its US constant price contract having fallen rapidly, the contracts needed to be renegotiated at a higher level of US dollars per barrel since the US dollar depreciated dramatically once floating exchange rates emerged. Blaming the victim here, by calling OPEC a monopoly that caused the 1970s inflation, might be easier than acknowledging that OPEC was being asked to honour contracts for oil at an increasingly lower real price; but it lacks any investigative assessment of the problem.

OPEC nations had provided a stable, low and competitive oil price tied to the US dollar through international cooperation and contractual obligation with Western nations at least since 1960. The US inflation led their cooperation to be increasingly devalued. When the first Egyptian–Israeli disengagement agreement between the United States and the warring nations was signed on 18 January 1974, the price of oil rose from $4 a barrel in December 1973 to $10 a barrel in January 1974. The OPEC oil embargo and the regional war both ended in March 1974.

The oil price was gradually stepped up to $16 a barrel by 1979, in a fashion that allowed for steady economic adjustment, almost like the way a wage contract can be indexed to inflation. In essence, a contract renegotiation during wartime allowed the US dollar pricing of oil contracts to reflect the post-Bretton-Woods devalued US dollar as a result of rising inflation. Yet, instead, the 1973 oil price increase was called the first oil shock of the 1970s to have been caused by OPEC monopoly power, leading to US inflation.

There are many stories as to what causes inflation and deflation, and about who the victim is and what the crime was. Friedman (1990) takes relish in debunking "the crime of 1873". After the Coinage Act of 1873 allowed coinage only in gold, rather than also in silver, many called the end of the US bimetallic era a crime, since it violated the interests of silver holders and producers. Friedman instead characterizes it as an economic crime, because the paucity of gold supply at the time led to sustained deflation after 1879, whereas retaining bimetallism with silver may have averted the costly deflation.

War against Israel, just like war against Ukraine, violates international law. The 1973 war might have been hastened by the end of the gold standard on which oil price contracts were based. It might have been avoided if the oil contracts had been renegotiated in a timely fashion to offset the declining real price of oil in the many years from 1955 to 1973, during the Vietnam War, that led up to the final breakdown of Bretton Woods.

In terms of oil prices, however, OPEC was the victim rather than the perpetrator a century after the 1873 Act. The oil embargo, which was treated as "the crime of 1973", did not cause the inflation era of the Vietnam War. The real crime was the unwillingness of oil purchasers to reset oil prices that were contracted in US dollars once those US dollars had become devalued by the Vietnam-War-induced inflation. Friedman (1994: 204) considers the 1970s OPEC oil price increases to be a one-off affair with no lasting consequence for inflation:

> The sharp rise in the price of oil in the 1970s lowered the quantity of goods and services that was available for people to use because everyone had to export more abroad to pay for oil. This reduction in output raised the price level. But that was a once-for-all effect. It did not produce any longer-lasting effect on the rate of inflation ... We return to our basic proposition. Inflation is primarily a monetary phenomenon that is produced by a more rapid increase in the quantity of money than in output.

Just as Figure 3.1 shows that oil prices and gold prices have moved together since 1973, it might be surprising that this co-movement can even be seen with diamond prices. Figure 6.1 shows the normalized path of the price of diamonds (import price) and the price of a barrel of crude oil (WTI spot price) for the first quarter of 1997 to the second quarter of 2021. Visibly there is a strong positive relation between the price movements, and in these data there exists a substantial positive correlation of 0.65.

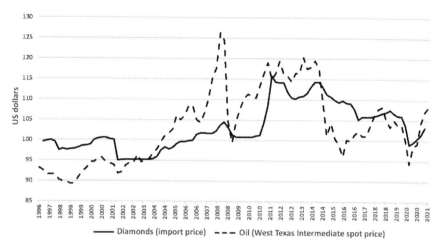

Figure 6.1 Diamonds and oil: the price mix over time, 1997Q3–2021Q2
Source: FRED.

What could possibly cause commodities as different from diamonds and oil to co-move? The answer is that markets compete to discern any policy change that affects types of "assets" such as diamonds, oil and gold. Government monetary policy is discerned through market prices.

What is the expected inflation rate from the government's supply of money? How does implicit bank insurance offered by the central bank after a bank crisis affect inflation? Markets need to anticipate this, so that they can build that inflation into the currency prices of goods.

When a lot of money has been printed, and the money supply growth rate has risen, markets naturally expect a higher inflation rate, given the predictions of the quantity theory of money. The markets' reaction is one of common-sense intuition backed by experience. A high growth rate of the money in circulation leads to high growth of the price level, which is the definition of high inflation.

Figure 6.2 shows how the US money supply and aggregate price level moved together from 1959 to 2008. Monetary aggregates are central bank definitions for groupings of what we consider the national money supply. For the United States and elsewhere, M1 is the most common. It sums together the currency in circulation – namely central bank money supply (public cash) – and the deposit accounts at private banks (private bank money). Starting when the Fed begins its historical data series for monetary aggregates in 1959, and going up to 2008, Figure 6.2 shows M1 (in billions of US dollars) and the CPI price index (normalized by being factoring by five).

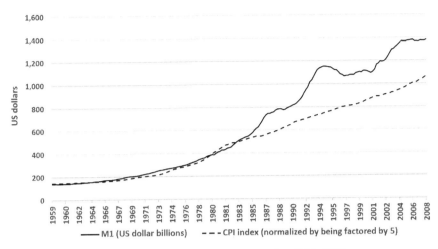

Figure 6.2 Money supply and price index moving together, 1959–2008
Source: FRED.

From 1959 to 1971, the end of the Bretton Woods gold standard regime, the M1 money supply and the CPI aggregate price index moved together very closely, with both rising at a slow rate. After 1971 both begin inflecting upwards, rising together at a faster rate with the beginning of the fiat money era. This reflects a rising inflation rate and a higher money supply growth rate to finance the Vietnam War.

In contrast to the Keynesian stagflation hypothesis of oil price change, the neoclassical theory is based on money supply increases causing both inflation and oil price movements. Supporting this, research by Alquist, Kilian and Vigfusson (2013) shows that oil prices can be predicted by the US M1 money supply growth rate and by the US CPI inflation rate. This uses economic statistical methods named after Nobel laureate Clive Granger as "Granger causality". Added to such findings, the expected US inflation rate, the actual US inflation rate and the US M1 money supply growth rate all have been found to "Granger-cause" – or, more accurately, "Granger-predict" – oil and gold prices (Gillman & Nakov 2009; Alquist, Kilian & Vigfusson 2013; Benk & Gillman 2020).

Granger causality, also presented as "Granger predictability", means that systematic movements in one historical series of data precede similar movements in another series of data. Applied here, changes in US money supply, inflation expectations and actual inflation precede similar changes in oil and gold prices. This upends the Keynesian theory of stagflation, by which oil prices are said to cause US inflation. Instead, "causality" evidence supports the reverse, with causality going from money and inflation to oil and gold prices.

Figure 6.3 The market price for oil versus the real price: dollars per barrel, 1947–72
Source: FRED.

Whether there is Granger causality of oil prices by US money supply and inflation has long been controversial. Hamilton (1983) published an influential article called "Oil and the macroeconomy since World War II", which determined that no macroeconomic variables Granger-caused oil prices. He used data on oil prices during the Bretton Woods era, when the oil price barely changed, which made the econometric findings questionable.

His data are for the period from 1948 to 1972, in testing the Granger causality of money and inflation to oil prices. Since prices changes little, this violates the assumptions of the estimation procedure. Hamilton later in the article included data for 1973 to 1980 and found Granger causality from oil to GDP output, but did not include this data period for showing results on causality from inflation to oil prices.

Figure 6.3 shows that the US dollar price of a barrel of oil (WTI) moved up somewhat in several steps from 1947 to 1972 and was nearly constant for long stretches of time. The finding that money and inflation did not Granger-predict oil prices during this period disregards the fact that oil and gold prices were closely tied to the US dollar under Bretton Woods. This constant nature of dollar oil prices is why such results are now considered to be invalid.

To see this movement in the dollar oil price, Figure 6.3 shows that the actual US dollar price of a barrel of oil rises from about $2 to $3.5 from 1947 to 1972. This price was $30 in 1980, $133 in 2008, above $70 in 2021 and above $100 in 2022. These prices from $2 to $3.5 are dwarfed by the price changes that occurred once Bretton Woods collapsed, as Figure 3.1 shows.

Also consider the oil prices in real terms once we take out the inflation impact from a rising aggregate price level. To do this, the real price is constructed simply by dividing any dollar price by the CPI index. Figure 6.3 shows that the real price of oil is about the same both in 1947 and in 1972, but with it having fallen for 15 years from 1957 to 1972. It makes clear that OPEC suffered from a continually falling real price of oil as a consequence of rising US inflation in the decades leading up to the oil embargo of 1973.

Regarding the 1983 findings of no causality from money and inflation to dollar oil prices, Hamilton (2008) notes that "challenges to the latter claim have recently been developed by Barsky and Kilian (2001, 2004)". Barsky and Kilian put forth the hypothesis that money growth caused the 1970s inflation. Using data starting in 1973, Alquist, Kilian and Vigfusson (2013) and others prove that Granger causality does indeed run from money, inflation and inflation expectations to oil and gold prices (both real and nominal).

Although Hamilton (1983) used data up to 1972, others use data after Bretton Woods broke down in 1973 and find strong evidence that money predicts inflation and expected future inflation, and that money, inflation and expected inflation all predict oil, as well as gold prices (Benk & Gillman 2020). At the same time, the stagflation theory of Keynesians cannot explain the large oil price increases from 2001 to 2015, since inflation remained relatively calm.

Moreover, the oil flow into markets was not being reduced from 2001 to 2015. Global oil production was rising as a result of "fracking" in the United States. This procedure enabled a technological revolution that lowers the cost of producing oil through a means of drilling into an oil and gas seam and cracking it open with pressurized liquid to release the oil and natural gas, rather than drilling straight into it. After falling by a half, from 10 million barrels of oil a day in 1970 to 5 million a day in 2005, the US supply increased to 9.5 million barrels of oil a day in 2015. This oil supply surge, while inflation was calm and oil prices had been rising, led to the repeal of the December 1975 ban on exporting US oil imposed by the Energy Policy and Conservation Act of 1975 passed that year. The Consolidated Appropriations Act of 2016, signed into law 40 years later, in December 2015, by President Barack Obama, repealed the 1975 ban on oil and natural gas exports.

The next step is to test the different hypotheses of oil and inflation causality with the new inflation and oil price increases starting in 2020. US oil production rose almost 40 per cent from its 2015 level to reach 13 million barrels a day in 2019, then fell back to 11.5 million barrels a day in December 2021. This means that the rising oil prices of 2020 took place when US oil production was near its all-time high, having started at 1 million barrels a day in 1920 – again, a facet inconsistent with the Keynesian perspective of a cutback in the supply of oil leading to higher oil prices. The US embargo of Russian oil imports, a demand-side embargo that is the opposite of the oil supply embargo of 1973, occurred well after oil prices were shooting upwards in 2022 along with inflation, and the Russian oil exports may simply be redirected to China instead, leaving world supplies unchanged.

In contrast to the stagflation theory, research has found that the oil price spikes of both the Vietnam War era and the post-2001 era were Granger-predicted by monetary factors. The 2022 oil price increase will no doubt be similarly tested. Controversy over money causality to inflation remains, however, because after 2001, and again after 2008, the money supply rose rapidly while inflation rose only somewhat. This no longer held after 2020, when money supply growth, inflation and oil prices all rose.

The experience after 2008 has been puzzling, and has put in doubt not only the monetary causality of oil prices but also the quantity theory of money, which forms the basis of the argument that oil prices are led by money supply growth. After 2008 money supply growth and both oil and gold prices rose, but inflation did not. The answer is that the money supply growth induced markets to expect higher inflation, which they then built into oil and gold prices.

The unusual result of expected inflation being built into oil and gold prices, but then experiencing a low US inflation rate contrary to expectations, was the outcome of the Fed's new, previously unknown, money and banking policy after 2008. For markets during the period from 2008 to 2019 the new Fed monetary policy caused higher inflation to be expected than actually emerged, with the actual inflation rate average remaining near to 2 per cent. In short, the new Fed policy sterilized the huge growth in the money supply by inducing much of the increase to be held as reserves remaining at the Fed instead of going into circulation.

After 2008 the lack of the expected inflation materializing led to new theories of the relation between money printing and inflation, such as "modern monetary theory". The latter argues that inflation is unlikely to arise from a large financing of Treasury debt through the central bank buying it and so printing more money. Based on having little inflation after the massive money supply increase, this perspective argues that the quantity theory of money tradition for explaining inflation is an anachronism.

This approach is like Keynes' (1930) repudiation of the quantity theory during the deflation after the 1929 stock market crash even as the government money supply rose slightly. This contradicted Keynes' (1923) full embrace of the quantity theory of money. Keynes (1930), as well as more recent theories in this vein, failed to distinguish between the government money supply and the amount of money in circulation, which is dictated in large part by private banks.

Recent theory ignores the fact that vast quantities of the money supply increase were sterilized continually by the Fed, for the first time in US history.

This money was the "excess reserves" that built up at the Fed after it started paying interest on excess reserves to private banks. The Fed in turn transferred inflation tax seigniorage directly to private banks, in return for banks building up the pot of excess reserves at the Fed. Markets had never experienced this, and only in 2014, just when excess reserves reversed their rise upwards and finally began to decline, did the market's inflation expectations and the market dollar prices of oil and gold finally begin to fall closely in line.

This was a confusing period for oil and gold price markets after 2008, which came after a culmination of events that marked a long sequence of increasingly relaxed regulations for the private banking sector. Before 2008 the closeness in Figure 6.2 of the M1 money supply and the CPI price index was evidence in direct support of the quantity theory of money exposed by Fisher, Friedman, and Volcker. Oil, gold and diamond prices reflected the inflation rate prior to 2008 as well as the anticipated inflation.

After 2008 these prices reflected the anticipation of inflation even though actual inflation rose little (until 2021). The switch from reflecting both the actual inflation rate and the expected future inflation rate to reflecting the expected inflation rate but less so the actual inflation rate occurred after 2008 as a result of the way in which the private bank sector was provided insurance against bank collapse by the Fed after this date. This insurance was instituted in a haphazard way after the market crash had occurred in 2008. It caused market turmoil, and came about after a gradual dismantling of the banking regulations and provided a form of bank insurance for the private bank sector.

As a result of the same high Vietnam War inflation that broke down Bretton Woods, caused the famous 1959 to 1969 "Phillips curve" (discussed in the next chapter) and caused oil and gold prices to rise continually with inflation and expected inflation, the US bank sector began to be deregulated. Starting in the early 1980s the question was whether to try to regulate the non-bank banks (as they were called) that were circumventing the normal bank regulation and insurance such as that provided by the Federal Deposit Insurance Corporation. The United States could either extend regulation to bring the non-bank banks into the bank insurance system of the FDIC or let them function under a less regulated banking system.

The United States and United Kingdom both decided to deregulate the bank sector. The United States started the deregulation by passing in 1980 the Depository Institutions Deregulation and Monetary Control Act. This eliminated the interest rate ceiling established in the 1930s ("Regulation Q"). During the zero-inflation trend of the gold standard, Regulation Q had set an interest rate ceiling of 5.25 per cent to avoid usurious rates deemed too high. This did not foretell the birth of the fiat standard, however, and its subsequent high and prolonged inflation rates during the Vietnam War.

Starting in 1978, investment banks had started to evade the Regulation Q interest ceiling. As inflation surged and market interest rates followed upwards, the investment banks devised new means of earning the market interest rate for savings. Much like standard deposit accounts that existed in the regular retail and commercial banks, which were restricted by the 5.25 per cent interest rate ceiling, the investment banks instead offered "mutual funds", which were equity holdings that provided a higher interest rate following market rates instead of being restricted by the Regulation Q ceiling.

After peaking at 12 per cent in November 1974, inflation had fallen to 5 per cent two years later in November 1976. But by 1978 it was back up to 8 per cent and climbing. This was well above the 5.25 per cent ceiling faced by commercial banks. And the high inflation could no longer be viewed as a temporary, short-term event.

It was sensible for the financial sector to devise a way for savers to earn a positive return on savings after taking inflation into account. The innovation of offering the mutual funds achieved this and made the financial sector more efficient at intermediating the savings of households to investment by firms. Nevertheless, it also began the long slide away from having the financial sector insured in an efficient way as the FDIC had envisaged.

In his "Requiem for Regulation Q: what it did and why it passed away", Gilbert (1986) describes the piece-by-piece dismantling of the interest ceiling, which he charts from 1978 to its final demise on 31 March 1986. In describing the shift of funds to depository institutions such as investment banks, he emphasizes that this took place because Regulation Q limited the interest rate that most banks then were subject to: "The Banking Act of 1933 established controls over deposit interest rates for commercial banks that were members of the Federal Reserve System. Nonmember commercial banks became subject to the same controls in the Banking Act of 1935. Mutual savings banks and savings and loan associations were exempt from the ceiling interest rates on deposits until the fall of 1966."

The Regulation Q interest limits imposed on regular banks led to the non-bank banks that could evade the interest rate ceiling. Interest rate ceilings during rising inflation in the fiat era were undoubtedly detrimental to the efficient intermediation of savings to investment through the banking sector. This did not mean that bank insurance for the financial sector as provided through government regulation was unwise in general. After the inevitable dismantling of Regulation Q, however, many argued that bank insurance for the investment banks was unnecessary.

In *The Evolution of Central Banks*, the former Bank of England chief economist Charles Goodhart (1988) states that greater regulation for the investment banks was unnecessary, since their assets were liquid, included much equity and could fully back up customer deposits in money market funds. The point was that they could be excluded from government efforts to provide forms of bank insurance. Goodhart argues that such regulation would simply result in less profit for investment banks without gaining additional insurance for the financial intermediation sector.

The Fed states that currently 38 per cent of the 8,039 commercial banks in the United States are members of the Federal Reserve System (Huntington Beach 2020), whereby they must hold 3 per cent of their capital as equity ownership at the Fed. Of these, the FDIC states that it "directly supervises" more than 5,000 banks (FIDC website: www.fdic.gov/about/what-we-do/index.html). The current amount of deposits insured per account by the FDIC is $250,000.

To take care of the glaring number of non-FDIC-insured banks, which in 1980 constituted 60 per cent of all banks, the 1980 Act also required non-FDIC banks to hold some reserves at the Fed. This latter provision doubled down on the lopsided approach to insuring the private banking system by requiring deposit insurance premiums for FDIC banks, while requiring at the same time that a fraction of deposits for all banks had to be held as reserves at the Fed.

Subsequently, the Garn–St Germain Depository Institutions Act of 1982 formally allowed the creation of accounts that were free of interest restrictions and held largely at investment banks. These money market accounts, and mutual funds, could be held at either FDIC-insured banks or non-FDIC-insured non-bank banks. Since more interest could be earned on the money market accounts than on savings accounts at the more regulated FDIC banks, the now legal status of money market accounts at non-bank banks accelerated the customer shift away from FDIC bank deposits into non-FDIC-insured investment banks.

One view of the shift is given by the relation between the money supply and the price level in Figure 6.2. From 1959 to 1980 the M1 monetary aggregate very closely followed the CPI aggregate price index. After 1980, as the depositors shifted funds to the money market accounts, the M1 aggregate began to rise erratically and more rapidly than the CPI price level.

An additional deregulation that increased the profit of banks, including non-bank banks, was the 1994 repeal of the prohibition of interstate branching by banks. Such prohibition was established by the McFadden Act of 1927, because of the competition between state-charted and nationally charted banks and the demand for protective legislation. By 1994 the repeal was simply a case of codifying into law the evasion of interstate branching that had already become well established. Banks circumvented the prohibition on interstate branching through the creation of bank holding companies that held banks located in different states. The Riegle–Neal Interstate Banking and Branching Efficiency Act of 1994 allowed interstate branching without the need for holding companies, which increased efficiency in banking, while allowing non-bank banks to benefit even more because of their relatively low regulatory burden from the 1980 and 1982 Acts.

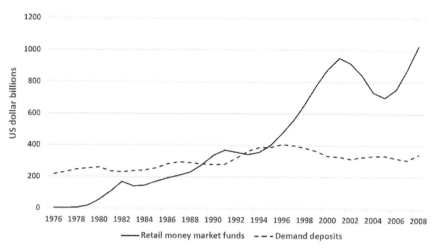

Figure 6.4 Money market funds versus demand deposits (FDIC banks), annual, 1976–2008
Source: FRED.

Finally, the Gramm–Leach–Bliley Act of 1999 repealed the part of the Glass–Steagall Banking Act of 1933 that separated commercial banking from investment banking. This had been part of the legislation that ended the Great Depression by also including the creation of the FDIC. It was designed to avoid bank imprudence, which could lead to bank crises and collapse by avoiding risky speculation in connection with depositor funds. Its repeal allowed investment banks to act exactly like commercial banks, again effectively codifying what the investment banks already were doing in roundabout ways and thereby increasing their efficiency.

Figure 6.4 provides a direct view of the rise of money market funds during the US bank deregulation period, versus the stagnation of demand deposits at commercial banks. Demand deposits started near to $200 billion in 1976. After modest growth to $400 billion in 1996, from then onwards demand deposits fell to $300 billion in 2007, just before the financial crisis of 2008. Meanwhile, money market funds went from essentially zero in 1978 up to $285 billion in 1989, which was about the level of demand deposits, where the lines first cross in Figure 6.4. Then money market funds more than trebled to reach $950 billion in 2001, and went on up to $1,025 billion in 2008.

In the United Kingdom, a related bank deregulation process took place, known as the "Big Bang" of banking deregulation. On 27 October 1986 financial trading restrictions were eased, with banks allowed to compete more freely both within the United Kingdom and internationally. This enabled greater efficiency in the finance sector, with far fewer restrictions (Clemons & Weber 1990).

Bank deregulation in the United States would have been fine in terms of greater efficiency if it really had been safe to have a giant part of the banking system outside the deposit insurance system of the FDIC-insured banks. In 2008 the sudden insolvency of investment banks caused depositors to dramatically withdraw funds from investment bank money market accounts and deposit them back in commercial bank deposit accounts. After 2008 it became clear that the bank system was not properly insured against insolvency and crisis.

Investment banks were without FDIC insurance on money market funds. They were also holding the hot potato of securitized home loans, or mortgages, when these went into a massive state of default during the crisis of 2008–09. Investment banks became insolvent, with assets less than liabilities. The Fed and central banks across the intricately connected banking system then scrambled to avoid a collapse of the international banking system of the type seen in the Great Depression.

Now we come to the way in which this deregulatory movement enabled the new policy that the Fed enacted in 2008, which led to the sterilization of the massive money supply growth. In 2006 another deregulatory banking law had been passed, called the Financial Services Regulatory Relief Act of 2006. It allowed interest to be paid on what at the time were only required reserves; this was to take effect in 2011. The idea was to let banks earn interest on the reserves that they were required to hold at the Fed, since earning zero interest on this was argued to be a tax on banks.

Then the investment bank panic hit, and the United States enacted the Emergency Economic Stabilization Act of 2008. This Act enabled the Fed to change the effective date on paying interest on reserves to 2008 instead of 2011. In 2008, when the Fed had run out of reserves and had to borrow from other central banks (through "swaps"), the Fed was desperate to draw in reserves. Thus the Fed began paying interest not only on required reserves, which were down to about 1 per cent of the deposits of all commercial banks, but, rather, on all reserves, contrary to the intent of the 2006 Act.

The intent of the 2006 Act was clearly deregulatory. The governor of the Fed, Donald Kohn, testified in hearings (Committee on Banking, Housing, and Urban Affairs 2006: 9) that

> [t]hese items would allow the Federal Reserve to pay interest on balances held at Reserve Banks, provide the Board greater flexibility in setting Reserve requirements, and permit depository institutions to pay interest on demand deposits. Together these changes would allow for a substantial reduction in regulatory burdens on banks and small businesses and an increase in the efficiency of our financial system.

The language of the Act talks about interest on reserves without specifying required reserves, although Kohn implicitly indicated that the interest was meant for required reserves. Senator Michael Crapo sponsored the bill and made clear in his statements that the interest was aimed only for required reserves, since required reserves were imposed more heavily on small commercial banks than on large investment banks. The Act was meant to rectify the imbalance by allowing smaller banks to earn interest on their greater burden of required reserves. In previous history, the only reserves kept at the Fed were required reserves, with excess reserves kept as close to zero as was possible through the "federal funds market".

Nonetheless, with the 2006 Act's wording being interest on "reserves" rather than on "required reserves", the Fed took full advantage of the legislative ambiguity to extend its reach and pay interest on any amount of reserves. This allowed the Fed to build up trillions of US dollars in excess reserves, which it held on behalf of private banks after buying Treasury debt and mortgage-backed securities from them. These excess reserves kept the new money from entering circulation and left inflation within the Fed's target range. This historic sequence of deregulation inadvertently gave rise to the myth that the quantity theory of money was dead, when in fact banks were paid to sterilize much of the new money by keeping it sitting at the Fed.

The bank regulation of the 1980s and 1990s, and right on up to 2008, ended with a crisis that turned monetary policy through money supply creation into bank insurance policy for uninsured banks during a severe banking crisis. The deregulation itself led to the crisis, since investment banks were self-insured, rather than federally insured, and more profitable because they could keep less in terms of reserves at the Fed relative to deposits and did not pay FDIC insurance premiums. The missing inflation after 2008 was caused by the missing money-in-circulation kept through excess reserves to help insure the bank system. Therefore, the monetary base, which includes reserves plus currency, for the first time ever after 2008 exceeded M1, which excludes reserves but includes currency plus demand deposits. Excess reserves at the Fed exploded rather than being zero, as they were before 2008. Unlike all previous history, the Fed's banking policy directly abutted its monetary policy, with the strange result being that the money supply accelerated dramatically but little inflation resulted.

When the money supply rose during the Vietnam War, so did inflation. After 2008 markets continued to build in the expected future inflation rates into the prices of all the things they considered, even though inflation did not result. The expected inflation eventually dropped in 2014, and so did oil prices. Excess reserves also began to fall after 2014, with the money supply finally entering circulation at a faster rate. Accordingly, the inflation rate then rose steadily form 2015 until 2018.

When excess reserves held at the Fed fell from $2.6 trillion in January 2015 to $1.8 trillion in July 2018 and they were lent out by banks, actual US inflation rose from 0.0 per cent in February 2015 up to 2.9 per cent in July 2018. Excess reserves continued falling until the pandemic hit in early 2020. In 2020 excess reserves began accumulating again, exceeding $4.2 trillion in December 2021, leaving markets to decipher when this ad hoc accumulation of reserves would be lent out, and actual inflation would rise again. The quantity theory of money is hard to escape. In fact, reserves began to fall, to $3.9 trillion in January 2022, as the inflation rate surged, to 7.9 per cent in February 2022.

The unexpected consequences of money supply financing of budget deficits have fallen on oil prices and other parts of the economy. The next chapter investigates another major economic debate arising out of the Vietnam War era of money printing, which broke down the Bretton Woods system. It describes an ongoing dispute about how inflation affects unemployment during certain periods, which can be characterized through Phillips curves. It illustrates evidence on these episodes with the daylight available now through our extensive databases, especially that of the Federal Reserve Economic Data of the Federal Reserve Bank of St Louis.

7

INFLATION AND UNEMPLOYMENT

A major issue arising out of the Vietnam War is the relationship between inflation and unemployment. This is known as the debate over the "Phillips curve". It has divided Keynesian and neoclassical economists since the 1960s.

New Keynesian models still build in a permanent positive relation between inflation and economic growth. They do this by assuming rigid prices, and monopoly price increases that lead to a relative price increase that they count as higher inflation. Because of the assumed price rigidity mechanism, the price increase is set so that it can raise output while inflation increases. In contrast, neoclassical work finds a negative relation between an inflation increase and economic growth.

The debate surrounds Phillips's (1958) findings for UK data showing episodes in which higher inflation was linked to lower unemployment, in sequential periods over time. Samuelson and Solow (1960) then applied this empirical finding to a policy suggestion. They argue that if, the Fed raised the inflation rate, the unemployment rate would fall, so we could choose a policy of allowing higher inflation to lower unemployment.

The new Keynesian school of economics has since assumed a permanent negative relationship between inflation and unemployment, although commonly with the substitution of economic growth for employment. Neoclassical economists instead argue that the inflation–unemployment negative relation is temporary, found only under certain conditions and with no foundation for conducting monetary policy based on it. Sorting out what has occurred between inflation and unemployment is important for deciding monetary policy going forward.

If there were a permanent negative relation, then a positive inflation rate might be warranted to push unemployment levels down. If there is no permanent relationship, then there would be no basis for trying to lower unemployment by increasing the inflation rate. Rather, it would be worthwhile to understand when exactly the temporary episodes have arisen, so that we can seek to explain them as they occurred historically.

Inflation does rise episodically at times, especially during wars and crises. Based on Phillips curve episodes, Keynesians argue that some inflation is good, and this bleeds into the debate on what the target rate of inflation should be. The 1978 US law binding the Federal Reserve states both inflation rate and unemployment rate targets.

As related to the original 1946 Act guiding the Fed, the 1978 Act allows for a higher inflation rate than the target level as specified by law if the unemployment rate target has not been met. The law remains agnostic but open to exploiting a Phillips curve relationship in the conduct of monetary policy. This means that the unemployment–inflation relation is still prominent in monetary policy debate.

For the decade from 1959 to 1969 a negative relation between the inflation rate and the unemployment rate was found, such as those identified by Phillips (1958) for an earlier period. During this decade the Fed printed more money and the Treasury employed more resources in fighting the Vietnam War. The money printing combined with the fiscal expenditure on war caused the inflation rate to rise as the unemployment rate went down.

Nobel laureate economists Milton Friedman (1968), Edmund Phelps (1970), and Robert E. Lucas (1972) argued that the trade-off was temporary rather than a permanent relation that could be exploited for monetary policy purposes. Solow's (1956) neoclassical growth theory and the related "real business theory" (Kydland & Prescott 1982) showed that productivity is the source of economic growth rather than inflation. Extensions to the Solow growth theory explained productivity through education (Lucas 1988), and included the government's money supply being used to finance expenditure. This gave the result that inflation acts as a tax that lowers economic growth (Gillman, Harris & Mátyás 2004).

Phillips was a New Zealander studying the British economy with UK data from 1861 to 1913 for his 1958 study. He identified temporary episodes of sequential, connected time periods showing inflation rising as unemployment fell, or, vice versa, periods with inflation falling and unemployment rising. Throughout British and American history, there are three types of readily identified Phillips curves that will be classified here (Gillman 2022a).

Phillips curves occur when there is a wartime build-up, as Phillips identified just before and during the First World War, from 1913 to 1918 in the United Kingdom. A similar wartime build-up curve exists for the United States, just before and during the Second World War, from 1938 to 1942. These episodes involve a movement up the curve to higher inflation and lower unemployment. This also characterizes the 1959–69 episode in the United States during

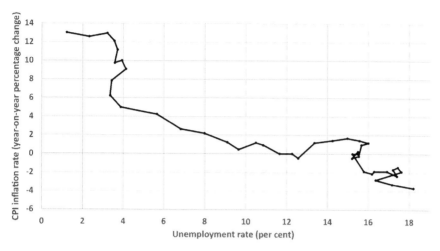

Figure 7.1 "Wartime build-up" US Phillips curve for the Second World War, October 1938–
May 1942
Source: FRED.

the Vietnam War. Then money was printed to expand military spending, the employment rate rose and so did inflation, as in all wartime build-up Phillips curves.

Figure 7.1 presents the wartime build-up Phillips curve for the United States from 1938 to 1942. The inflation rate (vertical axis) rises as the unemployment rate (horizontal axis) falls. This starts at the bottom right-hand point in October 1938, and moves up monthly, with each month connected to the next. This is what is meant by connected sequential time periods. To be clear, during such a wartime Phillips curve the money supply growth rate of the central bank accelerates to finance the increased government expenditure during the war, so that both inflation and employment rise, and unemployment falls.

The United States also had a build-up Phillips curve for the First World War, like the UK experience. Nonetheless, these wartime build-up Phillips curves, such as for the United States in the two world wars and the Vietnam War, are as rare as are major wars. In contrast, a frequent occurrence of Phillips curves exists during economic recessions.

Real business cycle theory explains how recessions are common, unavoidable and natural. So are coinciding Phillips curves common, as explained using the logic of Irving Fisher (1933) in explaining the Great Depression. In fact, the largest incidence of Phillips curves is evident during recessions, since these are recurrent and, in that sense, frequent compared to wars. The recession Phillips curves are characterized by a movement down the Phillips curve to lower inflation and higher unemployment.

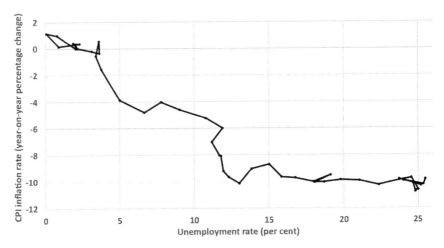

Figure 7.2 "Recession" US Phillips curve for the Great Depression, June 1929–April 1933
Source: FRED.

It may be surprising that, despite Phillips's contribution, Fisher (1926) is recognized as first identifying Phillips curves, doing so for the US recessions of 1906–07, 1912–14 and 1920–21. Most other US recessions also exhibit Phillips curves, with sequential movements downwards, as seen for 1929–33, 1948–49, 1970–71, 1980–82, 2001–02 and 2008–09. This collection includes both the Great Depression and the Great Recession, which featured banking panics.

From June 1929 to April 1933, Figure 7.2 presents the US Phillips curve during the Great Depression. As in Fisher's (1933) theory, the private bank money in terms of demand deposits at banks fell during the bank panic, while the price level was falling, and the inflation rate became increasingly negative. A decrease in the money supply growth rate caused the negative inflation rate here, but because of private bank money contracting during the recession.

Such a recession-based Phillips curve contrasts strongly with the central bank money supply expanding in a wartime build-up inflation episode, which gives a Phillips curve for a completely different reason. Now it is the private bank money supply growth contracting that causes deflation or a lower inflation rate. Fisher (1933) described how private loans default, banks go bankrupt, the bank deposits contract as loans are called in, the price level spirals downwards and unemployment rises. This could occur across globally interconnected economies through financial integration, and for the bank-panic-caused Great Depression and Great Recession there were Phillips curves appearing simultaneously in many nations.

Figure 7.3 presents the US Phillips curve during the Great Recession. It displays a movement down the Phillips curve for July 2008 to July 2009. The inflation rate

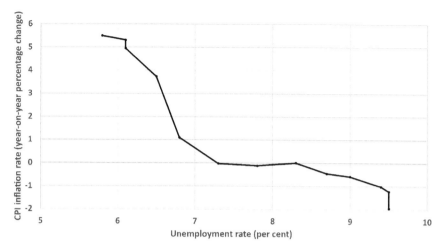

Figure 7.3 "Recession" US Phillips curve for the Great Recession, July 2008–July 2009
Source: FRED.

started above 5 per cent with moderate unemployment, in the top left of the graph, and fell as the unemployment reached almost 10 per cent, in the bottom right of the graph.

The third category of Phillips curves consists of "bounce-backs" of the financial sector after it has been repressed. When financial repression ends, the inflation rate and employment rate both rise, causing a movement up the Phillips curve. Private bank money expands its demand deposits and makes more loans for investment, the inflation rate rises and the unemployment rate falls.

From May 1933 to April 1934 in the United States a bounce-back Phillips curve is found after the FDIC was established. This reformed the private bank industry and provided for its normal functioning after the panic of 1932–33. Another example is when the United States started raising the rate of interest on excess reserves (IOER) in 2015. Figure 7.4 presents a Phillips curve for this US period, involving a movement up the Phillips curve from a low inflation rate near zero and an unemployment rate near 6 per cent, in the bottom left corner, to an inflation rate of 3 per cent and an unemployment rate of 3.75 per cent, in the top left corner.

The most recent example of a Phillips curve is of the build-up type during the Covid-19 pandemic, in which a war-style expenditure effort was undertaken to combat the economic havoc caused by the pandemic. From May 2020 to November 2021, Figure 7.5 shows a movement up the Phillips curve, as unemployment fell from 13 per cent to 4 per cent and the inflation rate increased from near zero

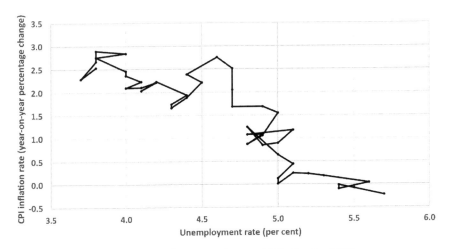

Figure 7.4 "Bounce-back" US Phillips curve, January 2015–October 2018
Source: FRED.

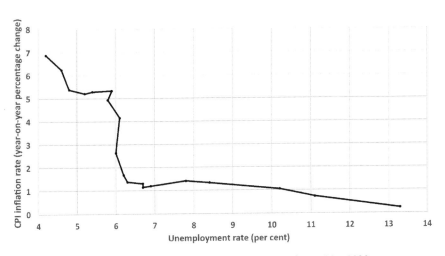

Figure 7.5 "Build-up" US Phillips curve for the Covid-19 pandemic, May 2020–November 2021
Source: FRED.

to 7 per cent. This was a rare crisis that forced the government to print money at an accelerated rate to finance rapid growth in Treasury expenditure and debt, like wartime. One can expect another burst of inflation and a new bounce-back Phillips curve to begin once the Fed starts deregulating capital markets again by raising the interest rate on reserves in 2022, as occurred in Figure 7.4.

Given a categorization of temporary historical types of Phillips curves, there is another exercise that has also been conducted to link inflation to unemployment. This exercise is computing over a long period of time the correlation between inflation and unemployment. Phillips (1958), as part of his study, did this for UK data from 1861 to 1913, and found a positive correlation.

Keynesians have evolved their theory to make this exercise of correlation between inflation and the output growth rate of real GDP, instead of unemployment. Again, carefully picking a time period can produce such a positive correlation between inflation and economic growth. This correlation was a side point in Phillips (1958), with the main idea being to identify episodes of temporary Phillips curve in sequentially connected time periods.

Taking Phillips' (1958) concept of temporary Phillips curves further, one can see if these episodes hold over a long period of time. For US data since 1959, graphing together all the unemployment and inflation rate sequences results in a blob of connected dots with no long-run Phillips curve evident. This was the essence of the point made by Fisher, Phillips, Friedman, Phelps and Lucas. Only temporary Phillips curve episodes between inflation and unemployment exist, without any such long-run relation.

In contrast to a positive relation between inflation and output growth, as new Keynesian models create, evidence shows how inflation acts as a tax that lowers the return on capital and the economic growth rate. This is found in repeated empirical evidence and is uncontroversial. Inflation lowers output growth in the long run.

Figure 7.6 shows a long-run statistical relationship in which higher inflation causes lower real GDP output growth rate. For the countries in the Organisation for Economic Co-operation and Development (OECD), with the real GDP growth rate on the vertical axis and inflation on the horizontal axis, as the inflation rate rises the growth rate falls. The figure is from Gillman, Harris and Mátyás (2004), using standard "panel data estimation", while also including "instrumental variables" (IVs), and estimating each segment of the graph separately in a contiguous fashion (spline).

In the clear light of evidence, as well as theory, we can be sure that, if inflation rises, we do not know what will happen immediately to unemployment and economic growth, although we may know the long-run effects of sustained inflation. Any effect of inflation depends on the cause of inflation in the first place. Recessions naturally lower inflation and raise unemployment, as private bank deposits decrease and firms fail. Increased government expenditure to fight a war has raised inflation and lowered unemployment in the past, causing wartime build-up Phillips curves. Sudden banking regulatory reform by the establishment of the FDIC in 1933 and the lifting of interest on excess reserves after

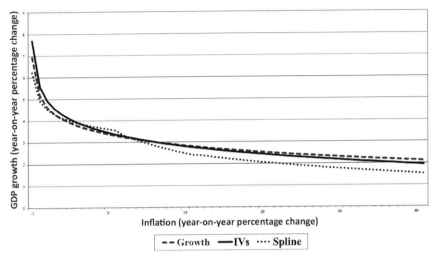

Figure 7.6 Effect of inflation on real GDP growth rate, OECD country sample, panel data estimation
Source: Gillman, Harris and Mátyás (2004).

2015 let the private banking industry rebound, increase its money deposits and give rise to the third category, bounce-back Phillips curves, as presented here.

The Federal Reserve has demonstrated since 2008 that it can sterilize the increased money supply by keeping excess reserves at the Fed, preventing them from entering circulation. If the Fed again deregulates capital markets by lifting the interest rate on reserves, as it did briefly from 2015 to 2018, the reserves will enter circulation as banks lend them out, causing investment to rise, unemployment to fall and inflation to rise. This would provide another rebound in the private banking system after the end of stifling regulation, which would probably give rise to a Phillips relation of the bounce-back type.

Phillips curves happen in nearly every economic recession. Fisher (1933) warned against "artificially reflating" the price level through the central bank increasing the money supply growth rate, since, he argued, it would not help bring economic recovery. Rather, the bank sector needs to recover naturally in normal recessions or be reformed in bank-crisis-led major recessions or depressions. Employment rates are determined by business cycle fluctuations and the level of the tax rate on labour and corporate income, while unemployment rates are determined both by business cycles and from the moral hazard effects of unemployment insurance policy that subsidizes being unemployed.

The inflation tax affects employment mainly by lowering real output growth, which in turn lowers the employment rate and raises unemployment. When moderate inflation is rising, as in the 1970s and since 2020, decreases in the government money supply growth rate can result in lower inflation, although possibly with a temporary increase in unemployment during recession. Friedman (1994: 233) summarizes the debate on inflation versus unemployment: "We have been led by a false dichotomy: inflation or unemployment. That option is an illusion. The real option is whether we have higher unemployment as a result of higher inflation or as a temporary side effect of a cure for inflation."

Monetary policy affects inflation and growth alike by determining both the level of the inflation tax and whether it is suppressed through the repression of real interest rates, as through IOER policy. In trying to provide bank insurance after a bank crash, capital markets can be repressed, economic growth lowered and the degree to which people enter the labour market to seek employment decreased. With efficient bank insurance in place, monetary policy can more easily promote a low inflation rate, a stable banking system and real output growth and high employment.

This first part of the book has described when simple principles guided policy under both gold and fiat monetary regimes. The next part describes early central banking, how central bank policy evolved to help bring the world's financial system towards collapse and the frenzied activity of central banks after the collapse that threatens us today. The next chapter starts with the origin of central banking, to begin the story of how central banks and their governments have been providing insurance against bank panic contagion in the private sector.

PART II

IGNOMINY: CENTRAL BANKS, INSURANCE AND INFLATION

8

THE RISE OF CENTRAL BANKS

Central banks conduct monetary policy for their governments and have oversight of the private bank system. Central banks evolved from private banking. The development of private banking hinged on how interest came to be a normal return on capital. It has a complex history, because religion has imbued interest with questionable morality. The main problem was that a lack of good regulation allowed "usurious" rates of interest to be charged that were considered too high.

For the first two centuries BC, Ancient Indian, Vedic, Sutra and Jatakas texts referred to usury as interest in a negative way. Religions and governments restricted or banned interest. Julius Caesar imposed interest rate ceilings, and in 349 AD all interest was banned in Rome. Pope Clement V banned interest in 1311 for Christianity. Judaism disallowed some forms of interest but was lax in regulating interest payments. Islamic law continues to ban interest to this day (Visser & McIntosh 1998).

Stable money during the Renaissance allowed private banking to flourish. This required innovative ways to avoid the prohibition on usury. Although the payment of interest was at first concealed, its use broadened steadily in ways that led to modern banking. In the fourteenth century the Genoese city state government borrowed money, creating public debt. The funding for such loans was provided by the private investors who helped build Genoa as a centre for transportation and trade. But, with the charging of interest prohibited by the Catholic Church, they resorted to indirect means for obtaining interest for loans.

A way to receive interest developed through the sale of "bills of exchange" between international branches of the same bank. The exchange of bills (debt owed by an entity) allowed them to be redeemed in a different currency in a different country for a set amount after a certain time, such as three months. Then the redemption was transferred back to the original branch, with the exchange amounts specified in the other country's currency such that a larger transfer was returned to the original branch than had left it. This incremental income acted as the interest payment for the length of the transaction. Although they were subject to the risk of international currency exchange rate changes, these transactions enabled interest to be paid in effect through a tangled web of transactions (Felloni & Laura 2017).

Banks spread in Europe during the Renaissance because they could earn interest. The Medici Bank was founded in 1397, a private Barcelona bank in 1401 and the Bank of Saint George of Genoa in 1408. The latter acted as a private bank that could lend to anyone. It also served as a central bank in making loans to the city state.

Providing interest through increasingly less costly ways, across a broad trading region even while interest was prohibited, was a key innovation leading to modern banks in the West. Another innovation was law granting limited liability rather than general liability for companies. This occurred in Renaissance Florence through a 1408 city state law (see Reinert & Fredona 2017). Goldthwaite (2009: 67) states:

> The only formal innovation of any consequence was the *accomandita*, a contract enabled by legislation promulgated by the commune in 1408 that allowed outsiders to invest in a partnership and share profits on the same terms as the other partners, without, however, risking anything beyond their investment. In other words, these investors were not subject to the personal unlimited liability characteristic of the classic partnership contract.

General liability partnerships allowed borrowers to take both the company assets and the personal assets of the partners of the company to pay off debt, even down to the silverware. Limited liability was an alternative way to form a company. It allowed merchant partners to be liable for debt only up to the amount of the company's assets, rather than also including the partners' personal assets.

Stable money, the provision of interest by private banks and the introduction of limited liability allowed private banking to flourish during the Renaissance. This enabled loans to finance development and economic growth. Parallel to the Genoa bank, the Medici Bank spread across Renaissance Europe from its deep links to the Lombardy ancestral clan that extended to Milan (de Roover 1963: 350): "The domain of the Italian merchant-bankers did not extend east of the Rhine. West of it, they were in exclusive control. While competition between Florentines, Genoese, and Venetians was strong enough to prevent the transformation of this vast area into a colonial territory, Italian hegemony had nevertheless the beneficial effect of welding it into something like a common market."

The Medici Bank spread to London and gave rise to the name of Lombard Street in that city, where international finance found a centre. Bagehot's *Lombard Street* (1873) references Adam Smith in describing how, by the early seventeenth century, banks were continuing to add functions. Banks first took in various coinage and provided a uniform amount that was given back to customers for a small fee (*agio*). As coin became risky to carry around, customers began depositing them in banks. With trust gained in the banks, customers began leaving their deposits for periods of time. Accumulating deposit accounts for customers allowed banks to begin lending money for interest to both governments and private companies (see also Dean 1884).

Bagehot (1873: 36) stresses how the first banks of Italy were just finance companies without the deposit system of modern banks: "Deposit banking is a very difficult thing to begin, because people do not like to let money out of their sight, especially do not like to let it out of sight without security still more ... The first banks were not founded for our system of deposit banking, or for anything like it. They were founded for much more pressing reasons, and having been founded, they, or copies of them, were applied to our modern uses."

The Bank of England came about formally in 1694 through the incorporation of the "Governor and Company of the Bank of England" by royal charter of the English Crown. The Bank was originally established to provide loans to the English government when its finances were depleted through war with France. With its incorporation, it obtained exclusive rights to hold the balances of the Treasury of the English government, a monopoly over issuing banknotes that could circulate and special limited liability as a joint-stock company bank, whereas all other banks had unlimited liability for any debts.

Limited liability allowed banks to leverage up their capital contributions without personal liability, by making more loans than their capital reserves. They could do this by calculating how much ready capital at hand would normally be needed at the bank, then lending out the rest. Taking this risk allowed for more loans and profits for the banks, without its owners being liable for loans beyond the amount of capital equity invested in the bank.

The benefits of limited liability for banking became increasingly clear over time. Bagehot (1873: 15) describes how general partner banks were at a competitive disadvantage, since they could make only loans that risked all personal wealth, while limited liability joint-stock banks could make a higher profit on their investment through lending out much more than their equity in the company: "The distinctive feature of the banker, says Ricardo, 'begins as soon as he uses the money of others'; as long as he uses his own money he is only a capitalist. Accordingly, all the banks in Lombard Street (and bill brokers are for this purpose only a kind of bankers) hold much money belonging to other people on running account and on deposit."

Nevertheless, it took a royal charter to obtain a joint-stock company status with limited liability, and, meanwhile, other banks were stuck with general partnerships. When bankruptcy occurred, general partners had to go through bankruptcy courts and incur the high cost of winding up the debts. The benefits of leveraging up loans relative to deposits plus the greater cost of bankruptcy for general partners created a growing demand for the limited liability corporate form, which selective grants through royal charter could not supply in sufficient quantity. Finally, the British government passed the Companies Act of 1862 (technically, the Act for the Registration, Incorporation and Regulation of Joint-Stock Companies: Evans 1908: 461), which allowed limited liability to any company through the joint-stock formation of a corporation – the predecessor to modern corporations (Gillman & Eade 1995; Carney 1998).

Foucaud (2011: 1–2, 26) relates how the Companies Act of 1862 in effect deregulated the capital finance industry by spreading limited liability to all firms, including banks, and launching modern finance:

> [T]he deregulation of 1862, which allowed any company to register as a limited liability entity, thus profoundly changing the behavior of entrepreneurs … Indeed, one part of the financial sector seems to have been more directly involved than others in the crisis: financial corporations. Having appeared in England in the early 1860s, their numbers increased very quickly in 1864 and 1865. All of them were formed as limited-liability companies. Initially they had no precisely determined function: they were to finance industrial or commercial activities, buy gilts, etc. … One of the leading consequences of the application of the Law of 1862 was to promote the expansion of new actors in the financial sector – the financial corporations.

With the Industrial Revolution taking place and creating a high demand for capital investment, the 1862 Act led to the growth of newly incorporated banks with limited liability. By being able to invest more capital through making loans than the amount of equity of the bank, limited liability banks increased the capital in circulation for funding investment. As the law enabled widespread use of this corporate form in Britain, which was absent in other countries such as France, with its undeveloped banking sector, British limited liability banks increased the capital investment in Western markets, with their international centre in Lombard Street in London. New capital loans made to customers appeared as new private bank deposits in the customer accounts and increased the private bank supply of money.

Over time, as more joint-stock banks were granted limited liability, the Bank of England's distinguishing feature was to be the only joint-stock bank that could issue banknotes in Britain. These later became currency as we know it.

They circulated with the implicit backing of the Crown, whereas other private banknotes had only the backing of the net assets of the bank.

Peel's Act of 1844 dictated that the Bank of England note issue had to be fully backed by gold reserves and a limited amount of Treasury debt. This kept the money supply under strict control. Bagehot's (1873) focus therefore turned to the other function of the Bank of England, which was keeping the reserves of the other private banks that gravitated towards the Bank, given its exclusive right to issue banknotes.

The Bank of England was a private bank that, at the same time, became the nation's central bank, within a system of private banking. As the only issuer of currency recognized as legal tender, Bagehot describes that the Bank of England's Issue Department was where it kept a full amount of reserves to completely back up its note issue, which circulated as a form of money in common use. The Bank of England's other element was called the Banking Department.

The Banking Department in practice held reserves for the entire private bank system. Other private banks would issue loans and make new deposits payable in the currency of the Bank of England. This meant that banks would need to be able to convert customer deposits into currency upon demand. To do this they kept reserves at the Bank of England.

The Bank of England held all the reserves for the entire private banking system, while those banks kept only a minimum reserve for daily needs of cash. The Bank of England was also a private profit-making bank. It would lend out its reserves from the private banks in order to make new loans, investments and profit. But, because of its role as a reserve for the other banks, it lent out a much smaller fraction of its reserves.

In lending out the private banking system's pot of reserves, the Bank had to keep a sufficiently large amount of reserves to meet any demands of the private bank depositors. With the Bank's owners not personally liable for loans, and seeking to maximize profit, it became a goal to lend out as much as was reasonable relative to the expected demand for redemption of deposits in the gold-backed currency. At the same time, the Bank had to keep a sufficient fraction of the deposits of the entire private banking system on reserve, to ensure a sufficient cushion in the event of a contagious bank crisis and to ensure the solvency of the Bank of England itself.

With this fractional reserve banking centred on Lombard Street and based in the security of the Bank of England, the private banks of Lombard Street could rapidly circulate capital to its most profitable use. Since other countries lacked the joint-stock framework and subsequent centralization of finance, Bagehot finds that this made Britain the centre of international finance, with which other nations could not compete. The fractional reserve banking system was a technological innovation in banking that allowed more capital to circulate and be invested.

The reach of this banking technological advance resulted from allowing interest on loans, deposit-taking by private banks, the sole legal note issuing authority of the Bank of England and limited liability, which permitted banks to raise more private equity capital and provide more loans for investment. Essential to Britain becoming the financial centre of the world was the emergence of the Bank of England as the central bank for a system that allowed for a minimal amount of capital to remain as reserves at the Bank. This enabled the rest of the capital to circulate from savers to investors through the system of private banks, which circulated wealth more rapidly than any other country and so drew international investment from around the world.

Bagehot attempted to determine the amount of reserves the central bank should keep. With a smaller fraction of the capital held in the Bank of England's reserves relative to the amount of loans and investment of the entire private banking system, profits were higher. This made for a greater yield on capital investment made in the banking sector. But, as the yield increased, so did the risk that defaulted loans could lead to financial ruin for the Bank.

Similarly, a single bank faced failure if its borrowers could not pay back loans. In this case, as default began to become likely and of public knowledge, depositors of the private bank would begin withdrawing their deposits. The bank would then withdraw all its reserves held at the Bank of England to pay off depositors. If only one bank failed, the Bank of England could easily cover the withdrawal of reserves. If customers at other banks worried about their bank also failing, however, there could be a "bank run", or bank panic. Then all the banks would begin taking out reserves, as in a contagion.

Bagehot (1873) states that the Bank of England would have to insure the depositors by freely giving out loans to banks as needed, so that their finances could be shored up and a bank run avoided. During a contagion, the Bank again would have to lend out reserves freely, although Bagehot specifies this should be at reasonably high interest rates and should include good collateral. Although not fully accepted at the time that Bagehot wrote, as he details, this main role of the Bank was as lender of last resort.

The Bank of England had to keep enough reserves at all times to be able to ward off a bank panic among the private bank sector. Otherwise, if the Bank ran out of reserves to lend out, it might have to draw upon the reserves held in the Issue Department for currency backing. Bagehot describes how the Bank had depleted its gold reserves that backed up its currency several times in the past when a bank panic struck, thereby violating the ruling in Peel's Act that the currency be fully backed by the gold and Treasury debt reserves. Depleting the reserves that backed the official notes issued by the Bank threatened confidence in the both the currency notes and in the private banking system, which, if left unchecked, could cause the collapse of the entire central bank and private bank system and lead to drastic deflation.

Bagehot (1873) suggests that, in order to avoid running out of reserves, the Bank needed to hold an "apprehension minimum" of reserves that would maintain confidence in the entire banking system. This might be 40 per cent of reserves relative to the whole amount of private bank deposits, or one-third as others had suggested. A main issue for Bagehot, in fact, was deciding what fraction of deposits to keep as reserves at the Bank of England.

Alternative bank systems were in operation in other nations, in which, essentially, each bank held a calculated quantity of reserves necessary to meet its own needs. Bagehot (1873) argues that, if every private bank held some similarly high fraction of reserves, the amount of new loans would be reduced for the entire system. He describes how French private banks each held reserves on their own, rather than relying on the reserves of the central bank, with the result of earning less profit and drawing in less of the potential customer deposits.

Bagehot shows that the total French reserves were much greater in proportion to total deposits, as compared to the British system. Bagehot (1973: appendix, note A) calculates the reserve fraction of total liabilities at the time for Britain to be 11 per cent, versus 25 per cent for France, 47 per cent for Germany and 12 per cent for the United States. The result was that the financial system in France was less profitable and had proportionately less capital investment.

An aspect of the American system at the time that Bagehot liked was that each bank had a required amount of reserves. He tentatively suggested that the Bank of England might likewise consider such a policy. The idea was that the Bank should decide whether the apprehension minimum was 40 per cent, or some other percentage, and then perhaps adopt that reserve ratio.

As the insurance system for the British banking system, the Bank of England's job was clear. Bagehot's entire enquiry into the Bank is a treatise adjudicating how best to supply such insurance. Although it had long been a private bank, the UK government nationalized the Bank of England in 1946 and made it wholly owned by the government. It is both the central bank of the United Kingdom and a full part of the UK government. The Bank of England Act of 1998 instituted an inflation rate target of 2.5 per cent that guides its monetary policy, but not its bank insurance policy. That policy is still much as Bagehot described it – at least, until the bank panic of 2008.

In the United States, the Fed came into being after a banking panic in 1907. Congress established a commission to consider a solution to banking panics, which then led to the establishment of the Federal Reserve System. As described in the Fed's web pages: "The Aldrich–Vreeland Act of 1908, passed as an immediate response to the panic of 1907, provided for emergency currency issue during crises. It also established the National Monetary Commission (NMC) to search for a long-term solution to the nation's banking and financial problems." The NMC deliberated from 1909 to 1912 and provided recommendations. Congress modified these into what became the Federal Reserve Act of 1913, with the Fed being established in 1914. The Federal Reserve was implicitly expected to stop bank panics.

Perhaps it was thought that the Federal Reserve would automatically act as the Bank of England had in Bagehot's times. Alternatively, the Fed might use the model of the US private bank clearing houses, which emerged independently and pooled together private bank reserve funds for use during crises by distressed banks. Gorton (1985: 277) suggests that the Fed was designed exactly to take the place of the clearing houses and to function as an insurance agent for the bank industry:

> An essential feature of the banking industry then was the endogenous development of the clearinghouse, a governing association of banks to which individual banks voluntarily abrogated certain rights and powers normally held by firms. Behaving most of the time as the dominant authority in a market-like setting, the clearinghouse was capable of temporarily behaving as a single firm during banking panics. The powers and functions that clearinghouses developed most resembled those of a central bank. In fact, it is almost literally true that the Federal Reserve System, as originally conceived, was simply the nationalization of the private clearinghouse system.

Nonetheless, the Fed did not act in the same way as the clearing houses or the Bank of England historically to stop the bank panic that arose during the Great Depression. It held reserves to back up the currency, as required through the gold standard. But it did not pool reserves from private banks and lend these to distressed banks during the crisis, even though it was expected to do so after the United States had previously suffered a sequence of bank panics. Its bank insurance role was not well defined, and this failure became evident with the US bank contagion of the Great Depression.

The Great Depression led to a temporary suspension of the gold standard for about six months, then to a temporary gold regime between the two world wars, on to the Bretton Woods regime based on the US dollar and, finally, to the fiat standard since 1971. Since the fiat standard began, the Fed has decided how much money to print by buying Treasury debt, along with recently buying additional classes of assets such as housing loans. After abrogating the bank insurance role during the Great Depression, since 2008 the Fed has attempted to provide insurance for the fractional reserve banking system, using excess reserves held at the Fed, in a vague semblance to Bagehot's Bank of England.

The modern problem of central banking is twofold. First, it supplies sufficient money to meet the demands of the private economy while also financing government deficits, both of which are accomplished through buying Treasury debt. It returns the interest on debt to the Treasury. Through the interest on Treasury debt, it collects both the natural seigniorage plus an additional amount of inflation tax revenue. It normally returns all such revenue to the government for use in its expenditure.

While printing money, providing finance for government expenditure and causing inflation, the US Fed also tries to ensure that the private bank system functions smoothly. One way to do this is through its reserves, although how it might do this is not specified in any Fed mandate. After the 1930s disaster of allowing private banks to collapse rather than using the concept of gathering reserves at the Fed to stop that bank panic, the Great Depression was brought to an end through the 1933 Banking Act and its creation of a revolutionary new system of bank insurance, to be administered by the Federal Deposit Insurance Corporation.

The FDIC system is still in place today, with revisions to it recently enacted. It originally insured private bank customer deposits in return for the bank paying a flat fee per dollar of deposits that were insured. A 2006 Act improved the efficiency of the FDIC's insurance system by specifying that the premiums paid per dollar of deposits should vary on the basis of the riskiness of the bank's assets. This was designed to eliminate the "moral hazard" of a set insurance premium, which could induce banks to take on more risk, as the depositors were still FDIC-insured. Risk-based insurance premiums reduce the incentive for banks to take additional risk, which, in turn, can minimize the hazard of the insurance system itself causing undue risk in banking.

At the same time, the Fed has long required each bank to hold a set fraction of deposits on reserve at the Fed. This means that the United States enjoys a strange mixture of two systems: FDIC-insured banks already have reserves sufficient for bank runs held by the FDIC, but the Fed then requires additional reserves for both FDIC- and non-FDIC-insured banks, which adds a second layer of reserves for FDIC banks. This mix endured up until 2020, when, during a short but serious bank crisis in March and April of that year, the Fed eliminated reserve requirements completely. The Fed continued to hold trillions of dollars in reserves from private banks, however, even as the FDIC has continued to operate normally.

This combination of two different systems creates an inefficient bank insurance system with many distortions. The inefficiency would not have been so glaring had it not been for the fact that, since 1980, "non-bank" banks have avoided FDIC insurance premiums, grown steadily and been the ones responsible for the bank panic during the Great Recession of 2008–09, and again in 2020. In 2008 the investment banks with deposits that were not FDIC-insured were holding mortgages as a major asset backing depositor accounts. When the mortgages went into broad default after the Fed raised interest rates rapidly in 2006 and 2007, the investment banks suffered a depositor run on their "money market" deposit accounts. These banks then tried to withdraw reserves from the Fed, which then quickly ran out of reserves, as it was holding only a nominal amount. Panic ensued across the international finance system.

The US system of bank insurance has devolved into two parallel operating systems: one outdated system, of the Fed holding reserves for the banks that are avoiding the efficient insurance system of the FDIC; and one for the rest of the banks, which are within the efficient FDIC system. The FDIC system is efficient because it can always adjust insurance premiums across the board if the "aggregate risk" of a run on banks warrants holding a bigger or smaller reserve pot.

The next chapter provides theory and evidence for how banking insurance can work well, and when it has failed because of a competing mix of methods by central bank authority. The result is fractional reserve banking within a fractured insurance system for banking.

9

FRACTURED INSURANCE

Bagehot describes how the Bank of England should use its reserves to stem bank panics. His rule was to lend generously, at higher than existing market interest rates, to any bank needing reserves. This dictum is that the Bank should act as the lender of last resort. To do this the Bank needs to keep gold reserves both for the money supply and for some fraction of the deposits of the entire private banking system, such as an apprehension minimum of 37 per cent, in his example.

Bagehot says this minimum level is arbitrary, subject to change and something of an art to identify. But, regardless of the minimum fraction of reserves that are held in relation to deposit liabilities, the total reserves held are fewer than they might otherwise be because the Bank of England acts to pool all the reserves together. The Bank pools risk so that it can direct reserves to banks in sudden need, so each private bank's reserves that are held at the Bank are smaller than if there were no such central bank, as in France and the United States at the time. Speaking of the joint-stock banks, Bagehot (1873: 107) says: "Not only did they keep their reserve from the beginning at the Bank of England, but they did not keep so much reserve as they would have kept if there had been no Bank of England."

Therefore, the British system of banking circulated more capital than other countries. In contrast, the "natural" banking systems of France and America at the time were designed around each bank keeping sufficient reserves to ward off its own individual bank failure. This natural, traditional system is equivalent to self-insurance by each bank rather than the pooling of risks of reserve demands into a central bank, as the Bank of England did. Bagehot (1873: 107) writes: "I have tediously insisted that the natural system of banking is that of many banks keeping their own cash reserve, with the penalty of failure before them if they neglect it. I have shown that our system is that of a single bank keeping the whole reserve under no effectual penalty of failure. And yet I propose to retain that system, and only attempt to mend and palliate it."

Bagehot warns that the ready reserves need to be sufficient for all institutions acting as banks, rather than those strictly defined as banks, since these non-bank banks likewise can lead to panics and bank failure. This is precisely what occurred in the United States in savings and loans (S&L) banks in the 1990s, and again with mortgages in the 2008–09 financial crisis. Similarly, although they were originally viewed as safe assets held within savings banks that specialized in commercial property loans, household loans and loans for house purchases, Bagehot (1873: 137–8) details the precarious reserves of Britain's savings banks in the late 1880s:

> I suppose that almost everyone thinks that our system of savings' banks is sound and good. Almost everyone would be surprised to hear that there is any possible objection to it. Yet see what it amounts to. By the last return the savings' banks – the old and the Post Office together – contain about 60,000,000 L. of deposits, and against which this they hold in the funds securities of the best kind. But they hold no cash whatsoever. They have of course the petty cash about the various branches necessary for daily work. But of cash in ultimate reserve cash in reserve against a panic the savings' banks have not a sixpence. These banks depend on being able in a panic to realize their securities. But it has been shown over and over again, that in a panic such securities can only be realized by the help of the Bank of England that is only the Bank with the ultimate cash reserve which has at such moments any new money, or any power to lend and act. If in a general panic there was a run on the savings' banks, those banks could not sell 100,000 L. of Consols [long-term government bonds] without the help of the Bank of England; not holding themselves a cash reserve for times of panic, they are entirely dependent on the one Bank which does hold that reserve.

Besides needing to cover such non-bank bank deposit runs, Bagehot (1873: 127, 132–3) suggests that instituting a fixed reserve ratio of, say, one-third or one-quarter should be avoided. Rather, there should be discretion based on the nature of the deposits, so that the ratio can be altered. In particular, the nature of the liabilities needs to be determined, and this can change over time: "The intrinsic nature of these liabilities must be considered, as well as their numerical quantity … Nor can you certainly determine the amount of reserve necessary to be kept against deposits unless you know something as to the nature of the deposits … a 'hard and fast' rule would be very dangerous … The old notion that one-third, or any other such fraction, is in all cases enough, must be abandoned."

For determining what the apprehension minimum should be for the ratio of reserves to deposits with discretion attached to this task, Bagehot (1873: 127) emphasizes the need to assess the quality of the deposit liabilities rather than fixing some set ratio: "Unless the quality of the liabilities is considered as well as their quantity, the due provision for their payment cannot be determined".

Bagehot (1873: 134, 136) then proposes that a governing body analogous to that directing the Bank of England could perform this task of assessing quality and determining a varying estimate of the apprehension minimum depending upon circumstances:

> There is no royal road to the apprehension minimum ... I shall perhaps be told also that a body like the Court of the Directors of the Bank of England cannot act on estimates like these: that such a body must have a plain rule and keep to it. I say in reply, that if the correct framing of such estimates is necessary for the good guidance of the Bank, we must make a governing body which can correctly frame such questions. We must not suffer from a dangerous policy because we have inherited an imperfect form of administration.

When the United States faced depression and banking panic in the 1930s, after the Fed had not provided reserves for failing banks, Irving Fisher (1932: 212–3) suggested recapitalizing US banks by having a commission provide them with short-term Treasury bonds as loans in proportion to bank deposits, so as to provide the needed liquidity:

> The commission to offer to every national and state bank and trust company, in proportion to its deposits, its quota of said bonds, and in return be credited with deposits ... The effect of the bonds as liquid assets for the banks would be to improve their position so as to enable them to increase their loans and investments, thus creating new purchasing power for the public, and raising the price level. The effect on the individual bank would be almost the same as pouring into a bank's vaults the equivalent of its quota of bonds in gold. Only 3 per cent is required as reserve against the time deposits. This strengthening of the banks' position can be accomplished by telegraph within a day or two, even before the physical delivery or even the printing of the bonds. After the price level has been restored to the legal normal, the commission to stabilize the price level by repeating or reversing the above operations, increasing or decreasing the amount of said bonds and deposits, as may be necessary, to maintain the stated level.

Not following Fisher's advice to recapitalize private banks by systematically lending them Treasury securities, the Federal Reserve had only 23 per cent of reserves against their deposits on 3 March 1933. The Fed then closed all Federal Reserve banks, on the basis that reserves had fallen below the stipulated 40 per cent ratio. The Fed waited to do this, however, until the day before the presidential inauguration of Roosevelt, on 4 March 1933, hoping to force him into action in terms of reforming the bank system.

According to the Fed's "Bank holiday of 1933" web page, the Fed shut down while urging a nationwide closing of banks:

> On March 1, 1933, [Federal Reserve Bank of New York head George L.] Harrison sent an urgent message to [Federal Reserve Board governor Eugene] Meyer and Secretary of the Treasury Ogden Mills: The New York Reserve Bank's gold reserve had fallen below the legal limit (Eccles 1982: 84–5). Reserve Banks were required to maintain gold reserves equal to 40 percent of the paper currency they issued, but foreign and domestic holders of US currency were rapidly losing faith in paper money and were redeeming dollars at an alarming rate (Wheelock 1992: 19) ... By March 3, the mounting toll of bank closures and failures had forced bankers and their regulators to recognize the need for decisive action. The directors of the Federal Reserve Bank of New York adopted a resolution requesting that the Federal Reserve Board urge President Hoover to proclaim a nationwide bank holiday ... Saturday, March 4, all twelve Federal Reserve Banks kept their doors locked, and banks in thirty-seven states either closed completely or operated under state-imposed restrictions on withdrawals.

This led to Roosevelt declaring the bank holiday almost immediately, after which banks were reopened and given Federal Deposit Insurance Corporation insurance on customer deposits up to a certain level, while other banks were kept closed and were merged with other banks.

This resulted in the reform that ended the Great Depression, in particular the initial establishment of the FDIC. Silbur (2009: 20) describes it in this way:

> Together, the Emergency Banking Act and the de facto 100 percent deposit insurance created a safety net for banks and produced a regime shift with instantaneous results, similar to Sargent's (1986) description of "The Ends of Four Big Inflations." This result would come as no surprise to Friedman and Schwartz (1963: 434), who observe that "Federal insurance of bank deposits was the most important structural change in the banking system to result from the 1933 panic, and ... the structural change most conducive to monetary stability since state bank notes were taxed out of existence immediately after the Civil War".

Although the FDIC insurance differed from Fisher's own 1932 plan to restore reserves by lending Treasury bonds as reserves in proportion to deposits, Fisher

(1933: 346–7) nonetheless emphasizes that FDR's actions ended deflation, bank panics and the Great Depression:

> Those who imagine that Roosevelt's avowed reflation is not the cause of our recovery but that we had "reached the bottom anyway" are very much mistaken. According to all the evidence, under that analysis, debt and deflation, which had wrought havoc up to March 4, 1933, were then stronger than ever and, if let alone, would have wreaked greater wreckage than ever, after March 4. Had no "artificial respiration" been applied, we would soon have seen general bankruptcies of the mortgage guarantee companies, savings banks, life insurance companies, railways, municipalities, and states. By that time the Federal Government would probably have become unable to pay its bills without resort to the printing press, which would itself have been a very belated and unfortunate case of artificial respiration ... If reflation can now so easily and quickly reverse the deadly down-swing of deflation after nearly four years, when it was gathering increased momentum, it would have been still easier, and at any time, to have stopped it earlier ... [T]he ways out are either via laissez faire (bankruptcy) or scientific medication (reflation), and reflation might just as well have been applied in the first place ... Finally, I would emphasize ... that great depressions are curable and preventable.

Many Americans tuned in regularly to hear Roosevelt. Just as Mervyn King, the then governor of the Bank of England, broadcast in 2008 that all deposits of the UK banking system henceforth would be insured by the Bank of England, FDR broadcast over the radio that the bank deposits were safe, and that banking could be resumed normally. They believed FDR about the integrity of the deposit insurance system being announced, the FDIC, which to this day claims not to have lost a penny of insured deposits. Silbur (2009: 19) describes this event as follows:

> After a month-long run on American banks, Franklin Delano Roosevelt proclaimed a Bank Holiday, beginning March 6, 1933, that shut down the banking system. When the banks reopened on March 13, depositors stood in line to return their hoarded cash. This article attributes the success of the Bank Holiday and the remarkable turnaround in the public's confidence to the Emergency Banking Act, passed by Congress on March 9, 1933. Roosevelt used the emergency currency provisions of the Act to encourage the Federal Reserve to create de facto 100 percent deposit insurance in the reopened banks. The contemporary press

confirms that the public recognized the implicit guarantee and, as a result, believed that the reopened banks would be safe, as the President explained in his first Fireside Chat on March 12, 1933. Americans responded by returning more than half of their hoarded cash to the banks within two weeks and by bidding up stock prices by the largest ever one-day percentage price increase on March 15 – the first trading day after the Bank Holiday ended. The study concludes that the Bank Holiday and the Emergency Banking Act of 1933 reestablished the integrity of the US payments system and demonstrated the power of credible regime-shifting policies.

Figure 9.1 presents the ratio of US demand deposits at private banks to the currency in circulation for the period January 1923 to July 1941. Demand deposits caused most of the change in the graph, as the currency was steady, with a slight rise over the period. This is before the Fed started accelerating the printing of money, as it was constrained by the gold standard. Deposits were rising in the 1920s as US investment increased. This reversed into a decline in deposits after the 1929 US stock market crash and the onset of the Great Depression.

The ratio of demand deposits to currency fell dramatically from 1930 to March 1933. People withdrew deposits as panic swept the banks. When the FDIC was established, the deposits were returned and the ratio rose. This turning point in Figure 9.1, which uses semi-annual data from FRED, occurred in the first half

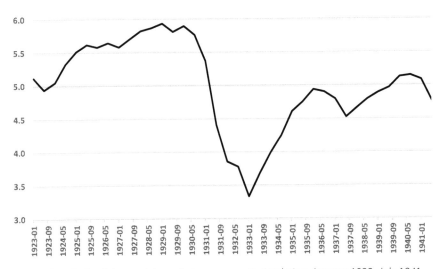

Figure 9.1 Ratio of demand deposits to currency in circulation, January 1923–July 1941
Source: FRED.

of 1933 (with monthly data, it is in March 1933), when the economy went from depression to recovery.

David Wheelock affirms (in the web page "The Great Depression" of the Federal Reserve Bank of St Louis) that the FDIC led to the end of the Great Depression:

> [T]he federal government set up a temporary system of federal deposit insurance and followed up a year later by creating the Federal Deposit Insurance Corporation (FDIC) and a permanent deposit insurance system. Roosevelt's policies restored confidence in the banking system, and money poured back into the banks. The money stock began to expand, which fueled increased spending and production as well as rising prices. Economic recovery was slow, but at least the bottom had been reached and the corner turned.

What is it about the FDIC deposit insurance system that is completely different from having a fraction of deposits held as reserves at the central bank, for times of bank failure? Are these two completely different systems or part of the same system? Why have both systems or only one or the other?

The concept of the Federal Reserve or the Bank of England as the lender of last resort is an anachronism, or, to put it more strongly, it should be an anachronism. This idea was based on a quantity of reserves as a fraction of deposits. Whereas Bagehot emphasized the quality of deposit liabilities in describing how the Bank of England served as lender of last resort, once formalized the concept of a fractional reserve banking system does not readily lend itself to a consideration of quality in the fraction of reserves to be kept.

The apprehension minimum of Bagehot was meant to include quality considerations, and these may have always behind the thinking at the Bank of England. But the Fed had no such quality considerations in place after its formation, as, basically, it performed only the Issue Department role of the Bank of England, which was to keep sufficient gold reserve for its currency note issue. The Fed had required a 40 per cent ratio of reserves to currency going into the Great Depression. This was not a banking insurance system, nor was it designed to be one, despite the intent of the NMC behind the founding of the Fed.

The FDIC provided the quality assessment by building up a reserve pot in direct proportion to deposits, and finally, as of 2006, as based on the quality of the liabilities being insured. With the quality issue added, as Bagehot advocated had to be systemically considered, the FDIC came to embody an efficient reserve pot that met much of Bagehot's criteria.

In contrast, before the FDIC, the American system of bank reserves evolved out of regulations related to state and nationally chartered banks. A certain fixed quantity of reserves was required. This evolved into a set of varying fractions of deposits to be held as reserves at the Fed, up to a certain amount of dollars. As deregulation of banking in the United States occurred after 1980, the amount of reserves in the Fed shrank ever more relative to deposits.

This American system of reserves never offered a quality assessment. It even acted to let the riskier forms of non-bank banks keep fewer reserves proportionately than safer FDIC-insured banks. Therefore, there was a movement to pay interest on reserves, as effected with the passage of the US 2006 financial deregulatory Act, to decrease the burden of reserves on small banks compared to non-bank banks.

With efficient bank deposit insurance, the "pot" of reserves is systematically built up, as in a private insurance system. The premium fee paid per deposit, in the FDIC, is specified by carefully weighing the risks of each member bank, assigning it a price for deposit insurance, then gathering funds from every bank to create a reserve of funds.

The only difference from a private bank insurance system is that a macroeconomic policy establishes government bank insurance, such as the FDIC. This is a macroprudential policy. The FDIC provides insurance that considers aggregate economic effects that can increase the risk of insuring the banking sector. This added risk is called aggregate risk. To include this factor in the FDIC deposit insurance system, the insurance fee per deposit must be enough to cover normal expected bank failures that occur during recessions plus bank failures that may arise during an occasional economy-wide bank panic.

Calculating the aggregate risk involves the correlation of the economy-wide recession with a widespread bank panic that makes for a greater risk of bank failures. The FDIC must build into its bank deposit premium structure not only the risk of failure of each individual bank, called idiosyncratic risk, but also the risk premium that must be levied as part of the deposit insurance fee for all banks, which includes an amount to cover the aggregate risk of failure that affects each bank. By charging a fee that includes both idiosyncratic and aggregate risk, the FDIC can run an efficient system by building a reserve fund that covers events of bank failure including any widespread panics.

Rather than being based on the amount of reserves, as in a fractional reserve system, the FDIC system since 2006 has been based on the riskiness of banks themselves. Each bank is assigned a different insurance premium per dollar of deposits insured, depending on the risk of the bank's assets and liabilities. This is how an arbitrary fractional reserve system of the Fed or Bank of England differs from an insurance system that, instead, builds a reserve systematically, consistent with what Bagehot was advocating.

Typically, an efficient bank insurance system would eliminate any widespread panic by the nature of it having a reserve to cover losses in such an event.

Through its reserve funds, collected through deposit insurance premiums, it would have sufficient reserves, as in Bagehot's apprehension minimum. But the reserves would be collected more efficiently, in line with the risk of each bank separately, as in private insurance systems.

With sufficient reserves, a panic would never ensue, and this propitious situation would be called a "no-default equilibrium". The implicit contract formed by payment of the bank insurance premium causes confidence in the bank insurance system and eliminates panics. In contrast, in a fractional reserve system, the varying risk by banks is considered only by having a different amount of total reserves as a fraction of total deposits without regard to the risk of each bank. The FDIC insurance system is refined to allocate the insurance cost to each bank according to its individual risk in building the reserve fund.

An efficiently collected reserve fund would automatically meet Bagehot's apprehension minimum. Bank customers would always have confidence, and the bank panic would not happen. The modern-day version of the apprehension minimum is precisely the reserve fund of the FDIC.

Debasing this efficiency, the FDIC reserve fund can never actually achieve this fortuitous equilibrium as long as a large fraction of the banking system lies outside the FDIC system. This fraction includes investment banking, as with Lehman Brothers and Merrill Lynch, which collapsed in 2008. But it also encompasses the casualty, property and life insurance system of the American Insurance Group, along with other financial companies, such as the General Motors Acceptance Corporation, which financed car purchases and which also collapsed in 2008.

It would be feasible to bring all financial intermediaries into the FDIC system, however, if it were done on a voluntary basis by such intermediaries. The risk premium on deposits of different maturities and with different assets behind them can be assessed. This can be done for deposits of pension funds, other deposit-taking financial intermediaries and life insurance funds; already there are US state insurance systems for life insurance companies in all 50 US states.

If this were done, in combination with the crisis-event FDIC liquidity provision that is described in the last chapter of this book, there would be no need for the Federal Reserve (or Bank of England) to scramble during a bank panic on behalf of the banks outside the FDIC system that suddenly have insufficient liquid reserves. This scramble has been called the unconventional money and banking policy of the Fed, as if it is a new innovative policy. But it is just plugging holes in the leaking dam of the government financial insurance system during a flood of needs for liquidity arising from years of letting banks grow outside the FDIC. This policy is in lieu of having an efficient bank insurance system for the whole set of financial intermediaries in place before the crisis. Instead, the central banks scurried to create very inefficient, and distortionary, bank insurance after the crisis.

Just imagine a private insurance company saying that it would insure you for your automobile crash after it had happened. It is impossible in private markets to receive an insurance payout for a bad event after the fact, unless you were insured before the bad event occurred. Getting insurance after the bad event occurs is contrary to the concept of an insurance system that collects premiums beforehand based on the probability of bad events happenings.

In contrast to private insurance, a government might have the power to subsidize any bank even after a crisis. The citizenry of such a government should not expect this insurance to be efficient. When asked at a Cato Institute conference[1] in 2016 why the FDIC did not bring into its system the investment banks and other financial intermediaries so as to create an efficient financial insurance system in advance of crises, Thomas Hoenig, as vice chairman of the FDIC, responded at the end of his presentation by saying that (paraphrasing) "it would be great to have more power. But I can just imagine all the lobbying that would go on from all the banks, and really I think it is better just to increase the reserve requirements that each bank holds."

The idea propounded by Hoenig and elsewhere, including in the 2010 Dodd–Frank Wall Street Reform and Consumer Protection Act, is that the government can create efficient deposit insurance by making each individual bank hold greater reserves. This is exactly the opposite of what Bagehot concluded to be the basis for the dominance of the British banking system in world finance at the time: holding the minimum amount of reserves in just one bank, the Bank of England, rather than in each individual bank, as in France and the United States.

The French and American systems in the late nineteenth century held a lot of reserves within every bank, making those systems must less efficient than the British one. Less capital was lent out for investment, and less investment was the result. Rather than forcing more reserves on every bank, the question should be how to collect efficiently in modern times the single reserve fund of Bagehot's Bank of England.

The FDIC collects a modern single reserve fund through a well-designed insurance premium collection of funds. From 1933 to 2006 the FDIC charged the same deposit insurance premium for every bank. This was said to cause moral hazard, since banks could take on more risk in their assets and pay the same insurance fee.

To reform the system in connection with such a lack of quality consideration and the potential moral hazard that can result, the FDIC in 2006 instead began charging risk-based premiums that took into account the risk of each bank. This became a system beyond reproach of the accusations of moral hazard. The only

---

1. www.cato.org/multimedia/events/34th-annual-monetary-conference-welcoming-remarks-key note-address

criticism now is that the FDIC cannot perfectly determine the risks; but neither can any private insurance system for each client, and so it also uses categories of risk – as does the FDIC.

People will hide risky driving behaviour by not informing their insurance company about how many stop signs they have ignored, just as banks will try not to reveal all the risk in their asset portfolio. But technology can be used increasingly to monitor risks. For example, the American Automobile Association (AAA), with the consent of customers, in 2020 began tracking every single mile driven by customers through their computer app, determining whether drivers speed, stop too suddenly or take other risks; after six months AAA gives a discount on the insurance premium based on the driving score from the app.

Any insurance company, including the FDIC, can continue to assess risks more accurately as technology advances, even as new financial instruments are created to share risks in the marketplace. The idea that the FDIC cannot encompass the entire financial intermediary system is outdated. But the approach of making the FDIC insurance coverage comprehensive is not what we currently take, nor what we took after the 2008–09 financial crisis. Yet there are ways to establish an efficient government banking insurance system.

The FDIC is now akin to the Maginot Line in the Second World War: an entrenchment that defended only France and allowed the German army, like the investment banks, to simply go around the defences (via Belgium) rather than going through them. After 2008 the investment banks withdrew their reserves held at the Federal Reserve, but that did not stem the run on the investment banks, and panic spread more broadly. Investment banks failed.

The bank run and withdrawal of reserves caused the Fed reserves to become a negative $50 billion in June and July 2008. The Federal Reserve had to borrow reserves from other central banks in what are called "central bank liquidity swaps". This obscure action meant that the Fed printed money and bought Japanese yen, for example, from the central bank of Japan, held the yen as reserves at the Fed and then sold back the yen to the Japanese central bank in return for the money that the Fed printed to buy the yen. This allowed the Fed's reserves during 2008 to rise above zero, to some $700 billion.

Having shored up its own reserves by printing money to increase its reserves, the Federal Reserve then "bailed out" the bank sector after the investment bank panic and failures. The Fed supplied bank insurance after the crash. It dramatically increased the money supply by buying Treasury bills and bonds, and, for the first time, mortgage-backed securities (MBSs). It lowered interest rates and gave the investment banks billions of dollars in "interest on excess reserves".

The Fed was desperate to gather more reserves for the non-bank banks' sudden need, since they had no single reserve fund in the way the FDIC has for the event of a bank crisis. The Fed bought all the available short-run Treasury "bills", and when they ran out started buying long-term Treasury debt, such as five-year bonds. The Fed's buying of Treasury debt led to a massive increase in the rate of growth of the US money supply. Markets expected the onslaught of money printing to cause inflation, based on the experience after the 2001 terrorist attacks.

After 2001 the Fed had sufficiently accelerated the money supply growth rate, by buying Treasury debt, to drive the interest rate down below the inflation rate for three years. Irving Fisher (1907) has demonstrated that, by subtracting the inflation rate (p) from the nominal market interest rate (R), one could infer the real interest rate level (r): $r = R - p$. This calculation is very simple, and is accepted by all economists, central bankers and market analysts. This means unambiguously that, after 2001, the real rate remained negative for several years.

Knut Wicksell (1936) focuses on the value of money, monetary policy and interest rates in the nineteenth century. He clearly states that he accepts the quantity theory of money but also describes how the central bank can temporarily push down the market nominal interest rate by increasing the money supply. He calls the temporary pushing down of the interest rate by increasing money supply the liquidity effect on interest rates, which he says will end once the inflation rate gets fully reflected in the market interest rate.

Wicksell (1936) also describes in the same passages that it is possible to create a persistent liquidity effect. This can happen if the central bank continues to increase the money supply for a prolonged period, continually pushing down interest rates with added liquidity, which is exactly what Alan Greenspan did as Federal Reserve governor after 2001. The money supply growth was accelerated for so long that the real Treasury short-term bill interest rate was negative for almost three years, from 2002 to 2004.

Greenspan served as governor of the Federal Reserve from 1987 to the early 2006. He targeted interest rates in the federal funds market while carrying out money supply changes through open market operations of buying and selling Treasury debt. This federal funds market is where private banks would borrow from each other to meet the reserve requirement for the Fed at the end of each week, without holding any unnecessary excess reserves.

For May 1999 to May 2011, Figure 9.2 plots the federal funds rate (FFR) and the CPI inflation rate. From May 2004 to December 2005 Greenspan raised the FFR from 1 per cent to 4 per cent. The FFR rose above the inflation rate in November 2005, just before Greenspan ended his term as governor, and remained above the inflation rate until the financial crisis began in 2008.

Ben Bernanke took over as governor in February 2006. He continued the increase in the federal funds rate, to 5.25 per cent, creating a significantly positive real interest rate. This established what was considered a "normal level" for interest rates relative to the inflation rate.

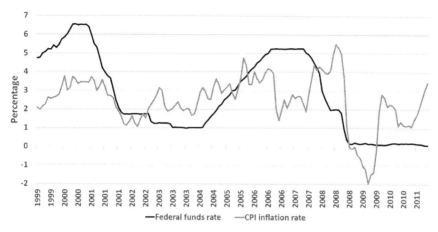

Figure 9.2 Federal funds market interest rate and inflation rate, May 1999–May 2011
Source: FRED.

There was just one problem. The normal rates should have existed all along. Suddenly ratcheting up interest rates to a normal zone after three years of abnormally low rates destroyed both savers and investors.

This normalcy occurs in most of US history, with short-term market interest rates above the inflation rate, so that the real rate of interest is positive. The real interest rate had almost always been positive, except when the central bank conducted sudden changes in monetary policy. Since the 1950s, only the 1970s had seen a sequence of negative real interest rates, until 2002.

The problem after 2001 was that the FFR had been kept below inflation for a long time and then rather suddenly increased. The Fed had induced a Wicksellian persistent liquidity effect of increasing the money supply and driving down the interest rate. In Figure 9.2, inflation then did begin rising after so much money printing, from 1.0 per cent in June 2002 to 4.7 per cent in September 2005.

The rise in the inflation rate then required an ever-increasing federal funds rate in order to get to a "normal" level that was greater than the inflation rate. This created a Catch-22 of deregulating the capital market while inflation was steadily rising – something akin to the 2015–18 Fed experience. This scenario is likely to unfold again in 2022, with the Fed raising the interest rate that it pays out on reserves. Trying to get back to a market-based competitive short-term Treasury bill rate that includes a positive real interest rate after inflation, which is really what is meant by "normal", required an increasingly high FFR after 2004 and after 2015, and probably will again after 2022.

For three years after 2001 mortgage loans had been taken out on variable interest rate policies when the FFR was 1.7 per cent, 1.4 per cent and 1 per cent, respectively. With rates below the inflation rate for three years, people were being paid to borrow, but then they saw their mortgage interest rates start to rise dramatically in 2004. Facing a one percentage point increase in your mortgage interest rate is difficult, while facing a four and a half percentage point increase can make avoiding default on the loan impossible.

The mortgage loan collapse and bank panic of 2008–09 by investment banks was a direct consequence of the Fed's policy from 2001 to 2007. After 2008 the Fed tried to clean up its own mess. The Fed assumed the role of providing ex post bank insurance to the large uninsured segment of the financial system. It was not equipped for the scale of the crisis, however, as Fed reserves as a fraction of the banking systems total deposits had steadily fallen to only 1 per cent of all commercial bank deposits by 2008. That meant that the Fed had close to zero reserves relative to the full deposit liabilities of the depository banks, while supposedly running a fractional reserve banking system, even as the FDIC continued its own efficient system for member banks.

The Fed decided to provide bank insurance while at the same time keeping to its illegal inflation target of 2 per cent, which was a self-made mark of its credibility. First, it accelerated money supply growth, as in historic wartime experience. Then the Fed took a set of steps beyond what the US Congress had intended (as with the 2 per cent inflation target).

This is where the interest on excess reserves comes into play. As mentioned above, the little-known law passed in 2006, the Financial Regulatory Relief Services Act (FRRSA), was designed to provide relief from unnecessarily burdensome regulation on financial intermediaries, by allowing the Fed to pay interest on required reserves starting in 2011. The 2006 Act resulted, on the basis of the view that requiring banks to hold reserves at the Fed without them earning interest acted as a tax on banks, even though reserves held at the Fed by that time were almost negligible.

The 2006 FRRSA law as passed allowed "interest on reserves" to be paid, the intent being for this to apply only to required reserves – which is how the language of the law should have been written. The Fed exploited the loose wording, just as it has continually ignored the 1978 zero-inflation-rate target law. The Fed paid interest on *all* reserves starting in 2008, when it had negative reserves on hand, without counting the central bank liquidity swaps. Then the Fed was faced with the next issue in its new ex post bank insurance plan: what interest rate should it pay on reserves?

The Fed made up a new interest rate for this, which it dictated by proclamation and called the "interest on excess reserves". Once the Fed had eliminated all reserve requirements during the 2020 pandemic, however, it started reporting this rate instead as "interest on reserve balances". It dropped the "excess" terminology completely, along with the pretence of conducting an efficient fractional reserve system of banking to insure the banks. Reserves were no longer required.

At first, in 2008, the Fed's IOER rate was high for a few months. Then the Fed dropped it to 0.25 per cent, for the next seven years. The banks selling Treasury bills to the Fed were credited with reserves at the Fed for the Treasury bill purchase that included payment for the interest stream on the Treasury debt. With the sale to the Fed, the banks were already paid for the interest stream and gave up the right to earn any further interest on Treasury debt that they no longer owned. The Fed payment of IOER to banks, on the reserves generated by the purchase on the Treasury debt from banks, was a double interest payment that acted as a brand new Fed subsidy for banks.

To be clear, the banks would traditionally sell Treasury debt to the Fed for the current value of the stream of interest payments on that debt along with the principal. The banks would be credited reserves, keep only the minimum required reserves at the Fed and lend out the rest, causing the traditional money multiplier of new loans and private bank customer deposits. Starting in 2008 the banks sold the Treasury debt, received reserves for the amount and then got paid interest on the reserves at the Fed account anyway, even though they no longer owned the Treasury debt that they sold to create the reserves.

Any such subsidy by the Fed violated its own stipulated by-laws stating that the Federal Reserve System could not favour any one industry over another. So what did the Fed do about this small problem? It eliminated the by-law. The Fed eliminated this provision during the 2008 crisis in order to subsidize the bank sector.

The other problem with this new subsidy was that it violated a most fundamental principle of the Fed's design. According to US law, all interest earned on Treasury debt is to be returned as seigniorage (inflation tax revenue) to the US Treasury, after deducting the cost of operating the Federal Reserve (including its gyms). The Fed violated this key foundation by instead paying out the seigniorage to the private banks through interest on excess reserves.

This double interest payment to banks violates the intent of the 2006 FRRSA law, which never intended for unlimited amounts of reserves to receive interest. Nor did Fed regulators allow for one sector to be favoured by Fed action. Nor did the law intend for the Fed to pay seigniorage to the private banks instead of returning the revenue to the Treasury, as required by law. As a result of these violations of its operating dicta, this is exactly why the revenue returned by the Fed to the Treasury dropped dramatically after 2008.

The Fed gave the seigniorage to private banks instead of the Treasury, which would otherwise have used it to fund congressional expenditure. This was a subsidy that, normally, Congress would need to allocate in congressional budget law. Congress never approved this subsidy, despite its sole US government role in legislating what taxes and subsidies are to be provided to any one sector of the economy.

The Fed conducts this bank subsidization while gathering reserves. This is related to how Milton Friedman (1994) explains that President Roosevelt's 1930s silver purchases subsidized silver producers while the consequent silver note money supply increase was sterilized by fewer standard notes being printed. The sterilization process was different, but both are examples of such a process.

The Fed's IOER policy allowed it to sterilize a vast portion of the money supply that it printed to buy up blooming Treasury debt and limping mortgage bonds. It did this by enticing private banks with interest on excess reserves to hold excess reserves, which amounted to almost $3 trillion by 2014 and $4 trillion in 2022. By sterilizing the reserves through the policy of paying banks not to make loans with the excess reserves, it could, meanwhile, keep to its 2 per cent inflation target.

A part of this sterilization occurred when, after 2008, the Fed also continually bought mortgage-backed securities. By doing this, the Fed also blatantly violated the congressional budget resolution process. The Federal Credit Reform Act of 1990 specifies that all federal government guarantees of loans, and all federal government direct loans, must calculate the expected loss implicit in the loans and then have it approved as expenditure by Congress. Congress must approve this in its annual budget process, including buying MBSs, since this is, in essence, providing a loan to the owner of the MBS in return for the collateral of the interest payments expected on the MBS.

Under President George W. Bush, in 2008 it was the Treasury buying up mortgage loans, not the Fed. The Treasury received approval of this through the congressional budget process. Once President Obama took office, Fed governor Bernanke bought the mortgages instead, so that the Treasury no longer had to have the expected net outlay from MBS purchases included in the annual congressional budget.

The Fed evaded the law by doing this. It received no congressional authorization for the MBS purchases, going against the intent of the Federal Credit Reform Act of 1990. The Fed circumvented this law because it directly bought mortgage loans without congressional budget approval, some $45 billion a month after 2009, and it is still doing it today, at varying levels. And note how vigorously the Fed officials proudly declare that they lost nothing on MBS purchases after 2008. That is a red herring relative to the law that requires that the expected loss at the time of the purchase must be approved by Congress before the loan purchases are made.

Throwing aside laws, by-laws and the foundations of Fed operations enabled the Fed to institute a bad system of bank insurance after disaster had occurred, creating the moral hazard that banks expect to be bailed out in the future. It also creates moral hazard if it results in less investment in the economy as banks are paid not to invest.

A problem arises with bad government insurance when it increases moral hazard. Moral hazard occurs when the probability of the bad state of affairs is increased by the policy actions of the government. Paying banks not to lend out money induces banks to not lend out money. This means that the Fed bank insurance policy causes less investment. In contrast, bank insurance policy is meant to create the most investment possible within undistorted capital markets.

Since the Fed policy was followed worldwide, the inducement against lending spread worldwide and led internationally to a "lost decade" from 2008 to 2017 because of low investment. After seven years with an IOER rate of 0.25 per cent, and then only one IOER rate increase from − 0.25 per cent to 0.50 per cent, in December 2015 − before Donald Trump won the 2016 presidential election, Trump's criticism of the Fed prompted it to raise interest rates much more regularly. The IOER rate increased in steps that continued once Trump was in office, and briefly exceeded the inflation rate in 2018, to reach "normal" levels more gradually than after 2004 and for the first time since 2007.

In contrast to the quantity theory of money, along with the persistent liquidity theory of Wicksell, Keynesian theory instead argues that it is natural to have low nominal interest rates as long into the foreseeable future as possible. The basis for this was the idea that the real rate of interest had been falling for 60 years because of global excess savings. The Keynesian (1936) thesis of international excess savings was widely used to justify an ongoing policy of a 0.25 per cent rate of IOER.

December 2015 saw an IOER rate increase for the first time since 2010. Until the pandemic inflation was averaging close to 2 per cent. This meant a significantly negative real rate of interest near to −2 per cent. Remarkably, such a negative real rate has been in place for all but three years since the 2001 terrorist attacks.

Keynesians advocate keeping interest rates low because the real interest rate is naturally low, to which Mervyn King (2017: xxiii) retorts: "Too many economists have run away with the idea that one model is all that is needed to guide policy." No economic theory, however, allows for a negative real interest rate forever. It violates necessary conditions for stationary equilibrium in both Keynesian and neoclassical economic models (time discounting in preferences is required to bound household utility, which in turn implies a stationary positive real rate of interest). King (2017: xix–xx) puts it this way: "Only economists could believe that negative real interest rates are the solution to the problem of restoring economic growth and only bankers could believe that our system of money and banking is fundamentally sound."

Evidence backs up King in his rejection of such policy. Looking at the business cycle, the real interest rate and investment rate move up together in expansions and fall together in contractions, over "normal" business cycles. The real interest had rarely been negative in the postwar period up to 2002, and, when the real return on capital was high, so was investment. More profit provides a higher real return on capital, or higher real interest rate, and allows more investment and economic growth in terms of output.

As the basis of the Fed's emboldened new policy, it dramatically increased the money supply growth rate. This tricked oil and gold markets, which were not expecting massive sterilization of the money supply through the Fed's policy of paying interest on excess reserves. Markets thought inflation would follow the massive surge in printing money. After rising after 2001 and then crashing during 2008, along with stock markets, oil and gold prices shot up again after 2008, for the second major "shock", and the larger of the two, in their history going back to the 1970s.

The expected inflation rate did go up, and drove oil and gold prices up. When the level of excess reserves finally stopped rising and then began to fall in 2014, oil markets realized that inflation was not going to materialize any time soon. The oil price dropped again suddenly, as did the market's inflation expectations. Inflation did not happen as expected because the Fed's policy-makers devised a way to sterilize the money so that it did not enter circulation, using their mix of (arguably illegal) means of paying interest on the reserves that they accumulated.

Monetary and banking policy became a murky mix after 2008, and has existed like that ever since, being renewed with great vigour when the pandemic crisis hit. Describing how inflation happens goes beyond a simple application of the quantity theory of money, if in fact the Fed prints the money to finance government deficit spending and keeps the money from entering capital markets. Predicting inflation becomes obscured when the Fed circumvents the intent of congressional law and the traditional by-laws that regulate the Fed. The results of the Fed's action were low inflation until 2020, moral hazard through low investment and non-bank bank expectations of being bailed out by the Fed after a bank panic – as occurred again in 2020 – and the worldwide repression of capital markets through negative real interest rates.

By setting the rate of IOER far below the rate of inflation, all the world's financially integrated economies had to imitate the Fed's policy of negative real interest rates or otherwise face currency appreciation relative to the US dollar and, subsequently, lower exports. Other central banks followed Fed policy by printing money or even explicitly setting negative interest rates on reserves held at the central bank (ECB, Switzerland, Japan).

The negative real rates worldwide had a major detrimental effect on the world economy and its political bifurcations. Savers provide more savings as the real interest rate goes up. With negative rates, private savers offer less in the way of savings for financial intermediation into private investment. Less private investment happens and leads to less economic growth, less government revenue and a growing political dilemma.

A negative real rate is "unnatural". The Fed's imposition of a negative real rate of interest on capital markets to provide ex post bank insurance has ended up taxing world capital markets. This has led to a lack of a recovery from the 2008 bank crash and Great Recession, as compared to normal business cycle recessions, just as the Great Depression led to a decade-long recovery in just the level of real GDP.

The threat from the distortions is real. Just as setting the Treasury bill rates below the inflation rate after 2001 led to the 2008 bank panic, an even more prolonged negative real interest rate policy has created enduringly bad effects. Institutions will continue to seek alternative ways to earn interest other than US Treasury debt with its negative real return. These other routes, such as MBSs, will look to have low risk but do so without factoring in the "aggregate risk" of financial collapse and the distortions in seeking higher-yielding instruments that have been caused by Fed policy. MBSs were relatively safe before 2001, until the Fed policy after that year made them go into default.

To avoid such a morass, an efficient insurance system run by the government can factor in both aggregate risk and individual bank risk by charging deposit insurance premiums based on both factors. The Fed has no real reserves except by paying banks to provide them. The FDIC, in contrast, is paid by the banks to build the reserves. With efficient insurance, government debt can earn a normal return continually and stop distorting the world's capital markets.

The FDIC holds the reserves in the United States that are poised to help save the depositors of failing member banks. The US Congress could strengthen that defence, if it chose to do so. It could redistribute banking insurance power from the Fed to the FDIC, while inducing the Fed to acknowledge the power of a competing agency for efficient bank regulation. The Fed could return to its principal role of ensuring a stable money supply through inflation rate targeting and stop its dreadful attempts at providing bank insurance to non-bank banks.

From Bagehot to FDIC insurance, the policy for keeping private banks healthy has always been rooted in the times in which banks succumb to widespread contagion that ideally an economy could avoid, as Fisher (1932) emphasizes. The next chapter describes how bank panics have occurred historically and continue to shape policy.

10

BANK FAILURE AND CRISIS

Inflation taxes your money because its value depreciates as price levels rise. Banks allow people to avoid part of that inflation tax. When banks provide credit cards to buy goods, and these are paid off at the end of the period, people can earn interest on their income deposits at the bank during the period. If that interest is as high as the inflation rate, they avoid some of the depreciation of currency that occurs from carrying around less cash during the period in which the price level rises.

Instead of carrying around currency that depreciates over the month, banks allow people to use private bank deposits for purchases and so avoid some of the inflation tax on public bank money in the form of currency. Having a well-insured bank system allows an optimal amount of inflation tax avoidance by people. Banking enables them to weigh the cost of the credit versus the amount of the inflation tax faced when using currency that depreciates.

When the bank system collapses in modern times, it can become harder to avoid the inflation tax. Even worse taxes can result, if the inflation rate is suppressed by bank regulators as they devise new means to provide insurance after the crash has already occurred. Having good bank insurance in place before a crisis is important because it can avoid the worse effects of bank panics.

Bank panics have long been a persistent feature of the US banking system. From 1873 to 1914, during the gold standard, the United States experienced a continual sequence of panics that decreased investment, leading to the creation of the Federal Reserve and, ultimately, the Federal Deposit Insurance Corporation.

The beginning of a US nationwide system of banking, in place until 1914, was created by the National Banking Acts of 1863 and 1864. Passed during the civil war to raise federal government funds, it allowed for the chartering of national banks that could issue the greenback notes, but in return for buying Treasury debt and depositing it at the Office of the Comptroller of the Currency. Banks also operated under state charters under these Acts, with their issuance of notes driven out in large part by the Acts imposing a new federal tax on state banknotes.

Both types of banks had capital requirements for backing the bank, with national banks having a larger one than state banks during this "free banking era". There were 7,473 national banks and about double that number of state banks by the time the Federal Reserve Act was enacted in 1913. At that time they had current (1913) dollar assets of $11 billion and $9 billion, respectively.[1]

Starting with the end of coinage to silver in 1875 up to the beginning of the Fed in 1914, Figure 10.1 uses FRED data to graph the percentage of deposits that had been made into loans, or the percentage ratio of loans to deposits, at US banks. As deflation occurred from the end of the civil war until 1900, there is a long trend downwards in the loan-to-deposit ratio, punctuated by banking crises. Figure 10.1 shows here one of the negative consequences of a prolonged price level deflation, which is reduced utilization of deposits for loans, indicating a decrease in the financial intermediation of savings into investment.

There were bank panic episodes in 1873, 1884, 1893, 1890 and 1907. Each of these resulted in a sudden drop of loans relative to deposits, as businesses failed, banks failed and loans went down. Bank panics increased economic distress by decreasing investment, employment and economic output.

Before the Fed, private bank groups called clearing houses helped pool the risks of a sudden demand for reserves by pulling together reserves for threatened banks. The New York Clearing House was perhaps the most prominent, playing

Figure 10.1 Ratio of state and national bank loans to deposits, as a percentage, 1875–1914
Source: FRED.

---

1. https://eh.net/encyclopedia/us-banking-history-civil-war-to-world-war-ii

a major role in the 1873 panic, for example. The clearing houses were private entities that acted like the Bank of England as a way to help ensure that reserves could be offered to a bank facing a run on deposits.

For example, reserves would be offered when the bank was still solvent, with assets exceeding liabilities, but having insufficient ready reserves for depositor withdrawal. Lacking ready reserves is a liquidity problem. Clearing houses also tried to pool sufficient reserves to help banks survive during a broader banking panic, although they were less equipped for such aggregate economy-wide risk.

In Figure 10.1, the loan-to-deposit ratio for US banks stabilizes after deflation ends in 1900. The subsequent bank panic of 1907 was severe and caused strong deflation, leading to the Fed's establishment. Despite the concept that the Fed would stop future bank panics, the Fed's reserves were equivalent only to those of Bagehot's Issue Department of the Bank of England, with gold and other assets backing up its currency.

The Fed did not have a Banking Department per Bagehot to keep an "apprehension minimum" of reserves accumulated from private banks. With only securities held by the government as required by charter, the US private banks did not have reserves held at the Fed for times of liquidity crises. Each private bank had to determine the optimal leverage of its total deposits relative to its own reserves, which is why Bagehot describes the US system as less efficient.

Having each private bank determine its own leverage ratio probably made the US bank national and state banking system subject to more bank panics than occurred in Britain, which Bagehot details in part. Although each US private bank would be likely to hold enough reserves for the event of itself going into partial default, it was less likely to hold the additional reserves required in the event of a contagious bank panic that caused a run on withdrawals of deposits across the banking system, in an event involving aggregate risk.

The aggregate risk of a run on banks would require more reserves at each individual bank than just that required in the event of the single bank experiencing a run on deposits as a result of that bank's assets going into default. In contrast, Bagehot's apprehension minimum was designed for both individual bank crises and idiosyncratic risk plus the contagion of a bank panic across the system. Such contagion constitutes the aggregate risk that would require additional reserves at every US bank.

The Fed by design was in no position to act like the Bank of England in supplying reserves for a panic, and did not serve the role of the private clearing houses that it had been envisaged to replace. The Fed's failure to insure the deposits of the private banking system was evident in the collapse in 1930 of the private Bank of United States. This bank was prominent, as it had originally been federally chartered, with that charter expiring in 1836 and later being replaced by a state charter (Friedman 1994).

Given the prestige of the Bank of United States, and despite being private, its demise in 1930 accelerated the run on banks in the Great Depression. O'Brien and Trescott (1992: 384) describe how the Bank of United States obtained a state charter in 1913 and joined the Federal Reserve System in 1919, and how its closure helped bring on the depression: "The failure of the Bank of United States plays a major role in the narrative of the economic downswing of 1929–33. The Bank, which closed December 11, 1930, in the midst of a heavy run, was the largest bank (in dollar terms) to fail in the country's history to date ... The Bank's failure was a significant element contributing to the economic downswing."

Many economic accounts of panic-induced contagion took hold, by which customers of one bank, seeing another bank failing, then withdraw their deposits in fear of their own bank failing. As Fisher (1932) stresses, however, a bank panic is never inevitable. Indeed, Gary Richardson (2013) in his online Fed article "Banking panics of 1930–1931" finds that, in 1930, US recovery was still within sight: "In the fall of 1930, the economy appeared poised for recovery."

Instead, the panic spread ever wider. In November 1930 the large US southern banking group Caldwell and Company failed across several locations. This induced panic in the financial centre of New York, "stoking fears of financial panics and currency shortages like the panic of 1907 and inducing jittery depositors to withdraw funds from other banks" (Richardson 2013). After the Bank of United States had collapsed, from panic, the crisis spread across the Federal Reserve System's 12 districts, but again it seemed to end in 1931.

Shortly afterwards, however, a bank panic took hold in Chicago. Calomiris and Mason (2003) detail the high rate of panic-inducing bank failures in Chicago from 1931 to 1932. Kristie Engemann (2013), in the Fed's online article "Banking panics of 1931–33", finds that the regional panics led to national panic: "The banking panics in 1930 and early 1931 were regional in nature. The nature of the financial crisis changed in the fall of 1931, when the commercial banking crisis spread throughout the entire nation."

Wheelock (1992) details the action taken by several of the Fed's individual regional branches then, which varied in form and fell short as the Great Depression saw a widespread bank panic across the nation. Like a set of dominoes, the bank sector fell after the Bank of United States did. Had that been averted, as Fisher (1932) said it should have been through banking insurance reform, the Great Depression might have been averted. The initial establishment of the FDIC in 1933 ended the Great Depression by providing deposit insurance guarantees using a pool of funds collected from each bank through fees charged per dollar of deposit insured.

The FDIC was a technological revolution for insuring the private bank system from banking panics in an efficient way. The "apprehension minimum" could be calculated through the fee for each dollar of deposits insured. This innovation enabled the systematic creation of the reserve pool relative to deposits, following Bagehot's suggestions.

The way the FDIC works is that it guarantees deposits at banks up to a certain dollar limit in return for a fee (insurance premium) per dollar of the deposits that are insured. The corporation collects these funds in a reserve from which to draw when a bank fails. The FDIC does not keep banks from failing but, rather, insures the failed bank depositors to avoid a contagious bank panic.

When an FDIC bank fails, the FDIC arranges a merger of the assets of the failed bank with another, prosperous bank. It uses its reserves to provide the funds to cover the guaranteed deposits of customers of the failed bank. This increases the asset value of the failed bank and facilitates the merger with another bank, such as one interested in the region covered by the failed bank. The customers of the failed bank find themselves in the newly merged bank with their deposited funds intact.

Since 1933 FDIC insurance has kept the US commercial banks it covers in good order. Beginning from just after the inception of the FDIC, Figure 10.2 uses FDIC data, retrieved from FRED, to show that FDIC bank failures have occurred historically in three separate waves. The first happened during the years after the Great Depression, when the unemployment rate still hovered between 10 and 15 per cent until the build-up to the Second World War began. The second tranche was in the late 1980s into the 1990s. The third was the set of failures during and after the 2008–09 Great Recession.

There were fewer than 100 failed banks each year just after 1934. From 1981 to 1994 there was a large spike in bank failures, with more than 500 at the peak in 1989. After 2008 failures peaked above 150 in 2010. Of these three sets,

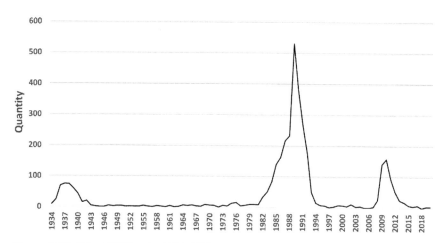

Figure 10.2 Failed FDIC banks, 1934–2020

Source: FRED, FDIC data, available at: https://fred.stlouisfed.org/series/BKFTTLA641N.

two involved global contagions – during the Great Depression and the Great Recession – whereas the wave in the 1990s saw a US recession but a lack of contagion internationally. Across these different experiences, the FDIC system remained resilient. But it became an isolated system after 1990 as money market funds, mutual funds and exchange-traded funds exploded across the shadow non-bank banks outside the FDIC.

The biggest episode of bank failures in the 1990s was well contained by the FDIC even as the non-bank banks arose. This set of failures was caused in part by the elimination of an obscure US government tax shelter for real estate investment. The US Economic Recovery Tax Act of 1981 tax act allowed limited liability partners to buy tax liability from general partners in real estate ventures. Investors in special real estate limited partnerships could invest, for example, $10,000 and receive in return income tax reductions by as much as $60,000 in losses that were incurred by the general partners. Effectively, this subsidized investment in real estate through the US tax code, by legalizing a market for sharing the liability of general partners among limited partners.

The US Tax Reform Act of 1986 eliminated this tax shelter and led to a collapse in the value of commercial real estate. This led to bank defaults that were concentrated in newly growing regions of the United States. According to the FDIC, the top two states by the number of bank failures were Texas, with 599, and Oklahoma, with 122 (FDIC 1997: 14–15).

The FDIC Division of Research and Statistics states, in its *History of the Eighties: Lessons for the Future*, that the elimination of the real estate subsidy dramatically lowered the demand for such real estate partnerships, created a flood out of investment in real estate and caused a collapse of the commercial real estate market (FDIC 1997: 141):

> The consequences of these provisions was to dampen the demand for commercial real estate investments during the late 1980s and early 1990s, and the dampening of demand helped soften real estate prices. The importance of these tax considerations is reflected in the rise and fall of real estate limited partnerships during the 1980s. According to data from the Roulac Group (a real estate consulting unit of Deloitte & Touche), the market for this investment vehicle had grown fivefold between 1981 and 1985. After reaching a high point of attracting $16 billion in new capital in 1985, real estate limited partnership sales fell precipitously over the next four years, gathering only $1.5 billion in new capital in 1989.

Outside the federal deposit insurance system, as the 1980s banking crisis unfolded, there was a 1985 bank run in a US Ohio state bank insurance system. Ohio had a savings and loans insurance system called the Ohio Deposit

Guarantee Fund, which was a state-chartered private insurance fund for the S&L banks of Ohio. Most US savings and loans banks, which specialize in mortgages, were part of the federal deposit insurance system that ran parallel to the FDIC, called the Federal Savings and Loans Insurance Corporation (FSLIC). The Ohio fund chose to operate independently, outside the federal banking insurance system.

It became bankrupt after the 1985 failure of the Cincinnati-based Home State Savings Bank, which caused a bank panic that Ohio state's insurance fund could not finance. The governor of Ohio closed all the Ohio S&Ls, as in the 1933 "bank holiday". They were reopened once they had managed to join the FSLIC deposit insurance system.[2]

During this period of the mid- to late 1980s the FSLIC itself became insolvent. The US Government Accountability Office (GAO) dates this as happening in 1987 (Sherman 2009). The FSLIC was then absorbed into the FDIC. Yet, coming out of these crises, Cooperman, Lee and Wolfe (1992: 936) use the Ohio case to illustrate how markets were well able to carry out risk-based pricing for different banks' savings accounts known as "certificates of deposits": "The finding of risk-based pricing during the crisis period indicates the public's awareness and concern over federal insurance fund problems as early as 1985."

Their work suggests that risk-based pricing was also possible within a federal banking insurance system. By the FDIC providing insurance at a flat rate per deposit, each bank would have some incentive to take on more risk in its loan and asset holdings, make more profits and return a greater yield to its investors. Even if the increase in risk causes a higher risk of default, its depositors would be covered and so would not be concerned by the greater risk position of the bank. A potential increase in risk taking with a fixed fee per deposit, across all insured banks, was a moral hazard problem of the FDIC that Kareken and Wallace (1978) emphasize.

If the FDIC insurance system induces more risky banking, while US banking spreads internationally, then the moral hazard raises the risk of panic in the entire global banking system. The nature of the problem suggests the solution of charging a "risk-based" deposit insurance fee for every bank, which the US Congress enacted in the Federal Deposit Insurance Reform Act of 2005, which became effective in 2006. Using a set of different risk categorizations, the FDIC now required deposit insurance premiums from each bank, determined on the basis of the degree of risk in the bank's assets, which can be adjusted as needed to try to accurately reflect bank asset risks.

The other issue is how the financial sector can obscure the riskiness of financial instruments, such as selling a group of mortgages in a pre-packed

---

2. https://ohiohistorycentral.org/w/Home_State_Savings_Bank%27s_Failure

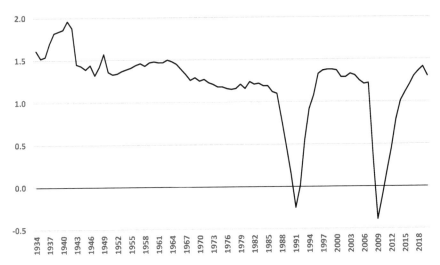

Figure 10.3 Ratio of FDIC reserves to insured deposits, as a percentage, 1934–2020
Source: FDIC (2021).

mortgage-backed security. If the banks do not reveal information or risk clearly, however, and the FDIC views the asset sheet as lacking detail about risk, the FDIC can simply be wary and put the bank in a higher risk category, with a higher fee. Clarity of the information revealed would remain in the interest of the FDIC-insured banks.

Sourced from FDIC data, Figure 10.3 shows the FDIC reserves collected from deposit insurance premiums, relative to the insured deposited funds, as a percentage for the period from 1934 to 2020 (FDIC 2021). This shows that FDIC reserves from collecting bank insurance premiums have trended near to 1.5 per cent of the insured deposits of the FDIC banks. During crises these dipped down below 0 per cent in 1991 and 2009, although there was no run on FDIC-insured banks during either period.

The 1990 recession and bank crisis led to a revision of the legislation as to how the FDIC could operate, which became relevant during the 2008–09 crisis. Like Irving Fisher's 1932 proposal, the 1991 FDIC Improvement Act granted the FDIC the ability to guarantee bank debt and to help banks facing default because of systemic (aggregate) risk. These provisions were designed to help during times of widespread bank failures.

During 2008–09 the FDIC used the 1991 law to guarantee bank debt, provide extended deposit insurance and support non-guaranteed institutions. According to the FDIC (2017: xi–xii):

> [T]he financial crisis that followed the housing market's collapse was so severe that, for the first time, the US government turned to a statutory

provision that had been put in place as part of the Federal Deposit Insurance Corporation Improvement Act of 1991 to help it deal with systemic risks. This provision prohibited assistance to failing banks if FDIC funds would be used to protect uninsured depositors and other creditors – but the act also contained a provision allowing an exception to the prohibition when the failure of an institution would pose a systemic risk. In 2008, by relying on the provision that allowed a systemic risk exception, the FDIC was able to take two actions that maintained financial institutions' access to funding: the FDIC guaranteed bank debt and, for certain types of transaction accounts, provided an unlimited deposit insurance guarantee. In addition, the FDIC and the other federal regulators used the systemic risk exception to extend extraordinary support to some of the largest financial institutions in the country in order to prevent their disorderly failure.

The 2008–09 panic affected FDIC banks, but they already had in place a system to keep guaranteed deposits safe by merging the asset of failed banks with other banks. One repercussion of the 2008–09 bank crisis that affected the FDIC was that the 2010 US Dodd–Frank Act required the FDIC to increase the minimum reserves from 1.15 per cent to 1.35 per cent of total insured deposits. Figure 10.3 shows that this adjustment was achieved when the ratio hit 1.36 per cent in 2018.

For the non-FDIC-insured "shadow banks", the banking deregulation of the 1980s through the 1990s in the United States and the United Kingdom led to the emergence of investment bank money market funds that competed directly with FDIC commercial banking. The investment banks prospered without FDIC insurance coverage while having the competitive advantage of not paying the FDIC premiums. This gives a permanent benefit of allowing a higher return for money market accounts within non-FDIC investment banks.

For the "shadow banks" in the United States that evolved outside the FDIC insurance system, however, a panic ensued in the bank crisis of 2008–09. This was like the panics before the creation of the Fed and the FDIC. Jon Moen and Ellis Tallman in their online Fed article on the "panic of 1907" (Moen & Tallman 2015) compare the crisis of 2008–09 to the US bank panic of 1907. Both panics started in New York and spread internationally, allowing the authors to conclude: "The Panic of 1907 had many elements in common with the financial crisis of 2007–09."

During 2008 some of the greatest US investment banking houses of the time suddenly failed. The Fed was ill equipped to stem the panic proactively, just as in the Great Depression. As a result, both the Fed and the US Treasury initially let these banks collapse, and a panic ensued.

The 2008 panic originated in the investment banks holding US-originated mortgage-backed securities. These went into default because the Fed dramatically raised the federal funds interest rate during 2005–06. Since the MBSs had been considered safe assets, they were sold throughout the global financial system.

The Fed ran out its reserves as investment banks withdrew them. The FDIC was there to insure banks covered by its insurance, which it did as many of them became caught up in the panic. Given the void for the non-FDIC-insured banks, the United States had to scramble and use both the Fed and the Treasury to stop the bank panic with a varied set of discretionary actions, as also occurred in the 1930s panic.

Investment banks could invest funds that they held in any asset, such as mortgage-backed securities. A failure of these assets was said to be unable to affect the value of money market accounts. Yet, when the MBSs went into default, this threatened investment banks with insolvency; depositors in the investment bank money markets suddenly withdrew their funds, and a panic withdrawal of investment bank deposits ensued.

The logic that investment banks could hold demand deposits and not be subject to a run was proved to be patently flawed. Many descriptions exist of the investment bank panic of 2008, with some context provided here. The crisis began when the mortgage loan company New Century Financial declared bankruptcy in April 2007, causing the nearly century-old investment bank Bear Stearns to lose a large quantity of its assets.

On 9 August 2007 the French bank BNP Paribas announced that it was closing several funds that were invested in mortgage loans. Shin (2009) marks August 2007 as the point when the global financial crisis first emerged. That summer the major UK mortgage lender Northern Rock approached bankruptcy and asked for help from the Bank of England. After a month of secret efforts on behalf of Northern Rock, the Bank of England decided against giving the bank funds and was also unable to find a bank to take over Northern Rock's assets.

Shin's (2009) article "Reflections on Northern Rock: the bank run that heralded the global financial crisis" attributes the Northern Rock bank crisis as spreading the banking panic internationally. On 13 September 2007 the BBC broadcast that Northern Rock was actively seeking Bank of England help. Queues formed along the street throughout the next day, a Friday.

One customer in the line was interviewed on television and asked if he was in a panic to withdraw funds. He replied he was not in a panic but "just preferred to put his funds elsewhere". Realizing that it had started a bank customer panic, that same day, 14 September, the BBC's *Newsnight* (2007) blogged online: "The UK's fifth largest mortgage lender, Northern Rock, has urged customers not to panic as a result of the announcement that it's to receive emergency funding from the Bank of England. The price of Northern Rock's shares have plunged – queues of people have formed outside many of the bank's branches; some have withdrawn their savings."

It may have been surprising that such an investment bank failure could spread to the neighbourhood commercial and retail banks. Yet Shin (2009: 101–2) finds that the "Northern Rock depositor run" was a result of the lack of a comprehensive national banking deposit insurance system: "Deposit insurance in the United Kingdom was a partial affair, funded by the banking industry itself and insuring only a part of the deposits."

During these two days, 13 and 14 September 2007, as the queues grew along streets towards the Northern Rock branches, the Bank of England's governor, Mervyn King, was preparing to host the Bank's conference "On the sources of macroeconomic stability". Cancelling his scheduled conference dinner speech on 14 September, King scrambled to deal with the Northern Rock crisis. He resolved it by authorizing the Bank of England to fully insure all the deposits of the mortgage lender, and in February 2008 the United Kingdom nationalized Northern Rock.

In 2008, with Bear Stearns then approaching bankruptcy, the Federal Reserve devised a way to act like the FDIC in its normal dealings with bankruptcy. Since Bear Stearns was outside the FDIC, and since the Fed had no powers to merge failing banks with others, it had to use emergency power to do this, despite having little precedent or authority to do so. The Federal Reserve Bank of New York created a company called Maiden Lane LLC, which bought up the assets of Bear Stearns, while arranging an equity stock exchange between Bear Stearns and JPMorgan Chase, which gave the latter ownership of the Bear Stearns assets.

The Fed manoeuvred beyond its mandate of inflation and unemployment targets to try to play the same role that the FDIC does routinely for its failing banks: providing reserves from its funds to merge a failed bank with another. The Fed had no insurance reserve for investment bank failures, so it just made up a "maiden" way to provide an insurance-type policy by creating a new limited liability private company to carry out its dubious deeds. The Fed had a vested interest, since it had long ago sanctioned investment banks to operate outside the FDIC system and wanted to avoid a widespread financial crisis.

Suffice it to say that these Federal Reserve actions did not stop a bank panic from occurring and spreading internationally. A year after the Northern Rock street panic, on 15 September 2008, after a merger negotiation for the famous Lehman Brothers investment bank had failed, it declared bankruptcy. On the same day perhaps the most famous investment bank, Merrill Lynch, went out of independent existence. Given that the BBC is funded by a licence fee tax, the UK government fostered this progression of days "as the worst crisis in 80 years built to its terrible climax" (Vigna 2008).

With its trademark "bull" standing as a statue on Wall Street in New York City, Merrill Lynch was taken over by Bank of America. This occurred as in an FDIC merger, after Merrill Lynch had sold off $31 billion in assets at a price of 22 cents per dollar of assets being sold, according to Morgenson (2008). The difference is that, once again, this occurred only after it had been induced by the Fed and US Treasury. In lieu of having FDIC-type insurance for the investment bank, "[b]oth Treasury Secretary Hank Paulson and New York Federal Reserve President Timothy Geithner ... pressured Bank of America to purchase Merrill Lynch", as the Seven Pillars Institute writes in an online article entitled "Bank of America's takeover of Merrill Lynch".[3]

The result was assessed in a legally binding judgement to be an ethics violation. Bank of America was ordered to pay $2.43 billion to settle a class-action lawsuit with the Merrill Lynch investors. In effect, both the Fed and the US Treasury engendered an illegal transaction that was far beyond the bounds of congressional law guiding the Fed, as the Fed tried to insure non-bank banks after the crisis had already occurred. This questionable policy was characterized as being a case of "too big to fail".

One might think that the collapse of investment banks would not spread to other financial intermediaries that provide a range of services including life insurance. In other words, the collapse might have involved only the investment banks and go no further. It did indeed spread more broadly, however.

For example, the private Reserve Primary Fund was simply a private money market fund, albeit one of the first. In September 2008 its dollar per share funds became worth less than a dollar, leading to a sudden withdrawal by customers and its ultimate demise by that autumn. With such a name and history, its failure in 2008 was noticed.

American Insurance Group (AIG), which operates in 80 countries, also insured money market funds while being primarily a "causality and property" insurance company, along with providing life insurance. In 2008 AIG ran out of funds, so that it became illiquid. The day after Lehman and Merrill Lynch ceased to exist independently, on 16 September, the US Treasury lent AIG "$85 billion in exchange for a 79.9% stake" (Vigna 2008).

In lieu of efficient bank insurance, after this discretionary US nationalization of AIG had occurred, on 3 October 2008 a US policy of nationalizing certain financial intermediaries formally was enacted as Public Law 110–343. This created the $700 billion Troubled Asset Relief Program (TARP). According to Webel (2013), TARP allowed the US Treasury to buy 92 per cent of AIG, 74 per cent of General Motors' GMAC/Ally Financial banking operation, 61 per cent

---

3. https://sevenpillarsinstitute.org/case-studies/bank-of-americas-takeover-of-merrill-lynch

of GM and equity ownership in both Citicorp and Bank of America. The US Treasury used its ownership power to restrict dividend payouts by these and a wide swathe of other banks, further distorting financial markets.

Nationalizing part of the financial system, as the United States and United Kingdom did during a bank crisis, enabled certain lucky companies to live while others were left to wither and die. This is a fragmented solution for when a government does not have an efficient bank insurance system. With efficient bank insurance, more banks could have survived, with banks in good standing allowing others facing insolvency to live on, using a pre-planned insurance reserve fund that allows systematic absorption of their assets into other banks – such as with the FDIC.

Without such a system, the whims of government select which banks survive. Since banks facilitate the avoidance of the inflation tax by offering bank accounts that earn interest, arbitrary government policy distorts the ability for households to avoid the inflation tax as well as the functioning of capital markets more broadly.

The next chapter details how, in 2008, the United States began a policy of collecting excess reserves that favoured large banks, failed to stem a subsequent bank crisis and continues today at enormous levels.

11

THE PROBLEM OF EXCESS RESERVES

Federal Reserve officials supply regulations to help banks. Although the information is difficult to find in Fed minutes, just ten banks hold almost all the excess reserves of the Fed system. These ten banks were in receipt of the new interest on excess reserves that the Fed decided to pay them from 2008.

Excess reserves are those reserves that are over and above what is required to be held at the Federal Reserve. Traditionally, banks had tried to keep the exact amount of required reserves, due at the Fed each week, with zero excess. From the second quarter of 1984 to the second quarter of 2008 excess reserves averaged $1.3 billion, a minimum that could be feasibly achieved.

Once the Fed began paying IOER, excess reserves averaged $1.75 trillion from the third quarter of 2008 to the third quarter of 2020. That is more than a thousand-fold increase, going from billions to trillions of dollars. This happened even though the interest rate paid was very low, and below the inflation rate.

Figure 11.1 shows how excess reserves quickly built up at the Fed, rising from zero to $2.7 trillion by the third quarter of 2014. They began to trend down after that, until rising again during the Covid-19 pandemic till the excess reserve data series ended in 2020. Since then these "excess" reserves are now just called reserves, and shot up to above $4 trillion in 2021.

The data series on excess reserves ends in September 2020, when the Fed changed its reserve requirement to zero. Therefore, reserves could no longer be called "excess reserves", since a reserve requirement no longer existed. In addition, the Fed's name of "interest on excess reserves" was officially changed in July 2021 to "interest on reserve balances" (IORB).

The Fed had required reserves for banks for over a century, from 1914 until 2020, with a continual decline in the requirement evident as banks avoided it. Feinman (1993: 570) describes how depository banks had to keep 10 per cent of

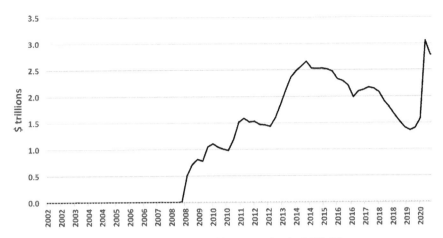

Figure 11.1 Excess reserves held at the Fed by private banks, 2002–22
Source: FRED.

reserves on "transaction deposits" that were viewed as being subject to immediate demand:

> Under current regulations, all depository institutions – commercial banks, savings banks, thrift institutions, and credit unions – are required to maintain reserves against transaction deposits, which include demand deposits, negotiable order of withdrawal accounts, and other highly liquid funds. Reserves against these deposits can take the form either of currency on hand (vault cash) or balances at the Federal Reserve ... At present, the required reserve ratio on non-transaction accounts is zero, while the requirement on transaction deposits is 10 per cent, which is near the legal minimum.

Historically, the US decline in reserve requirements began after the National Bank Act of 1863, which required national banks to hold reserves equal to 25 per cent of their total deposits and currency notes. Feinman (1993: 573) documents that there were lesser reserves required for banks "outside redemption cities", as the reserve amount became a continually evolving feature. After 1873 reserves for national bank currency notes, which were like the reserves held for banknotes in the Bank of England's Issue Department that Bagehot (1873) discusses, were eliminated.

In 1914 the Fed had variable reserve requirements for members of the Federal Reserve System. These depended on where the bank was located and the nature of deposits, varying from 18 per cent to 12 per cent for demand deposits and

5 per cent for saving account time deposits. Their rates subsequently declined over time while the geographic designation of banks was eliminated.

After the Second World War Federal Reserve member bank transaction deposits as a share of total such deposits dropped from 85 per cent in the 1950s to 65 per cent in 1979, after the Vietnam War, as interest rates rose and banks sought a higher return for depositors. State chartered banks were allowed to exit the Fed system and, instead, adopt reserve requirements that varied by state and were generally lower than the Fed system, which contributed to the decline of the percentage of reserves held at the Fed.

In response to these declining reserves at the Fed, the Monetary Control Act of 1980 required all depository institutions to hold reserves at the Fed even if they were not a member of the Fed system. Then reserve requirements were set at 12 per cent for transaction deposits and 3 per cent for non-transaction deposits. This dropped in 1992 to 10 per cent and 0 per cent, respectively, as non-bank banks with non-transaction deposits continued to grow.

Required reserves were viewed as a tax, because they could not be lent out or earn interest, such as through holding Treasury debt. This indirect tax incentivized banks to avoid it, which led to banks continually seeking ways to avoid holding reserves at the Fed, as Feinman (1993: 571) describes:

> Requiring depositories to hold idle, non-interest-bearing balances is essentially like taxing these institutions in an amount equal to the interest they could have earned on these balances in the absence of reserve requirements. This forgone interest, or reserve "tax," directly affects only the depository system and its customers, and not other parts of the financial system. Hence, it creates an artificial incentive for depositors and borrowers to bypass the depository system …

For the period from January 1973 to March 2022, Figure 11.2 shows the quantity of total reserves as a percentage of all commercial bank deposits, including both "transaction" and "non-transaction" deposits. This total reserve-to-deposit ratio declined from 5 per cent in 1975 to 1 per cent in 2008. After introducing interest payments on reserves, the ratio took off unevenly to almost 30 per cent in 2015, and remained above 20 per cent in 2020–22.

Paying IOER reversed the ever-declining reserve ratio, to create instead an uncontrolled large build-up of reserves starting in 2008. The purpose of these reserves is unclear. But what is clear is that they sterilized the money supply increase by the Fed, so that the inflation rate did not begin rising immediately once the Great Recession was over.

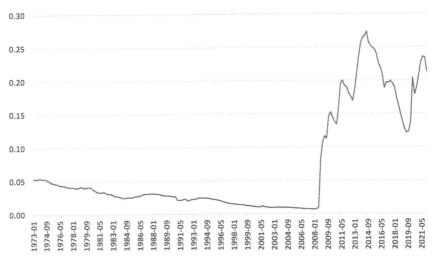

Figure 11.2 Ratio of required and excess reserves to total commercial bank deposits, as a percentage, January 1973–March 2022
Source: FRED.

The US system had used required reserves as a combined back-up for both its currency and deposits when on the classic gold standard, dropping this to reserves for deposits only when Bagehot's treatise appeared in 1873. Once the FDIC was in place, the need for reserves for deposits declined greatly. Currency was backed by gold again until the Bretton Woods version of the gold standard ended. But, once the Vietnam War commenced and interest rates rose, evading reserve requirements through non-transaction deposits became rampant through the growth of non-bank banks.

Paying interest on reserves was allowed under 2006 US legislation, and was meant only for required reserves so as to eliminate the incentive for banks to circumvent the reserve requirements of the Federal Reserve System, which they viewed as a tax, but not to allow interest payments on all reserves. Feinman (1993: 585) considers interest payment on required reserves to be better than eliminating reserve requirements: "Paying interest on reserves is a preferable alternative to eliminating reserve requirements. Specifically, if the Federal Reserve paid a market-based rate of interest on required reserve balances, the reserve tax would essentially be eliminated, as would the distortional effects of this tax on resource allocation."

Conversely, the reason the Fed did not want to pay interest on required reserves was because it did not want to reduce its seigniorage revenue from the inflation tax, which was remitted by the Fed back to the Treasury for its use in federal budget expenditure. Paying interest on required reserves would directly transfer the inflation tax from Treasury coffers to private banks. This in turn would subsidize those banks by increasing their profit (Feinman 1993: 572): "[I]f the Federal Reserve paid interest on all required reserve balances, the private sector would enjoy a net increase in after-tax income, whereas the Treasury would see its net revenues reduced."

The 2006 Act's authorization of paying interest on reserves was brought forward to 2008 during the bank crisis. The Fed's reserves were negative at that point, and it had to borrow from other central banks to bring its reserves up above zero. This was done through central bank liquidity swaps, by which the Fed printed money, gave it to other central banks in exchange for foreign currency, then counted that foreign currency as reserves at the Fed.

Since the foreign currency could not readily be given out to banks as they sought to use reserves held at the Fed to pay out depositors during the 2008 banking panic, the "swap" involved the Fed giving back the foreign currency to foreign central banks at a time in the future, such as within a year. This obscured the swap device in "smoke and mirrors", since the Fed could not print money and put it into its reserves directly, although it could print money, give it to a foreign central bank in return for its currency, then count the new foreign currency as reserves. In effect, the Fed printed money and put it into its reserves.

In desperate straits, to increase the excess reserves above what the Fed had borrowed from other central banks by printing dollars, the Fed then began in 2008 to pay interest on both required reserves and excess reserves. This way it could pay back the liquidity swaps to other central banks while building up its reserve pot. This began a new era of excess reserves, as the swaps that began the era surged in 2008, were used again in 2012 and were then used again during the 2020 bank crisis in the pandemic.

Figure 11.3 shows the level of the Fed's central bank liquidity swaps in billions of dollars. These rose to almost $500 billion in 2008, causing the first build-up of excess reserves (depicted in Figure 11.1) that was manifest through the swaps. Without counting as reserves the foreign currency obtained from the swaps, Fed reserves were –$50 billion in the middle of 2008, as noted above.

To see the interest rate paid for reserves from 2008 to 2021, Figure 11.4 plots the rate of IOER at a quarterly average rate. After initially being set at 1 per cent for several months in 2008, it was dropped to 0.25 per cent until December 2015. Then it rose in steps until the pandemic and dropped to 0.10 in 2020, with a slight increase to 0.15 per cent in June 2021 (not shown). The renamed interest on reserve balances rose from 0.15 per cent to 0.40 per cent on 17 March 2022, its first significant increase, while at the same time the inflation rate was already 8 per cent.

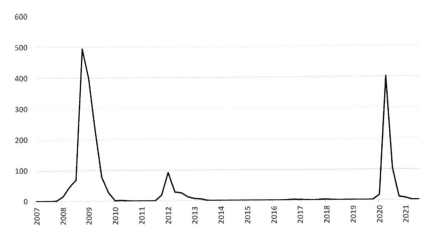

Figure 11.3 The Fed's central bank liquidity swaps, 2007–21
Source: FRED.

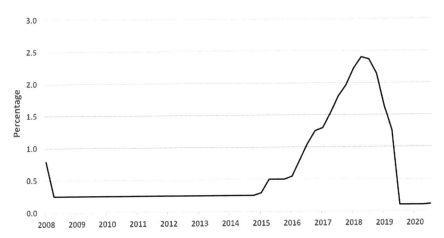

Figure 11.4 The rate of interest on excess reserves, 2008–20
Source: FRED.

Despite Fed concerns about redirecting inflation tax revenue from the US Treasury to private banks, the Fed paid about $11 billion directly to banks from 2008 to 2020. This is computed by taking the average IOER rate, which was 0.63 per cent, and factoring it (using 0.0063) by the average excess reserves held, which was $1.75 trillion. This $11 billion was given mainly to the ten largest banks.

By 2008 the reserve requirement was nearly zero, at 1 per cent of all commercial bank deposits. This means the Fed effectively had no reserves in the event of a bank crisis for non-FDIC-insured banks, which were continually growing in asset size. The Fed had in effect been eviscerated of its ability to raise reserves at a time when it suddenly faced a bank crisis of the FDIC-uninsured investment bank sector. Investment banks such as JP Morgan Chase, Citigroup and all the major ones with "nontransaction deposits" faced virtual bankruptcy, and so took from the Fed as many reserves as possible to pay out depositors as they withdrew their funds in a panic.

The Fed, as the leader of the international financial system, was faced with the dilemma of balancing financial stability, inflation stability and money supply stability. This had all begun with war after the 9/11 terrorist attacks and the Fed's subsequent three-year flooding of the money supply while driving down market interest rates below the inflation rate. The Fed was credited with handling that crisis well by avoiding a global financial crisis, even though its actions after 2001 directly caused the 2008 bank panic and concurrent global financial crisis.

The Fed's flood of new money after 2001 saw the inflation rate rise steadily to 4 per cent by 2006. It then fell briefly before climbing to 5.5 per cent in July 2008 as the financial crisis hit, and far above the Fed's illegitimate 2 per cent inflation rate target. After the Fed raised the federal funds rate from 1 per cent to 5.3 per cent between May 2004 and July 2006, the mortgages that had been taken out from 2002 to 2005 with negative real interest rates went into default en masse, and a run on reserves resulted. The Fed advanced the date, through Congress, for paying interest on reserves, and paid it on all reserves, so the private banks had a new option of earning risk-free income.

Looming over the entire bank sector after the 2008 crisis, however, was the fact that Congress had begun deliberating on imposing higher reserve requirements for each bank, including the shadow banks. The threat of increased reserve requirements may have contributed to large banks voluntarily holding trillions of dollars in excess reserves. The United States then passed the 2010 Dodd–Frank banking act, which formally raised capital reserve requirements for each individual bank, but especially for the "systemically important" banks, to levels similar to those stipulated in the international Basel III accord. Government officials designated which banks were systemically important, and the designation of the systemically important banks spread across Europe as it also moved towards Basel III standards on capital reserve requirements.

Despite Bagehot's (1873) view that increasing reserves at individual banks is inefficient, Vice Governor Thomas Hoenig of the FDIC advocated in 2016 that having a higher level of reserves by individual banks was better than expanding the FDIC insurance system coverage to investment banks. Mervyn King (2017) similarly recommended higher individual bank reserve requirements. It was difficult to find an economist who did not recommend more reserve requirements for each individual bank.

The reserves held by the banks that were declared "important" by the Fed remained far beyond what was required, until suddenly reserves for deposits were no longer required. The Fed's "monetary policy" website states: "As announced on March 15, 2020, the Board reduced reserve requirement ratios to zero percent effective March 26, 2020. This action eliminated reserve requirements for all depository institutions."

Despite sitting on over $1 trillion in excess reserves, a bank panic occurred again in 2020 across shadow banks, as depositors aimed to withdraw funds before restrictions on withdrawals were imposed. These restrictions were imposed by the 2010 Dodd–Frank banking act to slow down withdrawals and so avoid a panic. But this provision caused the panic. Anticipating the triggering of a limit on withdrawals during 2020, investors sought to beat the restrictions, caused a panic withdrawal of funds, and then "money market funds melted in pandemic panic" (Smialek 2021):

> [In] March, $125 billion was taken out of US prime money market funds ... One type of fund in particular drove the retreat... publicly offered prime funds aimed at institutional investors (think hedge funds, insurance companies and pension funds) ... totaling 30 percent of managed assets. The reason seems to have its roots, paradoxically, in rules that were imposed after the 2008 financial crisis ... which can temporarily prohibit redemptions once a fund's easy-to-sell assets fall below a certain threshold.

During the week from 18 March to 25 March 2021 the Fed was in a crisis as, again, it had run out of ready reserves. Even though excess reserves had been falling steadily since 2014, they still amounted to $1.7 trillion in February 2020. Yet these proved irrelevant to the liquidity need of 2020. The Fed resorted to more swaps again, borrowing $400 billion in March and April by printing money and giving it to other central banks in return for foreign currency, helping Fed reserves to rise suddenly to $2.9 billion in April 2020.

Banks had been willing to supply excess reserves in lieu of participation in an FDIC insurance scheme. The banks interact with Federal Reserve officials through any number of legal forums. Nobel laureate George Stigler (1971) calls this the "economics of regulation", through which government officials form discretionary policy for those being regulated so as to meet their demands.

Rather than a clear set of rules for bank insurance, this discretion allows banks to receive individual benefits and industry-wide benefits because of Fed policy.

Regulation and lawmaking requires a useful interaction between government and paid lobbyists of the financial sector arguing what laws should be passed in congressional staff offices of both the House and the Senate, and in the halls of the Federal Reserve itself to some extent. Lobbying is informational, and part of ongoing democracy in the United States. Nevertheless, it can give rise to inefficient policy that favours industry and causes the moral hazard of an increased probability of a bad state of affairs.

The moral hazard of bailing out banks after 2008 contributed to a similar bank panic in 2020. Banks took on risk, without deposit insurance, and found that the Fed had to rescue them once again during another bank panic. Rather than reining in the shadow banks within the FDIC, the easier regulatory path was chosen of trying to monitor any latent problem, then addressing it after it had arisen.

Most Federal Reserve officials restrain from openly criticizing the Fed in their official research reports, just as US military officers refrain from criticizing the government's military command structure under which they serve. Even so, as in the military, some brave Federal Reserve officials try to identify problems with Federal Reserve policy.

Craig and Koepke (2015) refer to the Fed's post-2008 policy as "excess reserves: oceans of cash". Ennis and Wolman (2011: 14–17), in "Large excess reserves in the US: a view from the cross-section of banks", name the few banks that held the vast quantity of reserves that received interest on reserves, and find that a broad spectrum of shadow banking became involved in this Federal Reserve excess reserve scheme. They list the largest seven banks in the system as of December 2007 as Bank of America, JP Morgan Chase, Citigroup Inc., Wells Fargo, USBancorp, HSBC and Suntrust, and describe how the large banks increased excess reserves (Ennis & Wolman 2011: 14–17):

> It is interesting to see that initially (in 2008q3) the top 10 banks are the main drivers of the increase in the proportion of reserves held by the top 75 banks ... According to Figure 5 then, large institutions hold a large portion of total reserves ... While Citi, Bank of America, and HSBC held more than 6 percent of assets in reserves during the period, the rest of the banks stayed at lower levels, around 2 percent of assets ... As was suggested by Figure 5, the largest banks held a disproportionately high amount of reserves at the peak of the crisis.

Rather than putting this capital into loans and investments, the excess reserves induced the moral hazard of less investment. Keister and McAndrews (2009: 1), in "Why are banks holding so many excess reserves?", acknowledge that the excess reserves are not being invested as they were in the entire pre-2008 history of near-zero excess reserves:

> Some observers claim that the large increase in excess reserves implies that many of the policies introduced by the Federal Reserve in response to the financial crisis have been ineffective. Rather than promoting the flow of credit to firms and households, it is argued, the data shown in Figure 1 indicate that the money lent to banks and other intermediaries by the Federal Reserve since September 2008 is simply sitting idle in banks' reserve accounts.

Adding to the excess reserve build-up was the other new policy of the Fed in 2008: to directly purchase mortgage back securities. Having eliminated its by-laws prohibiting favouring any one part of the economy, the Fed began buying – and still buys – an "ocean" of MBSs. Although Fed officials have asserted that all MBS purchases are high grade and do not subsidize the banking sector, this argument defies the principles of supply and demand.

If the demand for any fraction of the MBSs is increased by the Fed, then the demand for the whole market for MBSs is increased. This raises the value of all mortgages, whether being bought directly by the Fed or left to others in the private economy to hold. Just as the Treasury program of 2008 that bought a fraction of Citicorp, GM, AIG and a host of other banks raised the value of the rest of the equity in all those companies, the Fed's MBS purchases raised the value of all mortgages, which were the weakest part of bank assets and which were threatening widespread bank failure.

Implicit bank subsidies by the Fed in its post-2008 policy helped banks. Labonte (2018: 6–8) finds "purposeful ambiguity" in Fed policy before the crisis and an arbitrary Fed bailout after the crisis involving "too big to fail" banks:

> A Government Accountability Office (GAO) ... analysis found evidence of a funding advantage during the crisis ... sometimes referred to as the TBTF subsidy, although a subsidy typically implies a government willingness to provide the recipient with a benefit. Note also that a subsidy typically takes the form of an explicit direct payment, financial support, or guarantee, whereas in this case, if the funding advantage exists, it would derive from the expectation of future support that has not been pledged ... TBTF bailouts could be delivered through assistance unique to the firm or through existing government programs on a preferential, subsidized basis ... TBTF policy before the crisis could be described as purposeful ambiguity – policy was not explicit about what would

happen in the event that large financial firms become insolvent, or which firms were considered TBTF ... Policy during the recent crisis could be described as reactive, developing ad hoc in fits and starts in reaction to events. Ultimately, some banks and non-bank financial firms received federal assistance, despite the lack of an explicit safety net and federal prudential regulation in the case of non-banks AIG and Bear Stearns. In the absence of explicit authority to rescue a TBTF firm, as the crisis unfolded, broad standing authority was used ...

The Fed policy of continually buying MBSs increased the value of bank assets. The excess reserves provided an ongoing interest subsidy to banks of billions of dollars and a sterilization of the money supply increase to keep inflation in check. The Fed largely met its self-imposed inflation target, at least up until 2021, while obscuring the ability to predict when inflation would rise. Holding a huge amount of reserves and doling out Treasury inflation tax revenue to a few banks that they designated as systematically important, Fed officials claim that such a concentration of reserves and interest payments was never the intention but, rather, that it just happened that way. Milton Friedman may have laughed, and George Stigler may have smiled.

The haphazard Fed policy has created a permanent source of bank subsidization and moral hazard without any bank insurance policy having yet been articulated. The next chapter shows how the Fed has paid inflation tax to private banks instead of the Treasury, arbitrarily changed the definition of a main monetary aggregate while dropping reserve requirements and caused the new disconnect between the Fed's Treasury debt holdings and the money in circulation that causes inflation.

12
GIVING AWAY THE INFLATION TAX

The science of contemporary monetary theory arose to solve the problem of how the central bank should conduct monetary and banking policy under a fiat monetary regime. An important result was to provide an optimal amount of inflation tax revenue through inflation tax targeting. The inflation rate to target was found to be very low, such as that consistent with natural seigniorage.

Nonetheless, the Fed became typical of international central banks by financing significant US Treasury spending, especially during wars and crises. It also decided to try to maintain the growth of the global financial system. Although the conduct of the Fed's banking insurance role has become murkier, its inflation tax collection policy was clear up until 2008.

From Bailey (1956) to recent news headlines, economists have recognized the inflation tax as equivalent to a fiscal tax, enacted by the monetary authority through discretionary action to finance Treasury expenditure. Recently, Leeper and Zhou (2021) find that 50 per cent of new marginal fiscal expenditure in developed economies is financed by increasing the inflation tax. In its 13 October 2021 editorial "The inflation tax rises", *The Wall Street Journal* (2021) anticipates the high inflation tax episode that was experienced in 2022.

The Fed is unbound by the usual process for raising taxes. Article 1, section 7, of the US Constitution explicitly states: "All Bills for raising Revenue shall originate in the House of Representatives. The Senate may propose or concur with Amendments as on other Bills".[1] The House tax bills must arise in the Ways and Means Committee, which is the "oldest committee of the United States Congress, and the chief tax-writing committee in the House of Representatives", according to the Committee's website, which was "[f]irst established as a select committee on July 24, 1789 ... and was formally listed as a standing committee in the House Rules on January 7, 1802".

---

1. https://constitutionus.com

The US tradition of a tax-raising committee is modelled on that of the United Kingdom. UK Parliament web pages state that "Ways and Means is a traditional term for taxes or other charges levied on the public in order to fund Government spending". The United Kingdom had a formal Ways and Means Committee from 1641 to 1967 that originated proposals for taxes.

The UK tax committee was then abolished and replaced by granting the power to present tax code changes to the Chancellor of the Exchequer. As the UK parliament puts it, this means that taxes can be enacted much more quickly than in the US Congress: "Under the Provisional Collection of Taxes Act 1968, tax changes and tax continuations can be validated by a single Motion taken after the Budget Speech. This means that tax proposals contained in the Budget Speech may come into effect immediately."

In the United States, tax laws start in the Ways and Means Committee; go to the House floor for a vote; to the Senate Finance Committee, which can amend and revise them; to the Senate floor for a vote; and then to a House–Senate Reconciliation Committee, consisting of a hand-picked company of members, who devise a compromise bill. The bill then goes back to both House and Senate floors for another vote; then, finally, to the president, for signature. Taxes cannot be raised by the US Federal Reserve System or by the Bank of England.

Both central banks raise the inflation tax at will, however. The US Congress and the Bank of England alike have adopted inflation rate targeting to formalize this process. But the Fed can buy any amount of Treasury debt that it wants and fund Treasury spending to any degree that it wants, bound legally only by a zero-inflation-rate target, as established in a 1978 Act. The Fed then must transfer all profits after the cost of operations each year back to the US Treasury.

Private banks buy Treasury debt to earn a relatively "risk-free" rate of interest for customers, in that the government loan will go into default only if the government of the nation collapses and the new government does not honour past government debt. Investment banks especially supply their customers with options to hold a diversified portfolio of both risk-free government debt, which supplies a steady stream of interest, and ownership in risky private corporations, which pay dividends based on uncertain profits.

When the central bank buys up government debt from the private banks to increase the money supply, it earns the interest instead of the private banks and has to return this to the Treasury net of its operating cost. Given a zero cost of operating the Fed, the Treasury would get back all the interest payments it was required to pay on all the debt that the Fed purchases and owns.

Historically, the Bank of England operated in a similar fashion to the Fed in terms of printing money, by using the bond market for this scheme. In 2020, however, the Bank of England was allowed to directly buy UK government debt with freshly printed money. After all, why bother with "smoke and mirrors" in times of crisis? As the United Kingdom owns the Bank, it pays interest to itself, incurring a like expenditure and receipt.

Private markets and foreign nations usually hold most of the Treasury debt used to cover budget deficits, except for countries entering a period of hyperinflation. The central bank buys a considerable share of this debt in all countries. The Fed had held a steady share, which grew during the Vietnam War and again in the 2020–21 pandemic.

The Fed's share of Treasury debt tightly links together the money supply growth rate and the inflation tax, with divergence only if the Fed can "sterilize" some of the money supply increase. When FDR bought silver in the 1930s, the silver purchases could be effectively sterilized so that any inflation increase could be moderated. After 2008 the excess reserve build-up increased uncertainty about the inflation tax for households, as it was unclear when this money supply increase would enter circulation.

When a central bank is established, it issues a new currency that the Treasury uses to buy goods and services and to collect inflation tax. Every year more money is printed to buy Treasury debt, creating additional inflation tax revenue. But the imposition of the tax on households depends on when the money supply increase enters circulation and causes inflation. Collection of the inflation tax by the Treasury is distorted if the Fed gives away the tax by paying interest on these excess reserves.

During the 2008–09 Great Financial Crisis the collection of the inflation tax and the insurance of the banking system became entangled with the Fed paying interest on excess reserves and gifting the inflation tax to the private banks. Banks had already sold the Treasury debt to the Fed. The Fed then earned the interest on that debt and was supposed to return it to the Treasury as inflation tax revenue. Instead, the Fed gave the banks the US seigniorage revenue. Besides Treasury debt, the Fed also bought mortgage-backed securities and returned the interest on them to the Treasury as seigniorage – except that some of the MBS purchases added to excess reserves that earned IOER for private banks.

From 2000 to 2019, Figure 12.1 shows the seigniorage revenue "profit" of the US Federal Reserve that was remitted back to the US Treasury (black dashed line). Before 2008 the Fed bought only Treasury debt, and the total interest earned (black solid line) and the remittances moved together closely. After 2008 the total interest earned by the Fed included interest on MBSs, and the Fed began IOER payments (grey dashed line), starting at zero in 2005 and rising until 2018.

The Fed remittances to Treasury decline in tandem with the increase in the interest payments on excess reserves. To see that the IOER payments directly reduce the remittances requires only a comparison of the two lines, which move in opposite directions. Further, adding together the total remittances and the IOER returns the normal amount of remittances, aligning with the total interest earned.

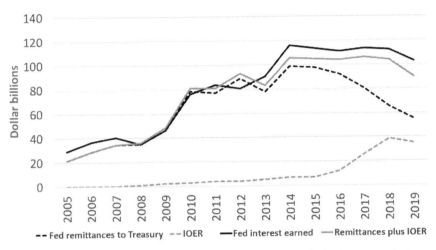

Figure 12.1 Fed remittances to the Treasury and the diversion of seigniorage to private banks, 2005–19
Sources: FRED; and board of governors of the Federal Reserve System, annual financial statements.

This quantifies how much inflation tax seigniorage the Fed is diverting from the US Treasury and giving to the private banks, which it regulates through the IOER payments. Not only is the Fed collecting a major source of tax revenue without going through the US constitutional process, it is giving it away, mainly to a select small number of private banks.

When the Fed allowed private banks to evade the FDIC insurance, starting in the 1980s, and then suddenly decided to build an unwieldy large reserve fund after the 2008 panic, it was presumed that this would supply some opaque form of bank insurance in the future. It was not sufficient for times of crisis, however, as the March–April 2020 bank panic showed. Instead, the excess reserves provided only a single clear result.

The excess reserves simply provided a way to directly subsidize private banks by giving them the US Treasury seigniorage, while generating the moral hazard of excessively low investment for nearly a decade, which stymied economic growth and stability internationally. The conduct of normal monetary policy became lost in the Fed's new role of providing bank insurance *after* the catastrophe, without having an insurance system in place before disaster struck. Despite assurances from many economists that the private bank mutual and money markets funds would not be subject to collapse, they did collapse in 2008, and again briefly in 2020.

First, the Federal Reserve determined how much money to print by deciding how much Treasury debt and related MBS assets to buy. Next, the Fed determined a Frankenstein form of Bagehot-type reserves for banks to hold at the Fed, unrelated to FDIC insurance. The Fed allowed the shadow banks outside the FDIC to prosper and devised a means to continually subsidize the banks through IOER payments after insolvency or the threat of insolvency. Finally, the Fed eliminated all reserve requirements in 2020, since the huge cache of excess reserves that it had accumulated to subsidize banks with IOER funding made required reserves look ridiculous.

After 2008 the Fed removed any notion that interest rates would be determined freely in the market and, instead, fixed market rates by dictating the interest rate on excess reserves. It set the IOER level such that market interest rates have been below the inflation rate and below normal market interest rates for more than 17 years. This allows the Fed to control the subsidy rate, given mainly to a few private banks, while suppressing inflation and distorting capital markets.

Paying banks to contribute reserves contrasts with Bagehot's reserve fund, to which banks contributed to voluntarily without being paid to do so. The Fed chose to subsidize banks semi-permanently, using wholly uncertain and excessive levels of idle reserves with little ability to insure the entire bank system. In contrast, in Bagehot's day, the Bank of England held a minimum of its reserves and insured the entire bank system.

This post-catastrophe bank insurance makes inflation targeting difficult, because banks can lend out the excess reserves any time that they think the Fed subsidy rate through IOER is less than what they could get, on a risk-adjusted basis, by investing the reserves through loans and direct investments. The Fed's questionable creation of the IOER policy has no end in sight, except for its renaming in 2021 as interest on reserve balances. This degrades the integrity of the Fed operations by further distorting, through monetary and banking policy, how the Fed's implicit system of taxes and subsidies constrains financial markets.

The Fed's obfuscation of policy has no limits. It includes new ambiguity on how the Fed defines inflation, how Fed officials signal to markets and how the Fed defines widely used money supply aggregates. The Fed began targeting a price index that excludes food and energy prices, the "core personal consumption expenditures" (PCE) price index, unlike the CPI index used across the world and in headline inflation reports. This excludes prices that build in the rising inflation rate expectations of markets, which consumers have to pay.

Households certainly pay the expected future inflation when they buy food and energy, but the Fed excludes it, because it usually makes the CPI inflation rate higher during any new inflation episode, such as in 2021–22. The CPI reflects the actual prices people face, including rising gasoline costs when oil prices build in future expected inflation. The Fed prefers to ignore the fact that expected inflation affects the prices people pay as they drive cars and trucks, fly in planes, heat their homes and offices and fire up their stoves, ovens and fireplaces.

The Fed also provides "forward guidance" on policy by announcing some decisions on its interest rate targets, while leaving hidden aspects of policy for markets to untangle as "news" (Nelson 2021). Some news includes that three Federal Reserve Bank presidents resigned from 2017 to 2021 for giving out inside information on Fed decisions, for trading securities sensitive to Fed decisions and for investing in MBSs of the kind that the Fed continues to buy to help private banks and build excess reserves.

The basic policy facets above about the Fed are fact. The Fed's motivation is unknowable, as the Fed regulates private banks and interacts with these banks that it subsidizes. It takes the markets considerable time to figure out the operations of the Fed, as it continually extends an arbitrary reach into markets.

Innovation in bank policy can be useful: just as the monetary gold standard innovated over time, so has the US Constitution. During the Great Moderation after 1983, as the bank deregulation period of the 1980s and 1990s continued, the money supply of the shadow banks, in the form of their commercial demand deposits, grew much more than traditional demand deposits. Banks innovated to be more productive in avoiding both the inflation tax and bank insurance regulations.

One outcome was that the growth of the shadow bank industry created confusion over how the money supply was changing, making it harder to predict inflation. The Fed omitted the majority of the demand deposits of the shadow banks from the M1 definition of money, which traditionally was seen as a main indicator of money supply growth. This made the M1 definition unreliable in showing the real money supply and money demand in markets.

Consider how the Fed then changed the M1 definition of money once it had abandoned the pretence of reserve requirements, and the possible ramifications of this. Reaping power from the chaos of the financial deregulation era starting in the 1980s, central bank research concluded that the M1 money demand was unstable, and so targeting the money supply growth was an infeasible way to target inflation. Instead, the new conventional wisdom became that money supply control should be abandoned and replaced by central banks regulating market interest rates. This led ultimately to the Fed setting global market interest rates through its fixed IOER rates, a tactic that was, effectively, copied by central banks around the world for more than a decade.

With its interest-setting power well in place through IOER, the Fed finally acknowledged that most of the deposits in non-bank banks should be counted as deposits in M1. This came about after the 2020 pandemic had begun. The Fed had accelerated both Treasury debt and MBS purchases to some $110 billion in Treasury debt and mortgage back securities each month, as compared to $85 billion a month during the years after 2008. In 2020 the Fed's M1 money stock appears in its FRED database to increase from $4 trillion to $17 trillion. We could be forgiven for concluding that the M1 money supply had jumped by $14 trillion, rising by more than 300 per cent.

Rather, most of the change in M1 resulted from the Fed changing the M1 definition to include non-bank bank money market accounts. When the Fed eliminated all reserve requirements on 26 March 2020, it faced little difference between the commercial banks and the shadow banks, since none of them had to keep reserves for deposits. Without the required reserve justification for excluding the largest amount of deposit accounts from the M1 definition, at a time when money market accounts had long grown much larger than standard FDIC-insured commercial bank demand deposits, the Fed decided to include these accounts in M1.

Instead of M1 being equal to currency plus demand deposits, the Fed redefined M1 in May 2020 to also include all deposits of shadow bank "money market accounts". FRED details the new definition of M1, but its major components became:

M1 = currency + demand deposits + money market accounts.

Confusingly, money market accounts are already included in M2, and had also been included in an experimental Fed aggregate called MZM, which the Fed discontinued after February 2021. To sort this data morass out, for the fourth quarter of 2018 to the third quarter of 2021, Figure 12.2 plots several different monetary aggregates in billions of dollars. The comparison shows that the Fed in effect changed the definition of M1 to M2, with M2 only slightly higher than M1 after 2020. By redefining M1 to include money market funds, the Fed is recognizing that the deposits of the shadow banking system should be counted as part of deposits that are normally defined to be part of M1, which, going forward, gives a more useful definition for M1.

In Figure 12.2, M1 appears to have jumped during the pandemic; this results purely from the redefinition of M1, however. By summing together three series – the "deposits held at all commercial banks", which include the traditional but discontinued demand deposits of FDIC banks, and the currency in circulation – this shows that, after the second quarter of 2021, these components add up to the M1 definition. Before 2019 this new definition of M1 coincides nearly exactly with M2, and it is only somewhat below M2 after 2019.

M1 money rose significantly during the pandemic, by about $2 trillion – but not by $14 trillion, as might otherwise be presumed by looking at the M1 data. The redefinition of money inadvertently obscured the link between money and inflation, as did the build-up of excess reserves. Conversely, it could be argued that now M1 has a new source of artificially induced instability, as seen simply by looking at the M1 data, so that controlling the money supply again looks

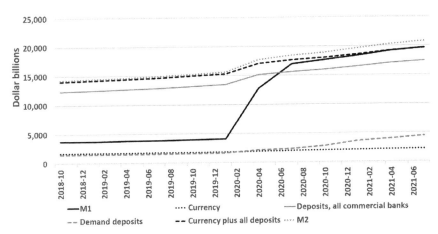

Figure 12.2 The effect of the M1 redefinition during 2020 after the elimination of reserve requirements, 2018Q4–2021Q3
Source: FRED.

implausible, since money demand apparently is "unstable". This could be used to justify the Fed's fixing of interest rates through IOER declarations as an ongoing policy. The user of FRED M1 data, like those evaluating how money may cause inflation, needs a *caveat emptor* and should study FRED's asterisk on M1.

Traditionally, either the monetary base of currency plus reserves or the M1 aggregate could be used to show the link between money and inflation. All but the small amount of required reserves had been lent out before 2008, entered circulation through higher deposits at commercial banks and allowed both the MB and the M1 aggregate to predict inflation according to how much either of these monetary aggregates grew. Once excess reserves had built up at the Fed, allowing seigniorage diversion to private banks, the use of the monetary base to predict inflation became difficult. Similarly, not knowing when the excess reserves would enter circulation made M1 less useful in predicting inflation. The amount of money sterilized as excess reserves held at the Fed broke the traditional link between monetary aggregates and inflation, which had been used to test the quantity theory prediction that the money supply growth rate determines the inflation rate.

Throughout 1953 to 1981, as shown in Figure 2.1, the Fed's purchases of Treasury debt to finance deficits through "freshly printed money" precisely equalled the currency in circulation. This changed once excess reserves were gathered. After 2008 Treasury debt bought by the Fed greatly exceeded currency, as much of this newly bought debt was held as excess reserves.

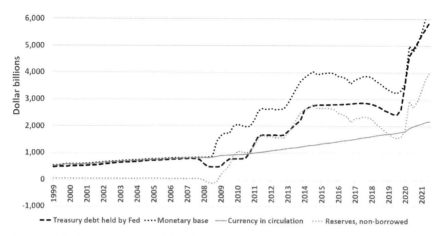

Figure 12.3 Excess reserves build-up breaks the link between money and the Fed's Treasury debt, 1999–2021
Source: FRED.

From 1999 to 2021, Figure 12.3 shows non-borrowed reserves held at the Fed, which exclude the reserves borrowed by the Fed from other central banks (central bank liquidity swaps). After being near zero between 1999 and 2007, the non-borrowed reserves turn negative in the first quarter of 2008 and reach –$143 billion in the third quarter of 2008. This shows that the bank panic eliminated any positive amount of reserves and required the Fed to borrow reserves through swaps. In turn, IOER was instituted as the Fed faced negative reserves.

From 1999 to 2007 all but required reserves were lent out, the monetary base moved in tandem with the Treasury debt purchased by the Fed, and currency in circulation rose, as did both the MB and the Fed's Treasury debt. All three lines moved together. Starting in 2008, Treasury debt held by the Fed and the monetary base diverged from the currency in circulation. Excess reserves built up, so that non-borrowed reserves and the MB moved in tandem and the Fed's Treasury debt moved nearly in tandem with the latter two, while, in contrast, currency in circulation grew steadily at a lower rate of growth.

Starting in 2014, the reserves began falling below the Treasury debt held by the Fed. The initially growing difference between the Fed's Treasury debt and the reserves represents a decrease in the amount sterilized and in the amount of reserves receiving IOER interest payments. As the reserves entered circulation, the inflation rate rose from 2015 to 2018. After 2020 the reserves rose dramatically, but again by less than the increase in the Treasury debt held by the Fed. As the reserves fell further below the Fed's Treasury debt purchases, the money supply was being increased through increases in the private bank money that is accounted for as deposits at banks.

The M1 aggregate is defined without reserves, but with currency in circulation and now, from 2020, with all deposits at commercial banks, including most of the non-bank bank deposits. Broadly defined M1, as it is now defined, is a way to predict the inflation rate, since it includes reserves that are lent out. Since excess reserves began accumulating, the monetary base, in contrast, can predict the increase in the money supply only by showing the amount of reserves created by the Fed buying Treasury debt. In the era of paying interest on reserves, building up the reserves and disassociating the traditional links between money, Fed-bought Treasury debt and the CPI price index, predicting inflation is made difficult.

In the past the reserves were all lent out, except a tiny fraction of total deposits, with practically no excess reserves. Now it is impossible to know in advance when the reserves will be lent out and when the money in circulation in terms of private bank money (deposits) will surge. Inflation now depends on when the banks choose to lend out their huge pot of reserves kept at the Fed.

The Fed has been implicitly insuring the shadow bank money market deposits that are now included in M1, while the shadow banks remain outside the FDIC. By making interest payments on reserves to shadow banks, the emboldened Fed has diverted seigniorage to private banks, made monetary aggregates confusing, made inflation prediction challenging, thrown away the pretence of a stable pot of Bagehot-style reserves in the central bank, encouraged the Fed-insured shadow banks to grow and reduced the scope of the efficient FDIC-insured banks.

The evaders of inflation taxes and FDIC insurance continue to grow. The Fed continues to handicap the "good" banks in the efficient FDIC system while favouring the "bad" shadow banks that earn more profits through non-FDIC-insured money market accounts. This encourages more diffuse forms of shadow banks to emerge and makes banking insurance as an efficient social insurance component ever more distant.

FDIC banks have a tough job competing against counterparts that can earn higher profits, are "systemically important banks" of the global finance system and receive billions of dollars of interest on excess reserves diverted to them by the Fed, away from the US Treasury and circumventing the intention of the US law guiding the Federal Reserve inflation tax revenue. The inflation tax is supposed to be given back to the US Treasury rather than being pilfered and hidden in the few largest banks through "IOER", which can be baffling to markets expecting inflation when the money supply increases. If the largest banks partially avoid the FDIC deposit insurance fees, get free taxpayer subsidies through interest on reserves and can successfully lobby for rescue when things go wrong for their risky assets that are held in place of negatively yielding Treasury debt, then the Fed's novel intertwining of money and banking policy is biased against the thousands of regular FDIC banks that play by the rules of an efficient bank insurance system.

Trying to predict the inflation rate after 2008 requires an understanding of how the Fed has cobbled together a bank insurance system. The post-2008 era represents a distorted system of Bagehot-type reserves along with FDIC insurance. Predicting inflation has become a matter of picking apart the different components of the monetary aggregates, along with how much Treasury debt the Fed buys.

The public Fed money in the form of currency has seen its growth rate inflect upwards in 2008, and again in 2020. The currency growth adds to inflation. The bigger source of inflation, however, since deposits far exceed currency, is the private bank money. When the reserves are lent out, the private bank money supply increases as deposits at banks increase and inflation rises, as in the 2021 surge.

This inflation surge resulted from reserves being built up at a slower rate than the Fed was buying Treasury debt. After 2020 the reserves created by the massive Fed increase in its purchases of Treasury debt have increasingly been lent out. If this trend continues, as is very likely, then a moderately high inflation episode will follow.

The last part of the book describes the consequences of this ongoing Fed banking policy for capital markets and for future inflation. The next chapter describes how the Fed has been fixing prices in capital markets, just as the Soviet Union used to fix the price of bread. And, in the same way that the Soviet economy collapsed, the chapter shows how Fed price fixing has caused negative real interest rates, threatening the collapse of global capital markets.

PART III

PURGATORY: CAPITAL MARKETS, INTEREST AND INFLATION

13

FED PRICE FIXING

Bad bank policy increases inflation rate volatility. Even worse bank policy causes inflation rates above market interest rates for decades. Savers suffer the consequences.

Without a comprehensive US bank insurance system throughout its history, except for that of the FDIC, Figure 4.3 shows that the US inflation rate was erratic with sharp fluctuations from 1774 to 1873, which marked the beginning of the gold standard. The US bank panics of the late 1880s experienced less inflation volatility until 1914, after which successive wars all coincided with highly volatile inflation rates. After the Balanced Growth and Employment Act of 1978 was passed, US inflation rate volatility decreased from 1983.

As capital markets developed after the civil war, private bank insurance began to shape itself through the clearing house system. After the failure of the Fed to provide similar insurance during the Great Depression, the FDIC was established, and the Fed maintained reserve requirements for banks, while mainly taking the role of financing fiscal deficits during war and crises through additional money creation.

The panic of 2008 revealed US complacency over bank policy. Financial market development saw increasing avoidance of both the deposit premium payment for the FDIC insurance and the reserve requirements of the Fed. Reserves in the Fed of 1 per cent of all commercial bank deposits in 2008 offered little support during the bank panic, and the banks experiencing panic were not covered by the FDIC.

In the good times, after inflation rate targeting took hold in 1983 up until 2008, the Fed entertained a "come as you are" party that left bank insurance policy in tatters. Its 2008 "macroprudential" banking policy launched a "Moonshot", with the Fed newly hoarding excess reserves in a haphazard attempt at bank insurance policy for those outside the FDIC. As a result of excess reserves mounting up irregularly, rather than all being lent out as in previous history, the Fed temporarily shifted volatility from the inflation rate to capital markets.

This new volatility has been in the ascendant the entire time since the Fed's attempt to establish a bank insurance policy through excess reserves. The consequent capital market volatility affects the whole economy, deserving the "macro" part of the "macroprudential" moniker, but leaving "prudential" questionable at best.

Starting with the 2001 terrorist attacks, the Fed's contribution to battling forces aimed at undermining capitalism and democracy has been to force the return on capital into negative territory for decades through excess reserves and IOER policy. This has caused highly volatile negative real interest rates. The Fed carried on this policy with the notion that it had been a success, because inflation remained close to its target. The recent increase in inflation has left the Fed scrambling but holding fast to its historically high reserves while fixing an IOER rate far below the inflation rate. This is what has become of the Fed's bank insurance system while international capital markets and inflation remain repressed and suppressed, respectively.

Ancient Rome faced ongoing military threats to its freedom, which it responded to by militarizing and levying ever higher taxes and regulation, which eventually led to the demise of its government. The modern United States has similarly compounded implicit taxes to such a level that it also faces an inflection point in global capitalist freedom.

The Soviet Union was the twentieth-century leader implementing the type of policy that the Federal Reserve created after 2008 as "macroprudential" bank policy. This policy is called fixing the price in a market. By owning nearly all capital and setting prices in all markets to the extent that it could, the Soviet system caused untold distortions in every market and undermined its own economic strength.

Supply and demand naturally determine market prices in a fashion that constantly changes as conditions change. Fixing a market price at its natural equilibrium is virtually impossible, since supply and demand are changing all the time. Setting a price too low causes the quantity demanded to be greater than that supplied, causing excess demand, and setting it too high causes the quantity demanded to be lower than the quantity supplied, causing excess supply.

Metallic monetary regimes implicitly set prices between silver and gold based on the implicit ratio of the supply of one metal relative to the supply of the other. These metal supplies changed only slowly over time, as they were based on mining the minerals. Demand for a means of exchange also changed slowly, following the growth of the economy, which would affect each metal equally.

The success of millennia of metallic standards was based on the limited conditions of a changing supply and demand. During peacetime this allowed fixed price ratios between metals for coinage that provided a near-zero trend inflation rate and a basis for modern banking to take root and blossom. War led to metallic standard inflation rate volatility around the zero-inflation-rate trend. The standard evolved to keep a fixed price of money in terms of gold, and of other currencies relative to each other under Bretton Woods.

When the Vietnam War brought the collapse of Bretton Woods, fiat money began, and fixed prices of currencies faded away. All the while capital markets freely determined the price of capital, with gold also a form of capital, and the central banks' gold stayed in place to implicitly back up fiat money. New stable price ratios arose under fiat money between the expected value of money and the market price of gold, as evidenced through the continuing relation between the expected inflation rate and the price of gold (and oil).

Capital markets trade "money" for use in investment. But they have to back up certain investments using capital that can be quickly turned back into ready "money", such as holding US Treasury securities rather than gold. US Treasury securities are the modern form of gold in terms of providing liquid value. In modern "money markets", as Bagehot referred to the activity along Lombard Street, US Treasury debt is the centrepiece that backs up the banking system's liquidity in decentralized international capital markets.

The key to global capitalism is a freely set price of capital supplied as savings and demanded for investment through ever-growing capital markets, including for US Treasury short-term debt. The capital markets supply money that can be reallocated to alter the "yield–risk profile" of the capital usage. This yield–risk trade-off is the basis of modern finance. Financial intermediaries choose the length of time for investments, or maturity structure, the mix of the yield between "riskless" US Treasury debt and private equity, or diversification, and the ease of commanding ready money for use in constantly adjusting the structure of capital investment across the world, or liquidity.

In contrast, the Soviet Union competed with global capitalism, for example, by fixing the price of bread below its equilibrium market price, with many other prices above their equilibrium market prices, just as fixing the US Treasury debt yield below its normal equilibrium pushes up the equity yield through more risky investment to offset the low US Treasury debt yields. If the fixed price of bread is set below the market price then the quantity of bread supplied will be less than the quantity demanded, and there will be an excess demand for bread, or scarcity. To satisfy basic needs at below-normal prices, while making other needs less accessible, the Soviet Union then had to command an industry to produce the extra bread by redistributing resources from other sectors in which the price was set too high.

This industry would normally be unable to supply the bread at such a low price, since its cost of production was higher than the price it commanded. The Soviet Union took control of the bread producers and produced the extra bread using Soviet government revenue to supplement the bread sales revenue. It set prices across markets, took increasing control of industry, eventually owned all of the private economy that it could own, then collapsed and spiralled towards a system of government selectively funnelling industry ownership towards individuals through corruption rather than free capital equity prices.

The use of price controls creates the danger of spreading market distortions from forcing down Treasury yields below their equilibrium level. This induces the government to direct revenue haphazardly to different segments of the economy suffering from the Treasury yield distortion. It induces devolution into increasingly corrupt government, which can ultimately become bankrupt if it tries to control capital markets with ever-increasing risk from more negative Treasury yields as inflation increases.

When the 2008 bank panic caught the Fed without a comprehensive bank insurance system in place, there was insufficient capital in the money market when needed because of mortgage loan defaults. Rather than fix the private bank insurance system in the Great Recession, as Fisher (1932) had implored during the Great Depression through emergency lending of US Treasury debt, the Fed chose increasing control of the "money market" by forcing down the market price of short-term capital used for liquidity internationally.

In 2008 the Fed followed a policy like that of autocratic governments by fixing the price of the main market in which it operates. This market is where the Fed prints an increasing supply of money over time by buying more Treasury debt than it sells. Since the Fed has to go through the middleman of private bankers to buy and sell Treasury debt, the natural market to use was the one in which bankers buy and sell capital from each other in order to meet their weekly reserve requirements due at the Fed, which is called the federal funds market. This is the market in which the Fed drove down the federal funds rate below the inflation rate for almost three years after the 2001 World Trade Center and Pentagon attacks, by increasingly printing money, which led to rising inflation.

When in 2008 the Fed began to set the rate of interest on excess reserves, its rules required the IOER rate to be below market rates. It was assumed by many that the IOER rate would be a below-market price of capital that would set a floor on short-term money market interest rates, which would still have normal equilibrium prices as supply and demand dictated. The normal equilibrium price of interest rates in the short-term markets such as the federal funds market and the three-month Treasury bill market was a price that exceeded the inflation rate in economic expansions and fell near to the inflation rate in economic contractions. This market price implied a normally positive real interest rate, which is the market rate minus the inflation rate, which would rise and fall with the business cycle at some varying but positive real level.

In contrast to expectations, ever since 2008 the IOER rate dictated by the Fed through its declarations set a maximum price across short-term debt markets. The Fed effectively set the short-term market interest rate in terms of the FFR and the three-month Treasury bill rate at levels slightly below the IOER rate from 2008 to 2018 and staying near to equality with the IOER rate right through 2021. In other words, to redirect reserves to itself, the Fed's IOER policy fixed the interest rates of funds across international capital markets. This has dictated a fixed nominal price of liquidity below its normal price to this day, with the result of less global capital market liquidity being supplied within the private world economy. This does not bode well for capitalism.

All central banks are familiar with this. Like Gandalf going into the Hobbit Shire, the unexpected guest that entered the realm of capital markets through the Fed's mysterious money and banking policy may have helped to avoid a world banking crisis meltdown in 2008, but the Fed did not leave capitalism in the hands of private finance. Instead, the Fed became the new controller of capital prices, directing capital to finance banks through IOER, and utterly failing to mould excess reserves into a new efficient banking policy that constituted a key component in the broader social insurance system of a nation. Gandalf's quest would have been branded a failure if it had ended with him taking control of Middle Earth; his quest was a success because he left Middle Earth in the end, giving control of it back to its citizens.

From when Volcker began as governor of the Fed, in August 1979, to October 2021, Figure 13.1 provides the federal funds rate and IOER rate, along with the three-month, six-month, one-year Treasury bill rates and the CPI inflation rate. The interest rates all huddle together above the inflation rate, which is the lower line from 1979 until 2001. The nominal market interest rates notably are highly variable up until 2002.

After 2002 the interest rates stayed semi-fixed as the Fed accelerated the money supply growth and first pushed down the FFR from 2002 to 2004. Then the Fed rapidly raised that rate to a steady level above 5 per cent, and dropped it back down during 2008. The new IOER rate was set at the "floor" of 0.25 per cent from December 2008 until December 2015, for seven years, as it proved to be a ceiling on other short-term rates rather than a floor.

Then the Fed raised the IOER rate in steps and dropped it down again in 2020, to 0.010 per cent and then 0.015 per cent. March 2022 saw the first significant step up in the IOER rate, to 0.40 per cent. Lamentably for capital markets, though, the IOER rate at 0.4 per cent was much further behind the inflation rate than ever in its ignominious history, since by now inflation had risen to 8 per cent.

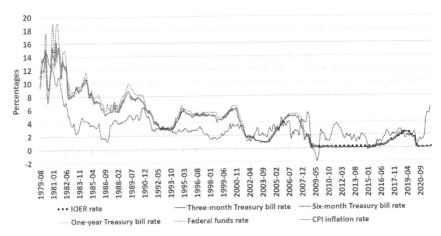

Figure 13.1 Post-Volcker interest rates and CPI inflation, August 1979–October 2021
Source: FRED.

Since October 1952, when the inflation of the Korean War era subsided and the new Treasury–Federal Reserve Accord of 1951 gave the Fed independence to set interest rates (see www.federalreservehistory.org/essays/treasury-fed-acc ord), negative real interest rates have been rare and short-lived, such as when inflation accelerated during the Vietnam War while the 1933 Regulation Q limited commercial bank interest rates to 5.25 per cent. Besides that wartime inflation, until 2002 interest rates were typically above the rate of inflation, and the real interest rate was positive across the spectrum of short-term rates. After 2002, however, with the inflation rate above the interest rate for most years, real interest rates were mostly negative.

Figure 13.2 focuses on the IOER rate and market interest rates for the post-2008 period. Not only was the IOER rate a fixed rate set by the Fed, but it also constrained the other short-term interest rates near to the same level. The IOER rate lies above all the other rates from 2010 until 2015. When Janet Yellen as Fed governor (2014 to 2018) began raising rates in December 2015, the one-year Treasury bill rate rose somewhat above the IOER rate. As the IOER rate continued to rise under both Yellen and then Jerome Powell as governor (2018 to present), the three-month and six-month Treasury bill rates also rose slightly above the IOER rate.

The IOER rate caught up with the inflation rate in 2018 for some months, ending the long reign of negative real interest rates. But then the IOER rate was quickly dropped starting in 2019, and it bottomed out near to zero from 2020 to 2021. Inflation had been tamed – or, rather, suppressed – through large excess reserve holdings, from 2008 to 2020, but then it began to quickly take off again

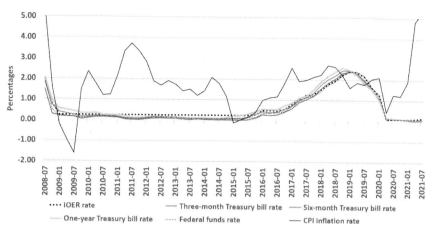

Figure 13.2 Post-2008 interest rates and CPI inflation, July 2008–October 2021
Source: FRED.

in 2021 and drive real interest rates into the deepest, most negative rates seen in US history since the fiat regime began.

What Figure 13.2 shows is that, once the Fed controls "oceans" of excess reserves and sets the interest rate return by diktat on these reserves, the rest of the short-term Treasury debt rates have had to follow suit. Just as the Soviet Union learned how to set prices in markets, and to cause inefficiencies within every market, the Federal Reserve has wielded a new method of control that has forced capitalism into a darkness that mocks the vivacity of Bagehot's "money markets" vision.

Karl Marx lived through a time of capitalism's injustice to the impoverished. From this came Marx's idea that a real return on capital was unnecessary. All that mattered was the return on labour, given the then prevalent labour theory of value. Marx deduced that the capital profit should be taken away from providers of capital and given to labour, thereby forcing the return on capital to zero or less.

Marx's plan, as enacted by the Soviet Union and communist China, was to take possession of all private capital so that the returns could be given to labourers. This drove out private suppliers of capital and instituted instead a government-only supply of capital. The Fed's huge purchase of Treasury debt after 2008, and again after 2020, led private suppliers of capital, who wanted a share of their portfolio in "riskless" assets, to give their capital to the government to meet its increased demand for capital.

The private market for capital faced the Fed-set IOER rate, which was constraining the Treasury debt rates in the short-term money markets below their normal equilibrium rates. The private capital suppliers thereby provided less in the way of savings for investment because of a continual negative real return. A negative real return also results when there is expropriation of capital, as occurred in the Soviet Union and as is seen in corrupt nations in modern times.

In contrast, a normal interest rate in capital markets occurs when the Fed continues to supply money to meet the economy's growing demand as it expands over time and fluctuates over the business cycle, without pushing market interest rates significantly away from their normal equilibrium, as was typical before 2001. Historically, the normal short-term maturity interest rates, such as for three-month, six-month or one-year Treasury debt, have been high enough to capture at least the inflation rate. During a typical down-swing of the economy the money market interest rates drop to equal the inflation rate, and the real return can be zero as a typical lower bound. This normalcy has held in general, except when the Fed significantly changed the amount of inflation tax levied through the money supply or when it began fixing market interest rates, with IOER policy now or with a similar policy in the Second World War.

The Fed price-fixing policy ultimately redistributes capital in a fashion that is similar to, but less extreme than, that of Marx's vision. Everyone ultimately loses by capital market distortions, but temporarily there are winners and losers. Shadow banking wins by manoeuvring on Capitol Hill to receive unending US Treasury inflation tax seigniorage instead of it being returned to taxpayers, to avoid the risk-based deposit insurance premiums of the FDIC bank insurance system, and to rationally keep expectations of future Fed bailouts. The losers are the people who save their money in banks, the pension funds that rely on Treasury debt to fund retirement, the insurance companies that need low-risk assets to manage long-term liabilities and all the other industrious savers who provide the foundation of the system of capitalism. These are the ones raked over by the "Moonshot" policy of the Fed pretending to protect the global banking system by fixing interest rates and collecting reserves as if we are in a war that will never end.

The Fed fixed interest rates after 2008 at similar rates to what the Fed had "pegged" them to throughout the Second World War. From November 1937 to October 1941 the three-month Treasury bill rate was near to 0.10 per cent, after which rates remained low because of Fed–Treasury collaboration. The Fed online history details its previous interest-rate-fixing practice when rates were also below normal market rates[1]:

> To keep the costs of the war reasonable, the Treasury asked the Federal
> Reserve to peg interest rates at low levels. The Reserve Banks agreed to

---

1. www.federalreservehistory.org/essays/feds-role-during-wwii

purchase Treasury bills at an interest rate of three-eighths of a percent per year, substantially below the typical peacetime rate of 2 to 4 percent. The interest-rate peg became effective in July 1942 and lasted through June 1947. The Reserve Banks reduced their discount rate to 1 percent and created a preferential rate of one-half percent for loans secured by short-term government obligations, substantially below the 3 to 7 percent that had been common during the 1920s. All the Reserve Banks implemented these rates in the spring of 1942. The rates remained in effect until January 1948.

In March 2020 the IOER rate dropped to 0.10 per cent, and stayed there until changing to the newly named IORB, at 0.15 per cent, in June 2021. These levels were even lower than the 0.375 per cent rate of the Second World War, whereas the March 2022 increase to a 0.4 per cent rate nearly matches it. Simply subtracting the inflation rate from the market interest rates, for the IOER rate and three-month, six-month and one-year Treasury bill rates, one can compute the level of the real interest rate. Taking a zero real rate of interest as the natural floor during a recession, the recession-equivalent degree of expropriation by the Fed can be seen by the extent to which the real rate is negative.

In both historical evidence and in mainstream macroeconomic theory, a negative real interest rate on capital savings and investment is rare. It can happen with unusual shocks. But it cannot be sustained indefinitely. In theory, a permanent negative real interest rate violates the assumptions required for the existence of a market equilibrium.

In Frank Ramsey's (1928) contribution on the theory of savings, which is the anchor of all modern macroeconomic and monetary theory, a zero real interest rate (after depreciation) cannot exist along the stationary path of the economy. Ramsey was a student of Keynes, and he provided our modern framework of analysis in which such a zero real interest rate implies "unbounded utility" for the consumer, the lack of any well-defined equilibrium and the ruling out of a zero real interest rate as a meaningful concept. Applied to our economy, it means that an equilibrium with a prolonged zero or negative real interest rate is abnormal. Rather, real business cycle theory builds on Ramsey's work (1928) to tell us that the real rate of interest goes up and down in the business cycle, while remaining positive throughout (Kydland & Prescott 1982).

From the third quarter of 2001 until the third quarter of 2021, Figure 13.3 shows that, by subtracting the CPI inflation rate from the IOER rate and three-month, six-month and one-year Treasury bill rates, the real rates were negative for all but three years up until 2018/2019. In 2018 the raising of the IOER rate led to

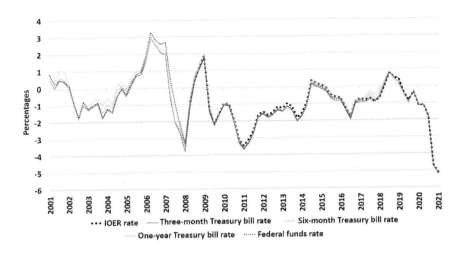

Figure 13.3 Post-9/11 real money market interest rates, 2001Q3–2021Q3
Source: FRED.

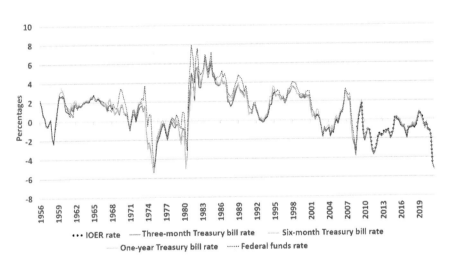

Figure 13.4 Long-run view of real money market interest rates, 1956Q3–2021Q3
Source: FRED.

steadily higher inflation and nearly another full year of positive real rates before the IOER, now IORB, was again set near zero.

Starting in the second quarter of 1956, Figure 13.4 goes back further for a longer historical perspective on real rates. It shows how healthy, positive and less volatile rates were in the 1960s and 1990s, compared to temporarily negative real rate spikes in the Vietnam era of the Fed-prolonged acceleration of inflation and the prolonged negative real rates in the post-2001 era of the Fed temporarily suppressing inflation. Fixing market rates below the rate of inflation causes volatile negative real rates.

Starting in 2008, the Fed fixed money market interest rates by setting the IOER rate and enforcing its level by gathering excess reserves. These reserves sat on top of money markets, and kept the nominal market interest rates below or close to the IOER rate ever since the policy began in 2008. The building of excess reserves enforced fixing the IOER rate below the level for the inflation rate, above which money market rates would normally climb and escape the level of the inflation rate itself to free capital investment at positive real money market interest rates.

Although the initial surge in reserves could be viewed as a reasonable response on the part of the Fed at the time, the long-term problem of Fed policy arose after 2010, when the Fed increased the reserves and money supply in three more surges while fixing the IOER rate. The first two surges after 2010 were given a new name in Fed parlance, namely "quantitative easing" (QE). The Fed's third foray into QE occurred during another bank panic in 2020, after the Covid-19 pandemic had begun. These three Fed surges in reserves weighed down the real interest rate and enforced the negative levels of capital return.

Figure 13.5 shows how the three post-2010 reserve episodes of QE followed remarkably closely the change in the level of the negative real interest rate.

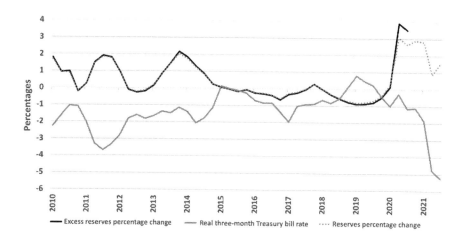

Figure 13.5 Effect of excess reserves on real interest rates, 2010Q1–2021Q3
Source: FRED.

Here the change in excess reserves and the change in all reserves held at the Fed were nearly indistinguishable, as required reserves were essentially negligible. The real interest rate for the three-month Treasury bill moved in nearly the opposite direction to the change in excess reserves, plunging as excess reserves surged, and was negative for all but five of the 46 quarters of the period from January 2010 to July 2021. This opposite movement in the gap between the change in excess reserves and the level of the real interest rate remained rather consistent throughout.

The Fed's price-fixing policy created capital market volatility, distortionary negative real rates and transfers of capital from savers towards the private banks. Without doubt, the Fed's enforcement of the IOER rate through excess reserves worked for a time to keep its self-prescribed inflation target in line on average. The cost of this Fed-centred government bureaucratic policy was the creation of world capital market distortions, which sludged up the engine of economic growth – the capital market investment that had driven democracy forwards. The Fed policy forbade savers from earning a positive real interest rate, caused them to pay for the privilege of being prudent rather than earn from it and left them to watch aggregate private savings and investment decline relative to output throughout a "lost decade" after 2008.

The upside-down world of negative real interest rates fomented discord across the globe reminiscent of earlier eras of populism, fascism and communism, and the bifurcations that arose after capital markets broke down during the Great Depression. At its own peril, Fed officials expressed content that the Fed had saved capital markets from worldwide collapse after the 2008 disaster – which the Fed itself had, arguably, induced. Through its price fixing of capital markets, the Fed turned a 2008 market collapse into a slow suffocation of the world's capital markets – its plan to save democracy by stifling its source of strength.

The next chapter provides evidence of the spread of negative real interest rates on a global scale. This includes developed economies and how their money supply policy helped institute this, as well as in developing markets. The latter are known as "emerging markets" when it comes to capital markets, and evidence of the spreading plague of negative returns is clear to see there as well.

14

A PLAGUE OF NEGATIVE INTEREST RATES

Central banks faced a dilemma after the 2008 debacle over how to keep the global financial system from the type of broad financial collapse experienced in the Great Depression. The prolonged US negative real interest rates after 2001 set the tone for the globalized capital markets. As they did during the Vietnam War, countries responded after 2008 by following US-centric negative real interest policy.

Bretton Woods members supported the United States during the Vietnam War by buying up the US dollars used to finance it. This stabilized the fixed exchange rates of the Bretton Woods era with the US fixed price of gold. After 2008 democratic, globally integrated countries around the world followed US real interest rate policy to stabilize the floating exchange rates of the fiat era.

International central banking innovated policy to mimic the United States on real interest rates. By maintaining the same real interest rates, exchange rates could remain stable. If real interest rates were higher in a country than in the United States, capital would flow into that country and cause its currency to appreciate.

Countries followed US real interest rate policy across both developed and emerging markets. For example, China followed the US policy until 2014, after which it disengaged from the democratic capital policies of the international financial system, while still holding trillions of dollars of US debt (Csabafi, Gillman & Naraidoo 2019). Other international central banks had to react quickly to induce negative real short-term interest rates so as to avoid currency appreciation through capital arbitrage.

Arbitrage happens when, for example, capital savings can earn a real return of 2 per cent in a European market and only −1.75 per cent in the US market. Then financial industry traders can move the capital from the United States to Europe to get the higher return on capital. Capital flowing into Europe would push down the return on capital in Europe. An equilibrium results whereby arbitrage possibilities are eliminated by equalizing the real return on capital, net of any arbitrage cost, across global capital markets.

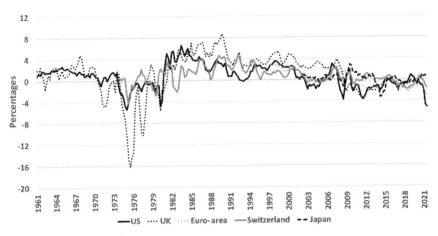

Figure 14.1 International money market real interest rates, 1961–2021
Source: FRED.

Investment capital flowing from the United States into the eurozone increases the demand for euros. The price of euros would rise relative to the price of dollars, as dollars are used to buy euros. The exchange rate between currencies would appreciate for euros relative to dollars, with €1 buying, for example, $1.16, instead of only $1.10.

Arbitrage is a natural part of how competitive markets prices are equalized through capital reallocation. A higher real return on capital relative to the United States in the eurozone would cause exchange rate appreciation of the "home" country currency, the euro, making its exports more expensive. The exports of eurozone countries would go down if the price of the euro rises relative to key currencies such as the US dollar. Because the negative real US interest rates persisted, international central banks created similarly negative real interest rates to avoid capital inflow, currency appreciation and a loss of export demand and domestic production.

From 1961 to 2021, Figure 14.1 demonstrates the real short-term Treasury interest rates for the United States, United Kingdom, euro-area, Switzerland and Japan. Overall, these move together rather closely, which helped to keep exchange rates stable. To focus on the period when the United States began making real rates negative, Figure 14.2 shows only the period from 2002 to 2021.

From 2002 to 2005 all but the United Kingdom are near to the United States' negative rates. After 2010 the UK, eurozone and US real rates move closely together, at negative levels, apart from in 2018–19. Japanese and Swiss real rates

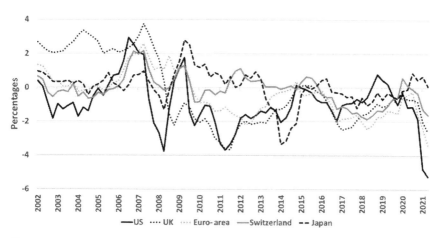

Figure 14.2 International money market real interest rates, 2002–21
Source: FRED.

begin converging to the others after 2014. This shows convergence after 2010, and, except for Japan, again after 2020.

To implement the negative real interest rate policies, the European countries and Japan increased their money supply growth rates to help drive down money market interest rates. From 2011 to 2021, Figure 14.3 shows the money supply growth rates for the United Kingdom, Switzerland, euro-area and Japan, using the M3 aggregate, which is defined similarly to the US M2 aggregate. The money supply growth moves in tandem in waves, with greater convergence in movement after 2014, through to the pandemic in 2021.

The UK, eurozone and Swiss money supply growth rates rise in three waves, like those of the United States. Japan had some waves like Switzerland after 2016, including after 2020. The eurozone's central bank, the European Central Bank, was faced with a new dilemma, since it had not even purchased any Treasury debt before 2008.

The European Union had to figure out how to buy the Treasury debt of different eurozone countries, if it were to follow the other developed countries. After first buying Greek debt in 2010, it broadened its buying of government debt through a new bond purchase programme called outright monetary transactions (OMTs), which entailed buying various eurozone government's debt in sec-ondary markets. The ECB head, Mario Draghi, said that the purchases were part of the European Union's newly forming bank insurance policy, then called the European Financial Stability Mechanism. This showed how government

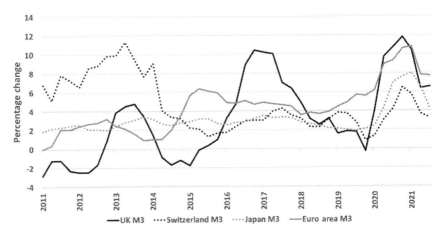

Figure 14.3 International money supply growth rates, 2011–21
Source: FRED.

bank insurance policy became intertwined with monetary policy innovations internationally.

Unlike the United States' IOER policy, however, which produced negative interest rates implicitly in markets, other countries supplemented their money supply increases by resorting to explicitly instituting negative interest rates for reserves held at the central bank. Rather than paying interest on reserves, as in the United States, the ECB required banks to pay to keep the required reserves by introducing negative interest rates on reserves in 2014 and keeping these in place, with the rate falling to −0.10 per cent in June 2014, and then further to − 0.5 per cent in March 2022. Other central banks followed the negative reserve rate policy, starting in 2015 in Switzerland and Denmark, from 2015 to 2019 in Sweden and in 2016 in Japan.

The result was that exchange rates did move together. From 2000 to 2021, Figure 14.4 provides the US dollar value of the foreign currencies of the United Kingdom, the eurozone, Switzerland and Japan. The co-movement is strong for the entire post-2000 period. Rising together after 2001, the exchange rates move together rather closely after 2009, and then converge more strongly and stabilize after 2014. This stabilization coincides with the real interest rate stabilization after 2014 and strong money supply co-movement.

After the collapse of the Soviet Union, global capital markets began spreading around the world, to the formerly Soviet-controlled eastern Europe, to the Baltics, and to all of the BRICS countries – Brazil, Russia, India, China and South Africa. Convergence to the negative real interest rates also occurred in these developing

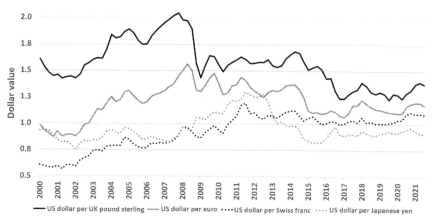

Figure 14.4 International US dollar exchange rates, 2000–21
Source: FRED.

countries. Along with the United States for comparison, the real short-term interest rates for the eastern European "Visegrád Group" – the Czech Republic, Slovakia, Hungary and Poland – plus Slovenia are shown from 2000 to 2021 in Figure 14.5. The eastern European leading nations gradually converged to the US real interest rate levels, with all the rates turning to negative levels after 2015 (see Gillman 2022b, from which part of this chapter is abstracted).

The real interest rates in the BRICS countries, and in the nations around them, also have converged since the Great Financial Crisis. Starting with Brazil, from 2000 to 2021, Figure 14.6 shows the real interest rates for the region around Brazil, with Mexico, Chile and Peru included with the US real interest rates. Although Brazil's real rate remains higher than others until 2018, there is close co-movement of the others with the United States throughout the period.

Taking Russia and the Baltic Sea nations around it, namely Lithuania, Latvia and Poland, as well as the United States for comparison, for 2000 to 2021, Figure 14.7 shows similar convergence of the real interest rates. The exception is that Russia diverges upwards after 2015 but then converges by 2020. Otherwise, the spread across the nations starting in 2000 generally becomes smaller among the Baltic group over time.

For India, the nearby countries of Turkey, Saudi Arabia and Pakistan are included, along with the United States. From 2000 to 2020, Figure 14.8 shows convergence to the United States starting in 2009, with Pakistan diverging some at the end of the period. Turkey has much higher rates while bringing its inflation rate from 70 per cent in February 2000 down to 8 per cent in April 2004, but then keeps lowering its real rate to converge with these other nations.

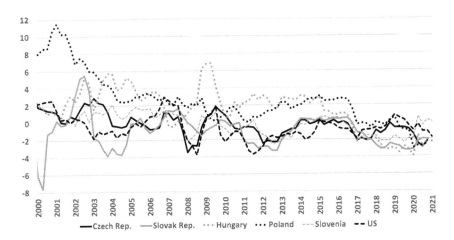

Figure 14.5 Eastern European real interest rates, 2000–21
Source: FRED.

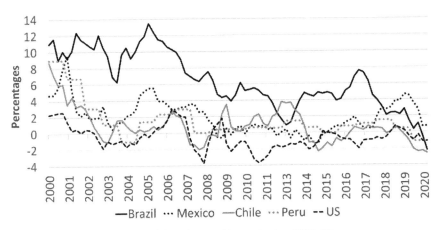

Figure 14.6 South and Central American real interest rates, 2000–20
Source: FRED.

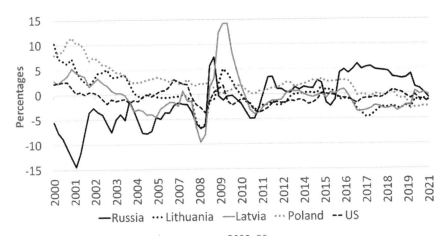

Figure 14.7 Baltic nations' real interest rates, 2000–20
Source: FRED.

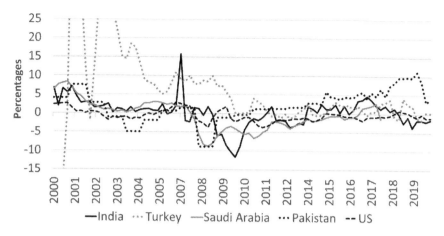

Figure 14.8 South-west Asian real interest rates, 2000–20
Source: FRED.

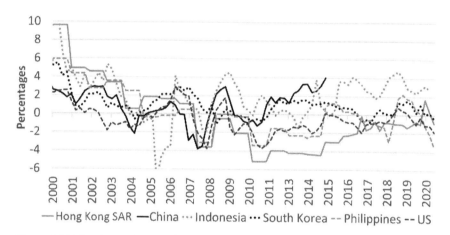

Figure 14.9 South-east Asian real interest rates, 2000–20
Source: FRED.

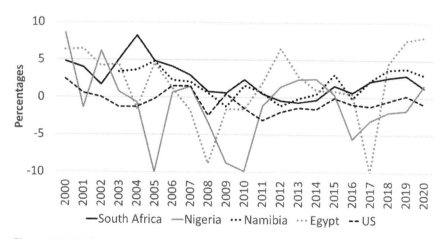

Figure 14.10 African real interest rates, 2000–20
Source: FRED.

For China, the nearby nations included are Hong Kong Special Administrative Region (SAR), Indonesia, South Korea and the Philippines, along with the United States. From 2000 to 2021, Figure 14.9 shows that most of the real rates co-move with the United States closely, with Indonesia rates remaining higher after 2015. China rates diverge upwards after 2014 and are no longer reported, while Hong Kong SAR has more negative real rates and then converges after 2017.

For the South Africa grouping, which includes Nigeria, Namibia and Egypt, along with the United States, from 2000 to 2020, Figure 14.10 shows more variability and less convergence. But there is some close co-movement with US rates, such as that seen for South Africa and Namibia.

International central banks induced convergence towards low, negative real interest rates across many nations, both developed and emerging. This shows the extent to which US Fed policy of fixing the rate of interest on excess reserves induced negative rates around the globe in financial markets. Central banks coordinated their monetary policy with the United States, especially in the more financially integrated economies.

During episodes of negative real interest rates just as during the chaos of hyperinflation, a demand for money can be seen – consistent with theory – that shows how distortions from the Fed's reserve policy cause the money demand to shift. The next chapter demonstrates this for the United States in money markets, reflecting how a positive capital market real return was killed off by Fed policy. It shows how the money market distortions spilled from capital into labour markets and lowered economic growth.

15

SHIFTING MONEY DEMAND

The Fed policy of price fixing in capital markets was part of an effort to bring reserves into the Fed. Required reserves of banks had been depleted to 1 per cent of all commercial bank deposits because of bank deregulation. With all but required reserves having been lent out before 2008, reserves had served as the foundation that the Fed provided for the aggregate money stock.

The monetary base is defined as "reserves plus currency in circulation". The aggregate M1 is defined without reserves but with deposits at banks plus currency in circulation. The M2 aggregate and the post-2020 definition of M1 essentially equal the old M1, which included standard demand deposits, plus the money market funds that had been a part of M2. The monetary base, M1 and M2 are useful, along with the reserves alone, for investigating the stability of money demand since 1959. Specifying money demand with these different aggregates shows how money was shifted about by the long financial deregulation and the sudden refilling of reserves after 2008.

Money is used for two main reasons: as a means of exchange for goods and as a "liquid" asset for deposited funds that are invested. The liquid form of money is closely related to the exchange form, since both come from Treasury debt. When the Fed buys the Treasury debt, it creates reserves in private bank accounts at the Fed that subsequently leverage those banks' deposits and investment when they lend out all except what is required – at least, until 2008, when the Fed's holdings of Treasury debt historically tracked the currency in circulation.

When money demand is stable, the use of it as currency, reserves and deposits is stable. With stable money demand, capital markets naturally hold less money when the cost of holding money rises. The cost of holding money rises when the inflation rate and market interest rates rise. This is especially apparent when money demand is presented as a ratio with respect to GDP output (Lucas & Nicolini 2015).

This practice is a common way to present money demand, since money demand tends to grow with output. Thus, the opportunity cost feature of money demand can best be discerned by looking at money as normalized by dividing by output. This gives a view of money per unit of output and how it changes with the implicit price of money, which is the nominal market short-term interest rate, such as the three-month Treasury bill rate.

Since currency, reserves and deposits can be invested in money markets and earn interest, the opportunity cost of money in terms of the three-month Treasury bill interest rate includes the sum of the real interest rate and the inflation rate that together can be earned when invested in the money market. The money market's nominal interest rate is the "price" of money, with a stable money demand showing how money relative to GDP falls as money market rates rise, and in turn rises when these interest rates fall.

Historically, with the Fed operating like the Issue Department rather than the Banking Department of Bagehot's Bank of England, it printed money both during the Bretton Woods era and as fiat money by buying Treasury debt. As non-required reserves were lent out, they caused deposits and the currency entering circulation to rise. A significant amount of the Fed-purchased Treasury debt was kept as reserves by commercial banks, although small relative to GDP, until the 1980s, when that reserve amount steadily shrank towards zero as a share of GDP. After 2008 the Fed purchase of Treasury debt no longer followed the growth of currency, as it targeted its policy on increasing reserves held at the Fed instead, acting more in the tradition of the Banking Department of the Bank of England. It distorted Bagehot's scheme, since the Fed paid banks seigniorage to get reserves and sterilize the large issuance of money rather than having banks offer reserves to the Fed without compensation in return for systematic panic insurance.

The normal fluctuations of reserves up to the deregulation of the banking sector kept US money demand stable. Once reserves began to fall through deregulation, the demand for money began to shrink. Commercial banks held less in the way of reserves and less money and, instead, put more liquid capital into less liquid, higher-yielding, riskier investment. After 2008, as investment banks were failing through a lack of liquid reserves, the Fed's subsidization for commercial bank holdings of reserves through its IOER policy induced more liquid money to be held as reserves, effectively distorting money demand.

Paying banks for reserves caused extreme volatility in the excess reserves held at the Fed. The shifting of money demand shows how the lack of control on excess reserves has been killing the free, normal working of capital markets. First, money demand was stable as Bretton Woods started, and it remained stable up to 1990. Financial deregulation and the sudden rebuilding of reserves by the Fed shifted down the demand for money, which can be seen differentially through the various monetary aggregates of the monetary base, M2 and reserves taken by themselves.

Cagan (1956) has shown how the demand of money works even during a period of hyperinflation. As the inflation rate rises, people avoid holding money because it becomes more costly. As they substitute away from money to other means of exchange, typically through banking, the price level rises more rapidly than the money supply.

If money is being taxed, and the government is issuing the tax, then taxpayers avoid the tax as far as possible, both legally and illegally. For a government that finances its expenditure by printing money, people avoid the tax by holding less money per unit of output as the price level rises. This means that the growth in the money supply pushes up prices at an ever-increasing rate, that the rise in prices outpaces the rise in money and that the demand for real money falls.

The real money held is derived by dividing the money stock by the price level, adjusting for the inflation component. Turning the nominal money stock into real terms is exactly like taking the current dollar nominal GDP and dividing it by the aggregate price level to get real GDP. The money per unit of output can be computed by dividing real money by real output, but since the price level cancels out in this ratio it is equivalent to dividing the nominal money stock by nominal output, with either way giving the same result.

For quarterly data from 1959 to 2021, Figure 15.1 plots the demand for the monetary base as a percentage of GDP, on the horizontal axis, as against the three-month Treasury bill interest rate, on the vertical axis. Each point is connected chronologically to the next, like a Phillips curve. The 1964 point starts at the end point in the middle of the graph, when MB/GDP in percentage terms is about 10.0. The 2021 third quarter point is at the far bottom right corner.

A normal money demand of Cagan's (1956) variety is downward-sloping with a similar degree of convexity to that found in Figure 15.1. The figure therefore shows normality while also including a major shift inwards towards the origin. After Bretton Woods established fixed exchange rates in 1964, the MB money demand was equivalent to approximately 10 per cent of GDP and then fell as the interest rate rose, by a half to 5 per cent of GDP in 1981, as the points move up and back around a rough curve.

In the third quarter of 1981 interest rates peaked and then fell under Volcker. Money demand fell but deregulation and the need to hold less in terms of required reserves pivoted the MB money demand downwards to a new, lower schedule. After 2008 the shifted-back MB demand flattened, and this extended up to 2014. It then reached 22 per cent of GDP, almost quadrupling in magnitude along this shifted-back MB demand curve.

Once the Fed began lifting the interest rate on excess reserves, money demand rapidly fell again while shifting outwards and up towards the "normal" money demand curve of the time, in evidence from 1964 to 1981. A new curve begins to form, starting from the bottom right-hand corner of Figure 15.1, that looked as

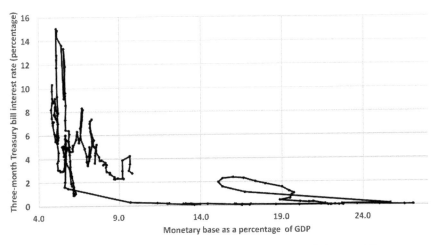

Figure 15.1 Demand for the monetary base and the three-month Treasury bill rate, 1964Q1–2021Q3
Source: FRED.

though it might connect with the old 1964 point on the money demand function were interest rates to continue rising. But then the Fed suddenly reversed the policy of lifting the IOER ceiling on interest rates, causing the money demand curve to circle back down to the zero-interest-rate floor again. It realigned back with the previously shifted-down money demand even as the ratio of the MB to GDP kept rising, to over 25 per cent.

For M2, splitting up the data sample in 1989 shows some similar features to MB demand and how broader money markets were affected. For the period from 1964 to 1989, Figure 15.2 shows in the left-hand panel that the M2 demand for currency and deposits of all commercial banks, including money market accounts, was a rather stable curve. The M2 ratio to GDP stayed between 62 per cent in 1964 and 52 per cent in 1981, rising and falling with the interest rate in an expected fashion.

From 1989 to the first quarter of 2020, Figure 15.2 shows in the right-hand panel that the M2 money demand started shifting down during the bank failures and economic recession in 1990, whereas the MB demand similarly shifted back but earlier in 1981. On the right-hand side of Figure 15.2, from 1989 to 2000 the M2 demand shifted down as deregulation continued, less in the way of reserves was required and more was invested in risky assets rather than in money market accounts, which, typically, are invested in less risky US Treasury debt. As the interest rate fell from 2002 to 2004, M2 demand rose towards the equivalent of 50 per cent of GDP along the shifted-back M2 demand schedule.

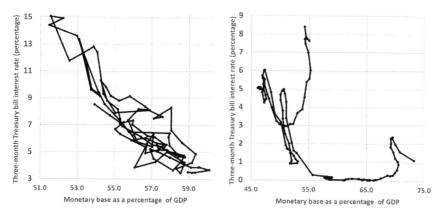

Figure 15.2 Demand for M2 and the three month Treasury bill rate, 1964Q1–2020Q1
Source: FRED.

Once the Fed began lifting the federal funds rate back up above the inflation rate from 2004 to 2006, with the three-month Treasury bill rate following, the M2 demand pivoted outwards in a shift towards the more normal demand schedule as Fed interest regulation was freed up. After 2008 the Fed's fixing of interest rates at bottom levels and below the inflation rate caused the quantity of M2 money demanded to rise steadily to an amount equivalent to more than 65 per cent of GDP.

When the Fed started deregulating markets by lifting the IOER rate in 2015 and up to 2019, like the MB demand the M2 demand started curling up to reach a more normal unregulated demand position of 70 per cent of GDP at an interest rate around 2 per cent. After 2019, as the Fed floored the IOER rate again during the first quarter of 2020, the quantity of M2 demand rose to an unusually high level, from 70 to 90 per cent of GDP in the third quarter of 2021 (not shown), following the shifted down demand schedule.

The Fed's IOER policy caused a shift towards holding more of the money market at lower interest rates, along an artificially induced, shifted-down money demand curve. With negative yields on money market accounts invested in US Treasury debt, portfolio managers invested in riskier equity to increase their portfolio return. In contrast, from 1964 to 1989 holding low positive-yielding Treasury debt through money markets was naturally diversified through a balanced holding of equity.

The money market distortions from Fed policy can also be seen through the demand for reserves by commercial banks. Compared to the monetary base, the M2 money demand was more stable throughout 1964 to 1989. The monetary

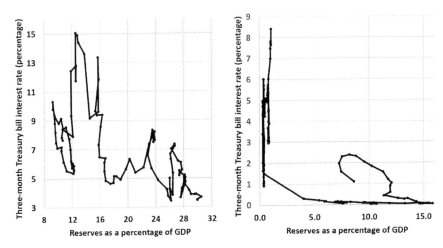

Figure 15.3 Demand for reserves and the three-month Treasury bill rate, 1964Q1–2020Q1
Source: FRED.

base demand had a nearly linear drop after 1989, whereas the M2 demand drop was graduated, rising by more than the MB as the interest rate fell. This was thanks to the large role of the falling reserves that emerged after the 1990 bank failures, and then the continually falling reserves as the deregulation of banking took hold and more banks avoided holding reserves.

From 1964 to 1989 (left-hand panel) and 1989 to 2020 (right-hand panel), Figure 15.3 shows the demand for reserves as a percentage of GDP, for all commercial banks over the same two periods as for M2. From Bretton Woods up until the bank failures in the late 1980s and 1990, the left-hand panel shows that the demand for reserves fell from 30 per cent of GDP down to as low as 9 per cent of GDP. The reserves demand curve was less regularly shaped than that for M2 was over the same period, more similar to MB demand in Figure 15.1 but relatively jagged as a consequence of changing reserve policy, from deregulation and then IOER.

From 1989 to the first quarter of 2020, in the right-hand panel of Figure 15.3, the demand for reserves shifted back from the equivalent of 9 per cent of GDP to between 3 and 4 per cent of GDP. As the interest rate fell the reserve demand became even more unlike a normal demand schedule, in which money demand rises as the interest rate falls. The low level of reserves occurred during the deregulation era, when it was thought that money market funds were always safe, with little in the way of reserves needed.

After 2008 the reserves in Figure 15.3 shoot outwards under the Fed's IOER policy. When the IOER rate was lifted from 2015 to 2019, the quantity of reserves demanded began falling along a new demand curve, which would conceivably be consistent with the "normal" pre-1989 demand curve. After 2019, as the IOER rate was dropped again, the demand began circling back once more, as it did for MB and M2 demand, and then shot out again, to an amount equivalent to 18 per cent of GDP, in the third quarter of 2021 (not shown).

The demand for reserves was volatile during the Bretton Woods era and under fiat up to 1989. It was consistent with a type of money demand, although less regular than for M2 during this time. The policy of letting banks escape both the FDIC and the holding of reserves at the Fed during the deregulation of banking led to an extremely small quantity of reserves being held at the Fed when the bank panic hit in 2008.

The Fed then pushed out reserves to make up for the declining reserves under deregulation. The Fed's increase in reserves through its IOER fixed interest rate policy disrupted the demand for MB, M2 and reserves. This policy enforced a shifted down money demand while forcing out the quantity of money demanded through near-zero nominal interest rates that forced distortions on capital markets because of the negative yields. Above this artificially low money demand curve lay the normal money demand, in which markets hold more money at any given market interest rate as part of a balanced portfolio mix.

A consequent distortion to bank investment from the IOER policy of negative interest rates is apparent in the amount of loans being made by banks out of their deposits. During the 1980s and 1990s the loan fraction of deposits rose and fell normally with real GDP over the business cycle. In contrast, after 2001 this pattern inverted to a negative co-movement, with loans falling relative to deposits during phases of expansion and rising during contractions.

For the post-Bretton-Woods years since 1973, Figure 15.4 plots commercial and industrial loans as a percentage of all commercial bank deposits, normalized by subtracting 25 per cent to make it comparable to the real GDP growth rate, which is also shown. This allows us to see the contrast with the business cycle, as represented by the rise and fall in the real GDP growth rate. An aberration from the normal co-movement, the data series move in the opposite way to each other in the 1970s, when real money market interest rates were temporarily negative as the volatility of the inflation rate hit markets.

Although the negative real rates in the 1970s were unplanned, after 2001 the negative interest rates were induced directly by the Fed fixing money market rates below the inflation rate. Then, instead of rising with real GDP growth, the loan ratio fell as the economy expanded and rose as the economy contracted, an inversion of the "normal" 1980s and 1990s experience.

After 2001 the percentage of deposits lent out fell rather than rising. Negative real interest rates induced a lower loan fraction of deposits, which fell as rates

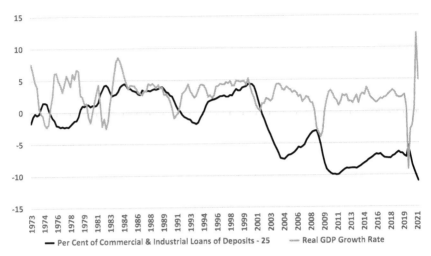

Figure 15.4 Commercial and industrial loans in relation to deposits versus real GDP growth, 1973–2021
Source: FRED.

became more negative but rose as rates became less negative. The Fed's control over real interest rates upended the investment rate out of deposits into a "counter-cyclic" co-movement over the business cycle rather than its normal pro-cyclical co-movement. An inverted rate of loans to GDP caused a lower investment rate in the economy, even as investment became skewed towards higher risks in order to offset the negative Treasury debt yield.

For the post-Bretton-Woods years, Figure 15.5 plots this investment as a percentage of GDP. This percentage was highly pro-cyclic, moving in tandem with fluctuations in the real GDP growth rate, which here is normalized in the graph by adding a constant 15 per cent. The value 17.7 was the average percentage of investment to GDP for the entire period from 1973 to 2021.

When the negative real rates were induced by the Fed after 2001, by pushing down the federal funds rate through heavy purchases of Treasury debt, the investment rate was halted in its fall relative to real GDP. It rose back up as the Fed deregulated money markets by letting the FFR in 2004 begin to rise back up above the inflation rate. Nevertheless, this deregulation of the FFR caused the rising investment rate to become slightly inverted relative to real GDP growth, which had already begun falling.

After 2008 the Fed worsened the distortions in loans and in overall investment by rigidly declaring fixed prices, which caused a prolonged below-trend investment rate. Investment in relation to GDP rose over more than 11 years but only up to 17.7 per cent, which was the average for the entire post-1973 fiat era. This

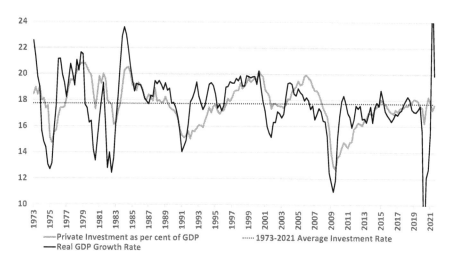

Figure 15.5 Gross private domestic investment in relation to GDP, 1973–2021
Source: FRED.

key investment rate never rose significantly above trend after 2009, as it had in previous, normal business cycle history. Unsurprisingly, real GDP growth also did not rise above trend, and this is why the period after the Great Recession is referred to as a "lost decade" of economic growth.

The policy-induced downward shift in money demand, the low rate of bank lending out of deposits and the low investment rate relative to GDP, all coupled with increasingly risky equity investment, are distortions caused by the negative real interest rate policy. The next chapter calls this policy what it is: a prohibition on earning a positive real return on capital. It provides some history on this prohibition, describes how this induces the need to find a positive yield in increasingly risky ways and makes clear that it helps explain far-ranging effects on labour markets, which coincide with these capital market distortions.

16

THE NEW USURY PROHIBITION

The Fed's money and banking policy of fixing interest rates below the inflation rate risks the global financial system's continued resilience. The system of efficiently allocating capital is called capitalism. Capitalism, with globalization, emerged through the international financial system, from Renaissance Italy to nineteenth-century Britain and into the modern era.

Global capitalism is a vital part of free trade. Adam Smith's *Wealth of Nations* (1904 [1776]) advocated free trade in goods and in capital. The British colony that was the precursor to the United States was well aware of the limits to trade through taxation of the markets engaged in trade. The 1776 Declaration of Independence coincides with Smith's 1776 statement of efficient allocation through free trade.

The US Constitution sufficiently innovated on England's Magna Carta to enshrine free trade in social, economic and political spheres, making the United States the centre of world democracy, freedom and capitalism. Milton Friedman's *Capitalism and Freedom* stresses these interconnections, with "economic freedom as a means to political freedom" (Friedman 1962: 8), whereas "capitalism is a necessary condition for political freedom" (1962: 10).

Adam Smith, as a student and then professor at the University of Glasgow in Scotland, essentially invented modern economics. A professor of moral philosophy at Glasgow, starting in 1752, Smith wrote a triad of treatises on free culture, law and economics, respectively.

The first book, published in 1759, followed the theme of his chair, *The Theory of Moral Sentiments* (Smith 1853 [1759]). This landmark achievement sets out how an equilibrium culture of norms arises through free social interaction and exchange. The treatise takes as given the legal and economic environment in which social norms flourish.

Smith next published, in 1763, his *Lectures on Justice, Police, Revenue and Arms* (Smith 1896 [1763]). This second treatise describes how the social and economic setting induces a demand and supply for law that results in legal equilibrium, provides the enforcement of property rights and creates the foundations for free social and economic exchange.

Smith's last treatise, published in 1776, was *An Inquiry into the Nature and Causes of the Wealth of Nations* (Smith 1904 [1776]), commonly known simply as *The Wealth of Nations*. This followed the Reformation, when interest on capital was allowed, and efficient work was promoted as the largely agriculture economy began its slow transformation towards incorporating other industries that required rather more capital.

Smith argues that the capital market requires free trade, just as the market for all goods does. In Britain, free trade in goods, and free travel of workers, had been written into common law through the final 1297 version of the Magna Carta, the "Great Charter". Binding the power of the king through law and made in agreement with the barons, this foundation of democracy, traceable back to the Charter of Liberties of 1100, stipulates that goods and people can move freely. It is still part of common law in England and Wales.

Although the Magna Carta focuses on freedom in terms of goods and labour markets, it omits free functioning of the capital market, which arose later. Smith's *Wealth of Nations* contributed to forming the consensus that charging interest on capital loans was necessary for an efficient capital market. This was a critical advance, since both capital and labour were the main factors in the production of output.

Going against historical convention, Smith (1904 [1776]) argues that prohibition against "usury" – the charging of interest for borrowing and lending capital – should be abolished, as free capital markets are a necessary part of production and efficient markets. Linking firm profit to a return on capital, as does Böhm-Bawerk a century later, Smith (1904 [1776]: 105–7) argues against restricting interest rates:

> According, therefore, as the usual market rate of interest varies in any country, we may be assured that the ordinary profits of stock must vary with it, must sink as it sinks, and rise as it rises. The progress of interest, therefore, may lead us to form some notion of the progress of profit. By the 37th of Henry VIII all interest above ten per cent was declared unlawful. More, it seems, had sometimes been taken before that. In the reign of Edward VI religious zeal prohibited all interest. This prohibition, however, like all others of the same kind, is said to have produced no effect, and probably rather increased than diminished the evil of usury ... All these different statutory regulations seem to have been made with great propriety. They seem to have followed and not to have gone before the market rate of interest, or the rate at which people of good credit usually borrowed.

Smith is supportive of the statutory ceilings on interest rates, which remained above the usual market rate, to avoid unjustly high "usurious" rates. Jadlow (1977) argues that this allowance of ceilings on rates above the normal rate was restrictive for high-risk ventures. Smith is careful, however, in emphasizing that ceilings should always exceed normal market rates, implying the inclusion of an allowance for a normal risk premium.

After centuries of usury prohibition, acceptance of interest on capital loans led to the development of modern capital markets, including London's Lombard Street. Henry George (1874) argues for better work conditions for labour, new expenditure and taxes such as a property tax to support labour. Bagehot and George were contemporaries pushing for better regulation of capital, through central bank insurance policy, and for better regulation of labour, respectively.

Modern capital markets work by dividing investment between loans that receive interest, such as the US Treasury debt, along with riskier loans of all sorts and private equity ownership of the economy. Loans to private companies can be as risky as equity ownership, in the sense that the enterprise might become insolvent. Riskier companies must pay a higher "loan premium" to compensate for the increased risk of default, just as the "equity premium" represents the higher yield from private stock ownership relative to government debt that, likewise, compensates for risk.

The equity return can be stated as a yield, expressed in percentage terms, that is like the interest rate return on a risky loan. The equity yield rate on a "portfolio" holding shares in companies has been significantly higher on average than the US Treasury yield. The US Treasury yield is normally set in competitive markets through the interest rate balancing the supply and demand for government debt.

The other risk to lending out capital or buying equity ownership in enterprises is that these investments are made in a certain currency, such as US dollars. If there is positive US inflation, and the yield on loans or equity dividends is based in nominal dollars, then the real return to loans or equity can be computed by subtracting the inflation rate, as in the Fisher equation of interest rates, which applies to any nominal yield.

Global financial markets depend on US Treasury debt as the most "risk-free" loan in the world. Portfolio managers across the world hold a mixture of government debt, including US Treasury debt. The rest of the portfolio can be in equity ownership of enterprises around the world, in real estate and in many diverse forms of capital ownership.

The Fed policy of regulating interest rates has, in effect, prohibited the earning of any real interest above zero for the last two decades. The Fed has created a global "casino financial" through negative real "risk-free" US Treasury interest rates. With capital markets denied positive real interest on the least risky and safest assets, riskier ventures are undertaken to offset that lack of yield, just as gamblers step up their appetite for risk after a loss.

The Federal Reserve's policy has reverted to the days when usury was prohibited for one of the biggest markets in the world, which is used in balancing returns on investment portfolios between riskless government debt and risky equity. Banning a positive return on the main risk-free asset, US Treasury short-term debt, has forced global finance, through competition, to balance the negative return on US Treasury debt with riskier options worldwide. This alternative investment has gone, for example, into Spanish condominiums along the Costa del Sol, commercial and residential real estate in the United States, the worldwide marketing of mortgage-backed securities, and high-technology companies with zero earnings and unknown potential.

With other governments following the Fed's prohibition on positive real money market interest rates so that their currencies do not appreciate against the US dollar, world financial markets have been taking on increasingly risky investments across the entire swathe of possibilities. After having let commercial banks' reserves decline for decades, the Fed's payment for reserves led to increasing global financial risk without the backstop of an efficient insurance system for the financial sector. Our households may well end up with empty pockets after this gambling spree, if ever-increasing risky investment causes global financial collapse.

After negative interest rates on Treasury debt for three years from 2002 to 2004, the investment banks constructed a very natural alternative vehicle for relatively risk-free investment. According to McConnell and Buser (2011), private mortgages first began to be packaged together by the US government agency the Government National Mortgage Association (GNMA) in 1970. Ginnie Mae, as it is called, then bestowed the bundle of securitized loans with the government's guarantee of repayment. It sold off the mortgage bundle as a security, of which people could buy a fraction. This process is called securitization.

The GNMA operates alongside Fannie Mae – the Federal National Mortgage Association (FNMA) – and Freddie Mac – the Federal Home Loan Mortgage Corporation (FHLMC). These all subsidize mortgages and have been viewed by markets as being implicitly government-guaranteed even if they are not fully guaranteed. This market doubled from $2.6 trillion in MBSs in 1996 to $5.3 trillion in 2002; it then jumped to $8.4 trillion in 2006 and to $9.5 trillion in 2008.

The government guarantee and higher yields made MBSs a good way to "rebalance" portfolios after negative real rates on Treasury debt began in 2002. When the Fed deregulated the money market by raising the federal funds rate rapidly, the traditionally low-risk MBSs became toxic, as homeowners defaulted on higher home loan rates. The investment bank collapse occurred without bank insurance being in place and without sufficient reserves at the Fed.

After the bank panic and the end of the Great Recession, the Federal Reserve decided to "do it again better", by fixing the rate of interest on excess reserves, sterilizing the increased money supply as excess reserves and subsidizing banks through paying IOER. For the first time the Fed then began directly buying MBSs, starting in 2009, and it continues to do so to this day. According to FRED[1]:

> On November 25, 2008, the Federal Reserve announced a program to purchase mortgage-backed securities guaranteed by Fannie Mae, Freddie Mac, and Ginnie Mae. The goal of the program is to provide support to mortgage and housing markets and to foster improved conditions in financial markets. Purchases of these securities began on January 5, 2009.

The Fed's holdings of MBS and Treasury debt was less than $800 billion in 2007. It rose by more than 400 per cent, to about $4.5 trillion, between 2014 and 2018. In the second quarter of 2021 this sum was up 700 per cent from 2007, at nearly $8 trillion.

After 2010 the Fed's usury prohibition on positive real interest rates took on an even stronger form than in 2002–04, through its IOER policy. Seeking yield, the shadow banks remain open to runs while holding risky investments through mutual funds, exchange-traded funds (ETFs) and hedge funds.

Mutual funds and ETFs are both pooled investment funds that have been devised by investment managers. Both can be invested in the stocks constituting a given stock index, such as the S&P 500 or the Dow Jones Industrial average, or many other new composite indices that have been devised. Some ETFs can be bought and sold in stock exchanges.

From 1990 to the third quarter of 2021, Figure 16.1 displays the growth of mutual funds and ETFs that lack any explicit banking insurance such as that of the FDIC. The total of these invested in corporate equities rose from nothing in 1990 to $20 trillion in 2021. This consists mostly of mutual funds, but with ETF investment up to $5 trillion in 2021. Meanwhile, the combined total of mutual fund and ETF investments in long-term US Treasury debt grew to $7 trillion.

The overall figure for mutual fund and ETF investments in equities and long-term Treasury debt was $27 trillion in 2021. This amount grew in unregulated shadow banks, which eclipsed commercial banks. In comparison, in 2021 the total assets were $23 trillion for all Federal Reserve System banks, of which $22 trillion was in FDIC banks that are part of the Federal Reserve System.

---

1. See the footnote to the table on https://fred.stlouisfed.org/series/WMBSEC

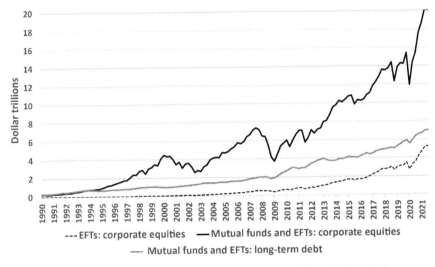

Figure 16.1 The growth of mutual funds and exchange traded funds, 1990–2021
Source: FRED.

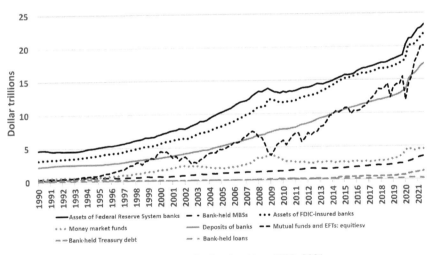

Figure 16.2 Commercial banks versus shadow banking, 1990–2021
Source: FRED.

Figure 16.2 plots the mutual fund and ETF investment in equities as compared to the total assets of both the Federal Reserve System banks and the FDIC-insured banks. The mutual fund and EFT investments in equities were almost as large as the assets of all commercial banks by 2021. Counting their investment in long-term Treasury debt, these assets were much larger than the assets of commercial banks.

The deposit liabilities of the commercial banks were equivalent to about 74 per cent of the assets of the Federal Reserve System banks. This gives the Federal Reserve System banks that are dominated by FDIC banks a ratio of equity to liability of about one-third. These banks held assets in the form of MBSs, Treasury securities, loans and Fed reserves. With the commercial banks in the Fed system having almost the same assets as those in the FDIC system, the Fed system has seemingly contracted to the FDIC system.

Meanwhile, the shadow banks grew with money market funds, mutual funds, ETFs and "non-bank payment systems", such as PayPal, Venmo, Apple Pay and blockchain payment systems such as Block. As these surpass FDIC banks, they have a shrinking share of liquidity in terms of a decreasing ratio of money market funds to the total equity assets of the mutual funds and ETFs.

New private credit markets are also active to achieve higher yields through direct loans by investment houses. For example, Wirz (2021) states:

> Investors often hold direct loans as substitutes for traditional fixed income, which has delivered dwindling returns as central banks have held interest rates low to spur economic growth and cushion market shocks. "More than anything, it's about low interest rates," said Kipp deVeer, head of Ares Credit Group. "A lot of investors are frustrated by the low yield in fixed income they've traditionally allocated to, whether it's loans or government bonds or high-grade corporates."

Besides this increasing risk and decreasing liquidity, as investors seek yield given the persistent negative interest rates on short-term Treasury debt, this capital allocation also slows the production of output. When the real interest rate on capital is low, producers substitute towards capital and away from labour in their relative factor intensity. Negative real interest rates lead to less labour employment and more capital employment by a substitution effect. This is compounded by a negative effect on both labour and capital demand, because of the reduced scale of output production from lower real GDP growth.

The substitution effect away from labour and the scale effect away from labour reinforce each other to cause employment to fall. The total labour effect in production is unambiguously negative from the policy of negative real interest rates, even as more capital is used relative to labour. This means that the remaining labour is complemented by an increasing proportion of capital used in production, so that the labour wage can rise when real interest rates become more negative.

Normally, the real wage rate would grow in tandem with real GDP growth, in a pro-cyclical fashion. After 2001 negative real interest rates instead coincided

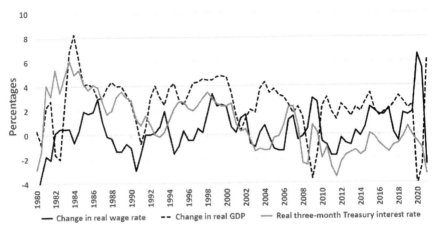

Figure 16.3 Changes in real wages, real GDP and the real interest rate, 1980–2021
Source: FRED.

with real wage growth, and both moved in the opposite direction to the business cycle. This created a "counter-cyclic" wage growth rate instead of a normal pro-cyclical one.

From 1980 to 2021 with semi-annual data, starting where the wage rate data begin, Figure 16.3 shows the change in the real wage rate, the change in real GDP and the level of the real three-month Treasury bill interest rate. From 1980 to 2001 the real wage change moved up and down broadly with the business cycle in terms of real GDP, which in turn was shadowed by the level of the real interest rate. This changes after 2001, when the real wage moved in the opposite direction to real GDP growth, while still moving with the real interest rate.

After 2001 real wage growth tended to fall as GDP growth rose, and to rise as real GDP growth fell. This is moving in the opposite direction to the business cycle rather than moving with it, especially during the Great Recession and the 2020–21 pandemic. As the real interest rate became negative, real wage growth continued to move with it – the opposite of real GDP growth.

The growth in the real wage changed atypically after 2001, trending down in economic expansions and up in contractions. The increasingly negative real interest rate caused a shift towards fewer workers while employing more capital. The increased capital raised the productivity of the remaining workers and increased the wage rate in a counter-cyclic business cycle fashion.

With workers being offered fewer positions, people left the workforce. The civilian "labour force participation rate" is the number of workers who are seeking work out of the total population. As real interest rates became negative, the labour force participation rate went down.

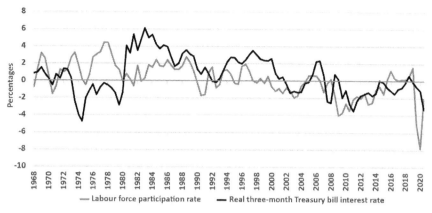

Figure 16.4 Changes in the labour force participation rate and the real interest rate, 1968–2021
Source: FRED.

From 1968 to 2021, Figure 16.4 shows how closely the change in the labour force participation rate moved compared to the level of the real three-month Treasury bill interest rate. Here the labour force participation rate is factored by three to normalize its change relative to the level of the real interest rate. The two data series moved together rather closely.

Starting out in 1968 the series moved together, and then their spread increased but still co-moved during the negative real interest rates of the 1970s. After 2001 the labour force participation rate fell and then rose with the real interest rate. The two series moved together throughout the Great Recession and pandemic.

The Fed's prohibition of a positive real interest rate after 2001 caused increasing risk within the shadow banking system, a growth of the shadow banking system, as that was where the yields were higher than in commercial banking, and a substitution from labour towards capital. The Fed policy caused a set of distortions that made the banking system subject to greater risk, thereby increasing its "moral hazard" of an increased probability of system-wide bank defaults and panics, while distorting the efficiency of production in the economy. The inefficient banking regulation, flight from the FDIC banks and economic inefficiency weakened the global capitalist system by making it more fragile, distorted and prone to panic.

The loss of labour and human capital, as labour leaves the workforce, causes human capital depreciation in the aggregate economy. Banning a positive real return for liquid capital causes a global increase in risky investment. The bank insurance system has been left in tatters while another global financial collapse could occur within the risky mutual funds and ETFs, just as a run on these markets caused the short-lived bank panic in 2020.

The distortions outlined here demand solutions. The final chapter starts by showing evidence of how inflation and the money supply growth rate remain linked as in quantity-theoretic tradition. This offers a means to anticipate future inflation. It then summarizes the bank regulation reform dilemma and provides a way to keep the spectre of inflation in the shadows, by bringing banking into the light.

17

MONEY, INFLATION AND BANKING REFORM

The inflation tax is caused by central banks financing government deficit spending. Inflation rose in the United States at such an increased pace during the Vietnam War that it broke the gold standard and caused a trend inflation rate above the zero trend of historic metallic regimes. The higher inflation trend of the fiat era put in place fluctuations in positive inflation instead of the more volatile price level changes of the metallic standards, with inflation during war and deflation after war.

The bank panics of the nineteenth century and the Great Depression brought about the establishment of the Fed and the FDIC. Today the inflation rate is tied closely by Fed policy to the threat of bank panics for those outside the FDIC. As the Fed buys Treasury debt and mortgage-backed securities, pays Treasury seigniorage to the private banking sector, prohibits positive real interest in money markets, suppresses inflation by keeping the newly printed money as reserves and attempts to provide sufficient liquidity for an ever more sprawling financial system, discerning the link between money and inflation is a challenge.

Although it has been said that inflation is no longer tied to the money supply, in fact the conflation of money and banking policy by the Fed simply makes the connection harder to uncover. The problem is not with the quantity theory of money. It has long shown the common sense of how the aggregate price level rises in tandem with the money supply.

There are important nuances. The price level rises more rapidly than the money supply because higher inflation rates normally increase interest rates and lower real money demand. And increases in economic growth can lower inflation, as more money supply is demanded for growth.

But the 2021 inflation increase had been declared by Ip (2021) as a "bout of inflation that defies old models". Supposedly this inflation episode cannot be explained by the centuries-old quantity theory. "Modern monetary theory" declares the quantity theory of money to be dead. Nonetheless, it omits, or does not seek to understand, that the increase in money by the Fed was sterilized by

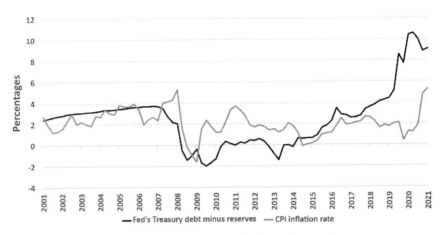

Figure 17.1 Reserves entering circulation and CPI inflation, 2001–21
Source: FRED.

the Fed's surge in excess reserves after 2008, which was enabled by its paying interest on excess reserves.

By sorting out how the Fed has been sterilizing part of the money supply, quantity theory is able to show how inflation is caused by the money supply that enters circulation. I have shown in this book that the increase in Treasury debt bought by the Fed rose directly in line with the amount of currency in circulation up until 2008. Then the Fed bought Treasury debt from banks at an accelerated rate that gave the banks massive amounts of reserves, which they in turn held at the Fed as "excess reserves", as if the Fed were the US Mint needing more gold. The amount of Treasury debt bought by the Fed, minus the reserves held at the Fed, is equal to the amount of reserves that have been entering circulation since 2008.

From 2001 to 2021, Figure 17.1 charts the difference of the Fed-held Treasury debt and the "reserves of depository institutions" held at the Fed, normalized by dividing by 200 to be comparable to the CPI inflation rate. Along with this Fed-held Treasury debt minus reserves is graphed the CPI inflation rate, with this inflation rate given on the vertical axis. There is a visible positive correlation between the two data series, with them moving together closely in a fashion consistent with the quantity theory of money. The quantity theory appears here as strong as ever.

As the banks took reserves from the Fed and lent them out, bank deposits increased the private bank money supply and the inflation rate rose. The change in the money entering circulation, defined here as the difference between the Treasury debt the Fed bought and the amount that remained "sterilized" at the

Fed as reserves earning interest, followed the change in the aggregate price level, which is the inflation rate. By accounting for the quantity of sterilized money that remains at the Fed as reserves, the application of the quantity theory of money shows the traditional link between the money supply and the price level, even for the post-2001 era of real negative interest rates.

After 2008 the excess reserves resulting from Fed purchases of Treasury debt were at first mostly sterilized, which is why the normalized difference in these was close to zero between 2010 and 2012. Yet the inflation rate and net reserve outflow still moved broadly together. After 2014 excess reserves dropped, the Fed raised its IOER rate, an increasingly less negative and then positive real rate of interest resulted, more reserves were used for loans and investment and real GDP growth rose.

Inflation did not rise in 2018 and 2019 as economic growth took off during IOER deregulation. Once the pandemic started, in 2020, real interest rates dropped as the Fed greatly accelerated its Treasury holdings. Inflation again began rising as the Fed's Treasury debt minus excess reserves shot up.

The 2020 surge in money entering circulation led to a surge in the inflation rate. Any relative price contribution to this inflation rate surge seems related to prices building in expectations of higher future inflation, as oil markets routinely work. Shortages arise when the prices of goods rises more rapidly than the wages of labour. The real wage falls, and labour shortages give rise to output shortages in the "supply chain".

The prospect of this new inflation rate surge being short-lived is dimmed by the surge in Treasury debt that was bought by the Fed and that has been entering circulation. The 2021 inflation increase appears to be the beginning of a prolonged inflationary episode. The huge growth in Fed-held Treasury debt, combined with these reserves being lent, means that inflation will be high for as long as these reserves continue to enter circulation. Wages and prices are likely to begin moving up together, as evidence already suggests, albeit in fits and starts, so that any relative price inflation will become overshadowed by a general aggregate price rise because of the higher growth rate of the money in circulation.

The Treasury has more than doubled its borrowing relative to GDP since 2001. The War on Terror after 2001, in Afghanistan, Iraq and Syria, combined with expenditure for banking insurance after 2008 and the pandemic in 2020–21, caused a major inflection upwards in US Treasury borrowing and in Fed purchases of Treasury debt. This expenditure connects war to inflation after 2001, and the Covid-19 pandemic expenditure comes into play after 2020.

Figure 17.2 shows that the US Treasury debt as a share of GDP rose steadily from 55 per cent in 2001 to 64 per cent in 2008. Then the ratio of Treasury debt

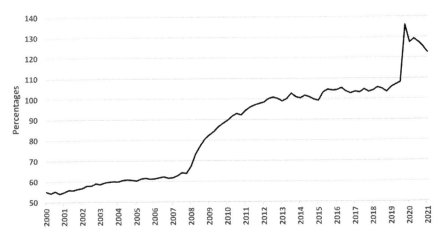

Figure 17.2 US Treasury debt as a share of GDP, 2000–21
Source: FRED.

to GDP accelerated upwards to 100 per cent in 2012, levelled off until 2020, then shot up to 135 per cent of GDP in 2020. It was 123 per cent in the third quarter of 2021, double what it had been in 2008.

Rising inflation creates a higher inflation tax, which is detrimental to welfare. Worse is the fact that the Fed's banking policy has suppressed inflation by inducing a build-up of excess reserves and an unending prohibition of positive real interest in capital money markets. Unleashing those reserves, enduring a full-blown inflation episode and eliminating interest rate controls are part of the necessary but not sufficient solution.

In addition to the growing government debt and inflation, the lack of a systematic insurance system for the financial intermediation industry is at the root of the problem. King (2017: xxvii–xxviii) writes:

> If bank "bailouts" were seen not as crisis intervention to save institutions in trouble, but as the payout from an insurance policy into which banks had been contributing regularly in normal times, then perhaps much of the understandable anger that accompanied the rescues of 2008 would have been tempered. It is all very well to throw the kitchen sink at the problem in the middle of a crisis, but is vital to think deeply about the incentives facing banks between crises.

The Fed's banking policy of prohibiting positive real interest and suppressing inflation precedes the Covid-19 pandemic. Yet the pandemic led to another bank panic in 2020 in the mutual funds market. The Fed's unregulated acquisition of

Treasury debt designed to provide liquidity to the banking system failed to avert another panic.

These banking fires may continue to emerge almost as they did with the bank panics of the late nineteenth century, which led to the 1908 Aldrich Commission and the creation of the Fed. With the banking system fragmenting and growing away from the FDIC and Federal Reserve System of banks, a redesign of banking policy is required, and this is not unlike the motivation behind the Aldrich Commission.

A solution to the problem of high inflation and a poor federal bank insurance system is to follow the advice that Fisher (1932) offered during the Great Depression: fix the liquidity problem of the banking sector, and thereby stabilize the change in the aggregate price level. The problem is more complex today because of the fragmentation, growth and innovation that has decreased the cost of various functions of banking. But the nature of the solution can be the same.

The entire global financial system depends on liquid assets in times of sudden redemption of its deposits across the array of funds invested. The base asset for this is the short-term US Treasury bill, because it is viewed as the least risky government debt in the world and is in large supply. The entire global financial world holds US Treasury bills as part of its portfolio of safe assets.

Short-term Treasury debt is to the fiat world what gold and silver was to the metallic standard world. This Treasury debt is the modern form of bank gold. This is because the payment of the debt is backed up by the value of the future stream of US government revenue, the most reliable expected stream of any government today. The gold reserves still held in central banks are a reminder of how Treasury loans and gold are fungible, since gold sales can pay off Treasury debt of equal value.

The holding of US Treasury bills as safe assets has become distorted, however, by negative real interest rates. The riskiness of the entire financial system has risen through its search for increasingly high-risk assets to offset the negative real rates dictated by the Fed's banking policy. This policy has led to a serious and persistent moral hazard problem in the supply of banking insurance.

Banking insurance is part of a social insurance system that demands the smoothing of consumption streams across time and across uncertain states of nature. By better smoothing consumption streams, aggregate uncertainty is decreased. When aggregate uncertainty is decreased, the human and physical capital that together comprise the wealth of nations is increased. This provides an increased flow of permanent income that funds consumption and investment.

The first step is to stop the paying of interest on excess reserves. By eliminating the interest on all but required reserves, money market interest rates will immediately rebound, as they did in 2019. They will rise to encompass the inflation rate and yield a positive real interest rate. This will stop the inducement to a distorted, higher-risk, higher-yield portfolio bias in all investments other than US Treasury debt. Continually prohibiting usury on the most risk-free asset on which the global financial system rests endangers the foundations of capitalism and, with it, the democratic roots of freedom in social and political spheres.

Then a new liquidity facility must be put in place for the entire financial system in a systematic way. The FDIC provides a reserve that supplies insurance against insolvency, but it cannot lend out the reserve for liquidity, other than exceptionally. The Fed has held reserves historically, and does so now, but supplies questionable and distortive bank insurance *after* the crisis has occurred. These reserves were irrelevant for the liquidity needed in the 2020 bank panic.

This endemic failure is evidenced by the flight of global finance from the FDIC and the Fed systems of bank supervision. The long-given solution, based on Bagehot's notion of reserves, is not to force or pay individual banking entities to hold more reserves. The Bagehot system was a voluntary holding of reserves in the then private Bank of England by the private banks in its network of international finance. The only question was how much of these reserves the Bank of England should keep itself as opposed to lending them out to make a profit. This concept of efficient global finance was prominently based on each individual bank voluntarily holding the smallest amount of reserves, which were pooled at the central bank, rather than forcing these banks to hold reserves.

Bagehot's argument was that having each bank hold sufficient reserves for a bank panic made such banking systems, as then seen in France, much less efficient than that in Britain. Forcing more reserves today is unfathomable given the fragmentation and ease of avoiding such "taxation" of banks. Once limited liability was available for all banks in Britain through the Companies Act of 1862, banks willingly held reserves at the Bank of England and facilitated an increased circulation of capital wealth that was previously unknown, marking the beginning of modern global financial markets.

The key to solving the liquidity and insolvency problems is to induce remedial voluntary actions by the global financial system in all its fragmented parts. Forcing this action cannot succeed, just as tax evasion can never be fully eliminated. The more that taxes are paid voluntarily, the better the governmental system of citizenship. The rights of citizens are established by the voluntary paying of taxes that they find fair. The citizen engaged in illegal tax evasion action weakens government and worsens the tax system.

The better the tax system is formulated, the more citizens view taxes as a competitive equilibrium price for the social insurance system that the government provides for them. Then citizens opt voluntarily to pay for that social insurance system by paying taxes as the law requires. This, in turn, provides steady revenue for a social insurance system of broad magnitude, as in the concept of it embodied in the 1942 Beveridge Report in the United Kingdom, in Friedrich

Hayek's and Milton Friedman's broad advocacy for it and in modern "social democracies" engaged in the global financial markets.

A premium charged for any particular social insurance policy that causes zero moral hazard by leaving incentives completely undistorted is a competitive equilibrium price for that insurance. By causing no change in incentives, and only decreasing aggregate uncertainty in a way that private markets are unable to supply, the government's social insurance scheme is not taxing and causes no distortions. It obliges citizens then to choose to opt into the scheme rather than trying to avoid the scheme, as when the insurance premium is viewed as a tax.

Providing bank insurance requires an insurance premium payment, which is more likely to be viewed as a tax if the bank insurance policy is poorly structured. The more that the various fragments of the global financial system find the bank insurance premium to be a fair competitive price in return for the benefit of the insurance coverage against aggregate risk, the more the fragmented banking system will voluntarily opt for that insurance coverage. The goal is to provide a banking insurance policy that covers both insolvency and illiquidity risk in an efficient way that least distorts incentives and causes the least amount of moral hazard.

The design of such an efficient bank insurance system for the global financial system is feasible. It requires a change in how the United States provides bank insolvency coverage through the FDIC plus ad hoc actions by the Fed and US Treasury. And it requires a change in how the United States provides bank liquidity during panics.

Money markets, mutual funds, exchange-traded funds, hedge funds and person-to-person payment systems do not have traditional deposits that can be insured by the FDIC. Nevertheless, the congressional laws guiding the FDIC, or the regulations made by the FDIC itself, can expand their reach and ensure solvency to investments across the spectrum of shadow banks. This can be done, first, by voluntarily allowing, but not requiring, any financial institutions that hold US Treasury short-term debt to apply to the FDIC for insurance coverage of some well-defined part of its deposited capital.

The FDIC can allow, but cannot require, any financial institution to seek insurance over some part of its portfolio of funds deposited into it by investors, just as people make deposits in commercial banks both for current exchange use and for savings. To cover more of the financial system, the FDIC needs first to drop the limit on the amount of deposits that it can insure. Then it needs to design a policy to evaluate the risk of covering the deposits of any financial institution.

The deposit limit for FDIC insurance is quickly reached under the current practice of a fixed premium on the limited insured deposits. Instead, this could be changed to a rising rate of premium as more investment deposits are insured. And a price of insurance for any financial institution could be offered by the FDIC.

The FDIC could offer a specifically determined risk-based premium, according to the FDIC's own assessment of risk, for different types of deposits across the financial intermediation spectrum, including pensions, insurance companies, investment banks and the host of new innovative financial institutions that are arising. This would simply allow any financial institution to apply for FDIC insurance. The institution could then pay the FDIC-stipulated premium and receive coverage, or choose not to participate.

With a well-formulated set of FDIC premiums, market competition would gradually drive investors towards the insured financial institutions, because they would be safer. This would work only if moral hazard were eliminated through bailouts that encourage financial institutions to flee FDIC coverage in the belief that they will be helped by the government in time of crisis even without FDIC insurance. This means that the FDIC insurance expansion would have to be carried out in tandem with the ending of the Fed's IOER policy.

The government would not have to help financial institutions in times of crisis, if enough of them were part of an efficient bank insurance system anchored by an expanded FDIC. This would make the expanded FDIC insurance policy a means of slowly halting the expansion of uninsured banking and begin pulling the fragments back into an insured centre of banking. This would simultaneously reduce the liquidity problem.

To work well, the FDIC would need to also drop the policy of a fixed risk-based premium for each insured financial institution. Rather, since the amount insured becomes increasingly risky as the amount of deposits increases, the FDIC premiums should also rise in accordance with the rising "marginal cost" of the amount of deposits insured. The FDIC-offered schedule for each risk-based premium for each financial institution should rise in segments as the quantity of deposits insured rises.

Supply by firms is offered at a lower price for each unit of a lower quantity supplied. When the price of each unit rises, firms offer more quantity at the higher price. Firms face an increasing cost of production for a higher quantity of units supplied because of constraints on resources, which become increasingly scarce as more resources are used.

This is also seen in private insurance. For a large excess (deductible) of the insured amount, the insurance premium is low. For a lower excess, and therefore a greater quantity of insurance provided, the insurance premium rises. These excesses are highly variable in private insurance markets, with the result that the cost of insurance rises as the quantity of insured dollars increases.

Insurance, just like the production of all goods, supplies the coverage or output of the insurance company, as in a normal upward-sloping supply of any good. The cost of insuring more goes up as the amount of coverage rises. This means that the "marginal cost" of additional coverage rises as the amount of coverage increases, giving rise to an upward-sloping supply of insurance that equals the marginal cost of the coverage.

The FDIC insurance policy could make the amount of insured funds almost unlimited for each type of institution insured by having tiered differentiated pricing, as in an increasing marginal cost of coverage that forms the "upward-sloping" supply of insurance coverage, or any output. Up to a certain quantity of funds supplied, the risk premium would be the base level. For the next additional set of funds to be insured, the risk-based insurance premium would rise, and this rise in the FDIC premium would continually increase as the amount of insurance of funds increases.

The other issue is information revelation. The FDIC would need to induce transparency in terms of the balance sheets of the institutions to which it offers insurance. The FDIC could do this by offering a higher insurance premium the more opaque the balance sheet is of the institution applying for insurance coverage, and by conducting (or outsourcing to other federal agencies) "stress tests" of financial institution resilience like those that began in the United States after 2008.

If the FDIC prices well, shadow banks would start joining the system. By giving investors confidence in the solvency of institutions, and with the institutions voluntarily allowed to join, then greater participation in the FDIC would decrease the liquidity problem. Once solvency is guaranteed more and more by the FDIC, liquidity becomes less of a problem – although it is still a problem.

The first problem of the current liquidity system is that the Fed operates it without any budgeting of the loans being offered and in any fashion it pleases. For example, there was a $1.5 trillion sale of mutual funds and ETFs in the first quarter of 2020 that caused a short-lived bank panic. The Fed intervened by providing massive liquidity in the short-term Treasury debt money market (Tooze 2021: 129):

> On 23 March, the Fed announced changes to both the Money Market Mutual Fund Liquidity Facility and the Commercial Paper Funding Facility that promised to ease the flow of credit to municipalities … All of these facilities were confidence building measures for the financial system as a whole. Indirectly, they served to relieve pressure on the Treasury market. The Fed did not stop there. The most direct way to support the market for Treasuries was for the Fed to buy them. By the weekend of 20–21 March, the Federal Open Market Committee had already announced purchases totaling $500 billion of Treasury securities and $200 billion of mortgage-backed securities. Powell now lifted even that ceiling. On the morning of 23 March, the committee declared simply that it would "purchase Treasury securities and agency

mortgage-backed securities in the amounts needed to support smooth market functioning and effective transmission of monetary policy to broader financial conditions and the economy." Over the week that followed, the Fed bought an astonishing total of $375 billion in Treasury securities and $250 billion in mortgage securities. At the high point of the program, the Fed was buying bonds at the rate of a million dollars per second. In a matter of weeks, it bought 5 per cent of the $20 trillion market.

The US Securities and Exchange Commission (SEC) has also tried to change regulations to help liquidity (Kiernan 2021):

> Other elements of the SEC's proposal include increasing the share of money-market funds' assets that are either cash equivalents or mature within one day to 25 per cent from 10 per cent and the share maturing in a week to 50 per cent from 30 per cent. The agency is also proposing to scrap rules it implemented after the 2008 crisis that allowed money-market funds to impose fees or temporarily suspend redemptions when liquidity started to dry up. While the objective of that change was to reduce the funds' susceptibility to runs, regulators and money managers now believe it simply encouraged investors to flee the funds when weekly-liquid assets approached the 30 per cent level in March 2020.

A line of credit can be added to the annual congressional budget for this liquidity provision. Irving Fisher (1932) wanted a facility to be devised that guarantees loans for banks in times of a liquidity crisis. The US Treasury can indeed provide this service by guaranteeing loans made through a designated facility, using the line of credit approved by Congress, to provide loans during a liquidity crisis.

For example, a facility already exists in the United States that is designed for exactly this purpose. Rather than having loans being made by the Fed in an ever-expanding way, uncontrolled and outside the US Congress's budget, the role can be taken over by the on-budget Treasury's Federal Financing Bank (FFB), which was established in 1973 for exactly such a purpose. The FFB's website describes its role thus:

> Congress created the Federal Financing Bank (FFB) in 1973 to help meet the demand for funds through Federal and federally-assisted borrowing programs, and to coordinate such borrowings with overall Federal fiscal and debt management policies. The mission of the FFB is to coordinate these programs with the overall economic and fiscal policies of the Government, to reduce the costs of Federal and federally-assisted

borrowings from the public, and to assure that such borrowings are financed in a manner least disruptive of private financial markets and institutions.

The US Treasury FFB could be allocated a credit line in the annual budget, including a special emergency catastrophe line of credit. The FFB could then coordinate with other agencies the allocation of loans needed in the event of a crisis in the global financial system. The FFB could use other agencies, including the Federal Reserve System and FDIC, to carry out any such operations, which would then be overseen by the Congress budget process and could include the buying of Treasury debt.

A complementary way to bring together Treasury debt for liquidity use, while also enhancing FDIC insurance against insolvency, would be to build a reserve of private Treasury debt directly within the FDIC. What would help bring shadow banking into FDIC insurance would be the provision of an intermediate step towards FDIC insurance.

The FDIC could offer to hold Treasury debt for any mutual fund, ETF or other financial entity, which it could add to or subtract from at will. The FDIC could then designate the financial entity as "FDIC-registered" rather than FDIC-insured. The FDIC registration could include a rating tied to the amount of Treasury debt deposited at the FDIC relative to the entity's total assets. This would work in the same way as the FDIC's current practice of offering a different deposit insurance premium based on its evaluation of the bank's asset risk.

The FDIC would thereby gather a pool of Treasury debt supplied voluntarily by shadow banks, just like the reserves of Bagehot's Bank of England. The FDIC would then allow the lending of pooled Treasury debt to any registered financial entity during a panic. Alternatively, the FDIC could provide pooled Treasury debt to the FFB as collateral for loans made by the FFB to banks for sudden liquidity needs, so that the FFB would incur almost no budget expense in making the loans under the Federal Credit Reform Act of 1990. This would encourage shadow banks to register their Treasury debt with the FDIC. With the Fed's IOER and IORB rates eliminated, the shadow banks would enjoy a normal interest rate yield on their reserves of Treasury debt held at the FDIC. There would be no distortion from such a liquidity policy, and no moral hazard.

In turn, the FDIC insurance would become more attractive to FDIC-registered financial entities, as in lodging Treasury debt the FDIC would be able to learn about the entity's risk structure and could offer a certain FDIC insurance risk premium. Competition between shadow banks would drive them through the door opened by the FDIC to obtain liquidity insurance and insolvency insurance through FDIC deposit liability insurance.

A twofold plan of voluntarily inducing insolvency coverage across the global financial system through FDIC insurance and offering special liquidity during crises through the FDIC's pooling of US Treasury debt would provide a global finance insurance system. By continually monitoring and adjusting accordingly, both the FDIC premiums and the pooled Treasury debt through FDIC registration would make the banking insurance system increasingly efficient and increasingly global in coverage.

The elimination of moral hazard in banking always remains a problem. A perfect global financial insurance system is impossible. But by basing the insurance in the United States, and building it around the use of US Treasury debt by financial institutions around the world, the global financial insurance system could be resurrected. This would decrease the frequency of financial crises, and even eliminate many of them.

There are country-specific deposit insurance systems in a vast number of nations around the world. The European Union is actively trying to design and implement an EU-wide deposit insurance system. Global flows across countries make national bank insurance systems difficult to manage.

All the individual national deposit insurance systems can complement the expansion of FDIC insurance and FDIC Treasury debt registration in a fiscally responsible way. A coherent Federal Reserve and international central bank policy after the Covid-19 pandemic is possible and desirable.

The Fed has tried to provide liquidity to the banking system through its reserves. The FDIC currently does not normally provide any use of its reserves for liquidity in the banking system. Therefore, the two systems have continued to operate in parallel and more haphazardly, while finance institutions grow outside both the FDIC and Fed systems of banks.

The solution is to bring together the ability to insure against both insolvency and illiquidity in an evolving and innovative financial world. A key to this is that the US Treasury short-term debt is the main source of liquidity throughout the financial system, including FDIC-insured banks, Federal Reserve System banks and the shadow banks engaged in money market funds, mutual funds, ETFs and person-to-person payment systems and blockchain coins. All the shadow banks have to resort to finding US Treasury debt for liquidity when their funds experience a sudden massive withdrawal, as Clayton (2021) describes:

> The most important financial market in the world, the US Treasury market, is a government market. Virtually all other financial markets, at home and abroad, have some tie to the US Treasury market, including the cash in our wallets and the entries in our bank accounts … More

than 95% of stablecoins by value are based on the US dollar. In other words, at the incipient stages of this global shift in financial technology, dollars – actually US Treasury securities – have remained the preferred liquid store of value for new and traditional markets.

Aggregate risk in the innovating financial sector, as based on US Treasury debt for liquidity, was the main concern recognized by the US Financial Stability Oversight Council, under US Treasury auspices, as Omeokwe (2021) describes:

> The rapid growth of digital assets, including stablecoins – digital currencies pegged to national currencies like the US dollar – is "an important potential emerging vulnerability," regulators on the Financial Stability Oversight Council, or FSOC, said in their annual report … While the report said addressing potential financial-system risks related to … nonbank financial institutions, such as money-market funds and open-end mutual funds, and Treasury market disruptions are the group's top priorities, it outlined several potential risks from digital assets and stablecoins in particular.

The evaders of inflation taxes and FDIC insurance continue to grow. The Fed continues to handicap the "good" banks in the efficient FDIC system by excluding the "bad" shadow banks that earn more profits through non-FDIC-insured money market accounts. This encourages more diffuse forms of shadow banks to emerge and makes banking insurance as an efficient social insurance component ever more distant.

After 2008 the world was still in a state of prolonged fear of global financial crisis. The 1978 zero-inflation-rate law had long been forgotten, and the Fed was operating at odds with several other laws through its new policy of massive purchases of mortgages and payments directly to banks. The Fed's mortgage purchases have continually violated the Congressional Budget Act of 1974 and the Federal Credit Reform Act of 1990, which together require the US Congress to budget for the expected costs of buying loans.

The Fed started paying interest to private banks in 2008 on all reserves they held at the Fed. This violated the spirit of the Financial Services Regulatory Relief Act of 2006, which allows interest payments on reserves (starting in 2011), with the legislative background statements making it clear that this was to be interest only on required reserves and not on reserves in excess of what was required. By paying interest on all reserves, the Fed essentially transferred US inflation (tax) revenue from the US Treasury to the private banks, which violates their original by-laws that all interest earnings must be transferred to the US Treasury after subtracting the cost of running the Fed.

After the 2008 bank panic the Fed further violated its own by-laws, which had historically required Fed actions not to favour any one sector of the economy, on the grounds that the Fed should be an unbiased foundation for conducting monetary policy. The Fed simply changed the by-laws to allow it to subsidize the bank sector through the interest payment to banks on all reserves and through buying mortgage-backed securities, which were the weakest asset group on bank balance sheets.

The gold standard had kept average inflation near zero. Dropping this basis for monetary policy, trying to reacquire the essence of the gold regime through a zero-inflation-rate target mandated by law in 1978 but then discarding this target drove the United States towards an increasingly disparate money and banking policy, with the efficient bank insurance system based on the FDIC becoming a shrinking enterprise.

Our central banks evolved during times of metallic standards for currency. They could keep only enough reserves as were likely to be needed in the event of a bank panic. Central banks suspended the metallic standards as wartime needs arose, and have long financed war by their governments by means of buying the government debt through new money.

Although the inflation tax is controlled by how much Treasury debt the central bank buys and does not sterilize, explicit income taxes require legislation. When the inflation tax goes up during a crisis, markets build in the expected inflation into energy prices, gold prices and government long-term debt interest rates. Sustained high inflation causes lower economic growth and higher tax rates on income.

Financial markets are highly flexible, adaptive and innovative. Risk can be diversified through capital allocation within a mixed portfolio. Markets strive to anticipate normal business cycle risk, financial volatility and the rare collapse of markets.

Financial intermediaries create the capital markets. These entities specialize in different types of capital risk. They act to create a high real return on capital given the laws and regulations in which they operate.

Aggregate risk, just like the aggregate price level, is the risk for the whole economy. Aggregate risk is different from individual risk to any one person or firm, or "idiosyncratic" risk, because of the inability to pool and eliminate aggregate risk through private, financial-intermediary-diversified capital holdings. The whole sector of financial intermediation provides a range of insurance against as much risk within capital markets as is possible, but it typically excludes aggregate risk.

Aggregate risk for private financial intermediaries is aggravated when competition drives these intermediaries to minimize consideration of this type of risk as long as the government covers aggregate financial risk. Whereas the global business cycle creates volatility for the globalized economy that is hard to insure, governments take on aggregate business cycle risk in a variety of ways, including unemployment insurance, health insurance and insurance of the financial sector.

A meticulous bank insurance policy gauges the normal business cycle defaults of financial institutions, along with the rare risk of contagion across a set of financial institutions as a result of their holdings of a common bad asset. Private insurance charges a premium in the good state and pays out the insurance in the bad state, and a comprehensive government bank insurance can be designed in the same way.

During the Great Depression, as the malaise it engendered continued throughout the 1930s, Keynes (1936) suggested the government step in and invest the savings that the private bank sector could not invest. This justified government intervention in markets in wide, unspecified, ways. Fisher (1932, 1933) instead stated that regulation of the bank sector needed to be reformed since it was the private bank credit that collapsed during the Great Depression, not the government money supply.

Today's central banks follow the advice of Keynes and not of Fisher. Rather than reforming the bank insurance system at its root causes of dysfunction, the Fed chose to intervene heavily in capital markets by fixing interest rates, without restraint or checks to its power to subsidize in extraordinary ways. The dysfunction led to growing sectors of the financial system finding themselves outside the bounds of the FDIC and the Federal Reserve System.

Reform can be enacted by inducing financial intermediaries back to the FDIC system. A tax through inflation is bad. A tax on the global economy through usury prohibition is worse.

When fringe benefits proliferated in the United States, so that companies could pay out more income in kind without employees or the companies facing taxes on that income, after a decade of effort the US Congress finally reined in this tax avoidance with title V, subtitle C, "Tax treatment of fringe benefits", of the Deficit Reduction Act of 1984, which specified what and how fringe benefits were to be taxed. This 1984 Act broke the impasse and allowed the US Congress to continue with tax reform, once the income tax base was well defined. The Tax Reform Act of 1986 followed by lowering tax rates further, inducing rising productivity and making both tax avoidance and tax evasion less worthwhile.

The US Tax Cuts and Jobs Act of 2017 lowered tax rates further. The world economy has been lowering and flattening out tax rates, albeit unevenly, as productivity rises steadily and tax evasion becomes less worthwhile. This has increased world development and wealth.

Bank insurance likewise needs to broaden the base of coverage through FDIC insurance premiums and FDIC registration, which pools Treasury debt for financial intermediation. The avoidance and what can be called evasion of FDIC insurance became apparent after the 2008 financial panic and global capital market repression of real interest rates. The repression of capital has led to the repression of capitalism and the rise of political regimes favouring the allocation of resources towards their own clientele rather than to their broad citizenry.

By offering bank insolvency and illiquidity insurance to all financial intermediaries, the arbitrary bank policy and capital market repression loses any justification and can simply be eliminated. In contrast, competition would drive financial companies into such a broad-based system, if they are otherwise left out of all government insurance. Broadening the base for bank insurance would lower the real cost to all financial intermediaries in the long run and stabilize global capital markets, capitalism and political systems on the basis of free exchange.

The story of inflation continues as the money supply increases in major nations aligned within the global financial system. The aggregate price level rises as the histories of money supply growth, inflation and wars coincide. Providing a reformed banking insurance system that efficiently safeguards against both global financial insolvency and illiquidity is the best way to tame inflation.

When the inflation tax goes up in markets with a broad-based, fair and transparent bank insurance system, there will be only the consequence of the cost of inflation. It will just be an increase in a single tax rate, perhaps in a new moderately high inflation episode. High inflation and hyperinflation will be different but less likely in a well-founded democracy with a fair and open tax system and with a well-insured financial system as part of an efficient social insurance policy.

After 2008 populist parties arose across the Western world and the Eastern world alike, as economies stagnated at the edges of the globalized financial system, just as had happened during the Great Depression of the 1930s. Repressed global finance threatens modern democracy, in which today's wars are fought over scarce resources, including technology financed through global capital. Allowing inflation to rise to a moderately high rate is better than allowing capitalism, democracy and freedom to fall.

REFERENCES

Alquist, R., L. Kilian & R. Vigfusson 2013. "Forecasting the price of oil". In *Handbook of Economic Forecasting*, vol. 2, G. Elliott & A. Timmermann (eds), 427–507. Amsterdam: North Holland.

Åslund, A. 2012. "Hyperinflations are rare, but a breakup of the euro area could prompt one", Policy Brief 12-22. Washington, DC: Peterson Institute for International Economics.

Bae, K. & W. Bailey 2011. "The Latin Monetary Union: some evidence on Europe's failed common currency". *Review of Development Finance* 1 (2): 131–49.

Bagehot, W. 1873. *Lombard Street: A Description of the Money Market.* London: Henry S. King.

Bailey, M. 1956. "The welfare cost of inflationary finance". *Journal of Political Economy* 64 (2): 93–110.

Barsky, R. & L. Kilian 2001. "Do we really know that oil caused the great stagflation? A monetary alternative". *NBER Macroeconomics Annual* 16: 137–98.

Barsky, R. & L. Kilian 2004. "Oil and the macroeconomy since the 1970s". *Journal of Economic Perspectives* 18 (4): 115–34.

Benk, S. & M. Gillman 2020. "Granger predictability of oil prices after the Great Recession". *Journal of International Money and Finance* 101: 102100.

Bernholz, P. 2016. *Monetary Regimes and Inflation: History, Economic and Political Relationships*, 2nd edn. Cheltenham: Edward Elgar.

Board of governors of the Federal Reserve System 2012. "Federal Reserve issues FOMC statement of longer-run goals and policy strategy". Press release, 25 January. Available at: www.federalreserve.gov/newsevents/pressreleases/monetary20120125c.htm.

Bordo, M. 1981. "The classical gold standard: some lessons for today". *Review Federal Reserve Bank of St Louis* 63 (5): 2–17.

Bordo, M., R. Dittmar & W. Gavin 2003. "Gold, fiat money, and price stability", Working Paper 10171. Cambridge, MA: National Bureau of Economic Research.

Bundesbank 2013. "1973: The end of Bretton Woods: when exchange rates learned to float". 14 October. Available at: www.bundesbank.de/en/tasks/topics/1973-the-end-of-bretton-woods-when-exchange-rates-learned-to-float-666280.

Cagan, P. 1956. "The monetary dynamics of hyperinflation". In *Studies in the Quantity Theory of Money*, M. Friedman (ed.), 1–25. Chicago, IL: University of Chicago Press.

Calomiris, C. & J. Mason 2003. "Fundamentals, panics, and bank distress during the Depression". *American Economic Review* 93 (5): 1615–47.

Carney, W. 1998. "Limited liability". In *Encyclopedia of Law and Economics*, B. Bouckaert & G. De Geest (eds). Cheltenham: Edward Elgar. Available at: www.elgaronline.com/view/nlm-book/9781782547457/9781782547457.xml.

Clayton, J. 2021. "America's future depends on the blockchain". *Wall Street Journal*, 16 December.

Clemons, E. & B. Weber 1990. "London's Big Bang: a case study of information technology, competitive impact, and organizational change". *Journal of Management Information Systems* 6 (4): 41–60.

Committee on Banking, Housing, and Urban Affairs, United States Senate 2006. "Consideration of regulatory relief proposal: hearing before the Committee on Banking, Housing and Urban Affairs". Washington, DC: Government Printing Office.

Committee on Finance, United States Senate 1975. "Effects of petrodollars on financial markets: hearings before the Subcommittee on Financial Markets". Washington, DC: Government Printing Office.

Cooperman, E., W. Lee & G. Wolfe 1992. "The 1985 Ohio thrift crisis, the FSLIC's solvency, and rate contagion for retail CDs". *Journal of Finance* 47 (3): 919–41.

Crabbe, L. 1989. "The international gold standard and US monetary policy from world war to the New Deal". *Federal Reserve Bulletin* 75 (6): 423–40.

Craig, B. & M. Koepke 2015. "Excess reserves: oceans of cash", Economic Commentary 2015-02. Cleveland, OH: Federal Reserve Bank of Cleveland.

Csabafi, T., M. Gillman & R. Naraidoo 2019. "International business cycle and financial intermediation". *Journal of Money, Credit and Banking* 51 (8): 2293–2303.

De Long, B. 1997. "America's peacetime inflation: the 1970s". In *Reducing Inflation: Motivation and Strategy*, C. Romer & D. Romer (eds), 247–80. Chicago, IL: University of Chicago Press.

De Roover, R. 1963. *The Rise and Decline of the Medici Bank, 1397–1494*. Cambridge, MA: Harvard University Press.

Dean, S. 1884. *History of Banking and Banks: From the Bank of Venice to the Year 1883, including the Establishment and Progress of the Present National Banking System of the United States*. Boston, MA: Pelham Studios.

Eccles, G. 1982. *The Politics of Banking*. Salt Lake City, UT: University of Utah Press.

Elliott, C. 2020. "The role of money in the economies of ancient Greece and Rome". In *Handbook of the History of Money and Currency*, S. Battilossi, Y. Cassis & K. Yago (eds), 67–86. Singapore: Springer.

Engemann, K. 2013. "Banking panics of 1931–33". Federal Reserve, 22 November. Available at: www.federalreservehistory.org/essays/banking-panics-1931-33.

Ennis, H. & A. Wolman 2011. "Large excess reserves in the US: a view from the cross-section of banks". Richmond, VA: Federal Reserve Bank of Richmond.

Evans, F. 1908. "The evolution of the English joint-stock limited trading company". *Columbia Law Review* 8 (6): 461–80.

FDIC 1997. *History of the Eighties: Lessons for the Future*, vol. 1, *An Examination of the Banking Crises of the 1980s and Early 1990s*. Washington, DC: Federal Deposit Insurance Corporation.

FDIC 2017. *Crisis and Response: An FDIC History, 2008–2013*. Washington, DC: Federal Deposit Insurance Corporation.

FDIC 2021. *Annual Report 2020*. Washington, DC: Federal Deposit Insurance Corporation.

Feinman, J. 1993. "Reserve requirements: history, current practice, and potential reform". *Federal Reserve Bulletin* 79 (6): 569–89.

Felloni, G. & G. Laura 2017. *Genoa and the History of Finance: Twelve Firsts?* Genoa: Riccardo Campanella Begliomini. Available at: www.giuseppefelloni.com/rassegnasta mpa/genovafinanza12primati_2017.pdf.

Fisher, I. 1907. *The Rate of Interest: Its Nature, Determination and Relation to Economic Phenomena*. New York: Macmillan.

Fisher, I. 1911. *The Purchasing Power of Money: Its Determination and Relation to Credit, Interest and Crises*. New York: Macmillan.

Fisher, I. 1920. *Stabilizing the Dollar: A Plan to Stabilize the General Price Level without Fixing Individual Prices*. New York: Macmillan.

Fisher, I. 1921. "The best form of index number". *Journal of the American Statistical Association* 17: 533–7.

Fisher, I. 1922. *The Making of Index Numbers: A Study of Their Varieties, Tests and Reliability.* Boston, MA: Houghton Mifflin.

Fisher, I. 1926. "A statistical relation between unemployment and price changes". *International Labour Review* 13 (6): 185–92.

Fisher, I. 1932. *Booms and Depressions: Some First Principles.* New York: Adelphi.

Fisher, I. 1933. "The debt-deflation theory of Great Depressions". *Econometrica* 1 (4): 337–57.

Foucaud, D. 2011. "The impact of the Companies Act of 1862 extending limited liability to the banking and financial sector in the English crisis of 1866". *Revue Économique* 62 (5): 867–97.

Friedman, M. 1960. *A Program for Monetary Stability.* New York: Fordham University Press.

Friedman, M. 1962. *Capitalism and Freedom.* Chicago, IL: University of Chicago Press.

Friedman, M. 1968. "The role of monetary policy". *American Economic Review* 58 (1): 1–17.

Friedman, M. 1990. "The crime of 1873". *Journal of Political Economy* 98 (6): 1159–94.

Friedman, M. 1994. *Money Mischief: Episodes in Monetary History.* New York: Harcourt Brace.

Friedman, M. & A. Schwartz 1963. *A Monetary History of the United States, 1867–1960.* Princeton, NJ: Princeton University Press.

Gavin, W. & A. Stockman 1988. "The case for zero inflation", Economic Commentary 1988-18. Cleveland, OH: Federal Reserve Bank of Cleveland.

George, H. 1874. *Progress and Poverty: An Inquiry in the Cause of Industrial Depressions and of Increase of Want with Increase of Wealth ... The Remedy.* New York: Appleton.

Gilbert, R. 1986. "Requiem for Regulation Q: what it did and why it passed away". *Review Federal Reserve Bank of St Louis* 68 (2): 22–37.

Gillman, M. 2002. "Keynes's treatise: aggregate price theory for modern analysis?". *European Journal of the History of Economic Thought* 9 (3): 430–51.

Gillman, M. 2020. "The welfare cost of inflation with banking time". *BE Journal of Macroeconomics: Advances* 20 (1): 1–20.

Gillman, M. 2022a. "Lucas's methodological divide in inflation theory: a student's journey". *Journal of Economic Methodology* 29 (1): 30–47.

Gillman, M. 2022b. "Emerging regions in the era of negative real interest rates: twenty years of convergence towards the United States?". In *Handbook of Banking and Finance in Emerging Markets*, D. Nguyen (ed.), 687–709. Cheltenham: Edward Elgar.

Gillman, M. & T. Eade 1995. "The development of the corporation in England, with emphasis on limited liability". *International Journal of Social Economics* 22 (4): 20–32.

Gillman, M. & A. Nakov 2009. "Monetary effects on nominal oil prices". *North American Journal of Economics and Finance* 20 (3): 239–54.

Gillman, M., M. Harris & L. Mátyás 2004. "Inflation and growth: explaining a negative effect". *Empirical Economics* 29 (1): 149–67.

Giovannini, A. 1975. "Athenian currency in the late fifth and early fourth century BC". *Greek Roman and Byzantine Studies* 16 (2): 185–95.

Goldthwaite, R. 2009. *The Economy of Renaissance Florence.* Baltimore, MD: Johns Hopkins University Press.

Goodhart, C. 1988. *The Evolution of Central Banks.* Cambridge, MA: MIT Press.

Gorton, G. 1985. "Clearinghouses and the origin of central banking in the United States". *Journal of Economic History* 45 (2): 277–83.

Hall, R. 1997. "Irving Fisher's self-stabilizing money". *American Economic Review* 87 (2): 436–8.

Hamilton, J. 1983. "Oil and the macroeconomy since World War II". *Journal of Political Economy* 91 (2): 228–48.

Hamilton, J. 2008. "Oil and the macroeconomy". In *The New Palgrave Dictionary of Economics*, S. Durlauf & L. Blume (eds), 2nd edn. London: Palgrave Macmillan. Available at: https://link.springer.com/referenceworkentry/10.1057/978-1-349-95121-5_2119-1.

Hetzel, R. 2013. "Launch of the Bretton Woods system". Federal Reserve, 22 November. Available at: www.federalreservehistory.org/essays/bretton-woods-launched.

Huang, A. 1948. "The inflation in China". *Quarterly Journal of Economics* 62 (4): 562–75.

Huntington Beach 2020. "Statement of investment policy 2020". Huntington Beach, CA: City of Huntington Beach.

Ip, G. 2021. "A bout of inflation that defies old models". *Wall Street Journal*, 9 December.

Jadlow, J. 1977. "Adam Smith on usury laws". *Journal of Finance* 32 (4): 1195–200.

Kareken, J. & N. Wallace 1978. "Deposit insurance and bank regulation: a partial-equilibrium exposition". *Journal of Business* 51 (3): 413–38.

Keister, T. & J. McAndrews 2009. "Why are banks holding so many excess reserves?", Staff Report 380. New York: Federal Reserve Bank of New York.

Keynes, J. 1923. *A Tract on Monetary Reform*. London: Macmillan.

Keynes, J. 1930. *A Treatise on Money*, 2 vols. London: Macmillan.

Keynes, J. 1936. *The General Theory of Employment, Interest and Money*. London: Macmillan.

Kiernan, P. 2021. "SEC seeks to prevent one cause of investor runs during financial panics". *Wall Street Journal*, 15 December.

King, M. 2017. *The End of Alchemy: Money, Banking, and the Future of the Global Economy*. New York: Norton.

Kydland, F. & E. Prescott 1982. "Time to build and aggregate fluctuations". *Econometrica* 50 (6): 1345–70.

Labonte, M. 2018. "Systemically important or 'too big to fail' financial institutions", Report 42150. Washington, DC: Congressional Research Service.

Leeper, E. & X. Zhou 2021. "Inflation's role in optimal monetary-fiscal policy". *Journal of Monetary Economics* 124 (C): 1–18.

Long, T. 2008. "Oct. 17, 1973: angry Arabs turn off the oil spigot". *Wired*, 16 October.

Lucas, R. 1972. "Expectations and the neutrality of money". *Journal of Economic Theory* 4 (2): 103–24.

Lucas, R. 1976. "Econometric policy evaluation: a critique". In *The Phillips Curve and Labor Markets*, K. Brunner & A. Meltzer (eds), 19–46. Amsterdam: North Holland.

Lucas, R. 1980. "Equilibrium in a pure currency economy". *Economic Inquiry* 18 (2): 203–20.

Lucas, R. 1981. "Discussion of: Stanley Fischer, 'Towards an understanding of the costs of inflation: II'". *Carnegie–Rochester Conference Series on Public Policy* 15 (1): 43–52.

Lucas, R. 1988. "On the mechanics of economic development". *Journal of Monetary Economics* 22 (1): 3–42.

Lucas, R. & J. Nicolini 2015. "On the stability of money demand". *Journal of Monetary Economics* 73 (C): 48–65.

Lucas, R. & N. Stokey 1983. "Optimal fiscal and monetary policy in an economy without capital". *Journal of Monetary Economics* 12 (1): 55–93.

Mabro, R. 1984. "On oil price concepts", Working Paper 3. Oxford: Oxford Institute for Energy Studies.

McConnell, J. & S. Buser 2011. "The origins and evolution of the market for mortgage-backed securities". *Annual Review of Financial Economics* 3: 173–92.

Machemer, T. 2020. "Spanish conquistadors stole this gold bar from Aztec emperor Moctezuma's trove". *Smithsonian Magazine*, 14 January.

Mankiw, N. 2015. *Principles of Macroeconomics*, 7th edn. Boston, MA: Cengage.

Marshall, A. 1920. *Principles of Economics*, 8th edn. London: Macmillan.

Milne, J. 1945. "The economic policy of Solon". *Hesperia* 14 (3): 230–45.

Mincer, J. 1983. "George Stigler's contributions to economics". *Scandinavian Journal of Economics* 85 (1): 65–75.

Moen, J. & E. Tallman 2015. "The panic of 1907". Federal Reserve, 4 December. Available at: www.federalreservehistory.org/essays/panic-of-1907#:~:text=Moen%20and%20Tallman%20(1999)%20argued,companies%2C%20institutions%20outside%20their%20membership.

Morgenson, G. 2008. "How the thundering herd faltered and fell". *New York Times*, 8 November.

Nelson, E. 2021. "The emergence of forward guidance as a monetary policy tool", Finance and Economics Discussion Paper 2021-033. Washington, DC: Federal Reserve Board.

Newby, E. 2012. "The suspension of the gold standard as sustainable monetary policy". *Journal of Economic Dynamics and Control* 36 (10): 1498–519.

Newsnight 2007. "Credit crunch". BBC, 14 September. Available at: www.bbc.co.uk/blogs/newsnight/2007/09/friday_14_september_2007.html.

O'Brien, A. & P. Trescott 1992. "The failure of the Bank of United States, 1930: note". *Journal of Money, Credit and Banking* 24 (3): 384–99.

Omeokwe, A. 2021. "Regulators press for stablecoin oversight". *Wall Street Journal*, 17 December.

Phelps, E. 1967. "Phillips curves, expectations of inflation and optimal unemployment over time". *Economica* 34 (3): 254–81.

Phelps, E. 1969. "The new microeconomics in inflation and employment theory". *American Economic Review* 59 (2): 147–60.

Phelps, E. (ed.) 1970. *Microeconomic Foundations of Employment and Inflation Theory*. New York: Norton.

Phelps, E. 1972. *Inflation Policy and Unemployment Theory: The Cost–Benefit Approach to Monetary Planning*. New York: Norton.

Phillips, A. 1958. "The relation between unemployment and the rate of change of money wage rates in the United Kingdom 1861–1957". *Economica* 25 (3): 283–89.

Prescott, E. 1987. "A multiple means of payment model". In *New Approaches to Monetary Economics*, W. Barnett & K. Singleton (eds), 42–51. Cambridge: Cambridge University Press.

Ramsey, F. 1928. "The theory of savings". *Economic Journal* 38: 543–59.

Reinert, S. & R. Fredona 2017. "Merchants and the origins of capitalism", Working Paper 18-021. Cambridge, MA: Harvard Business School.

Richardson, G. 2013. "Banking panics of 1930–1931". Federal Reserve, 22 November. Available at: www.federalreservehistory.org/essays/banking-panics-1930-31.

Rockoff, H. 2015. "War and inflation in the United States from the Revolution to the First Iraq War", Working Paper 21221. Cambridge, MA: National Bureau of Economic Research.

Rosen, S. 1993. "George J. Stigler and the industrial organization of economic thought". *Journal of Political Economy* 101 (5): 809–17.

Samuelson, P. & R. Solow 1960. "Analytical aspects of anti-inflation policy". *American Economic Review* 50 (2): 177–94.

Sargent, T. 1986. "The ends of four big inflations". In *Rational Expectations and Inflation*, 38–110. Princeton, NJ: Princeton University Press.

Sargent, T. 2015. "Robert E. Lucas Jr's collected papers on monetary theory". *Journal of Economic Literature* 53 (1): 43–64.

Sargent, T. & N. Wallace 1975. "'Rational' expectations: the optimal monetary instrument, and the optimal money supply rule". *Journal of Political Economy* 83 (2): 241–54.

Schwartz, A. 1973. "Secular price change in historical perspective". *Journal of Money, Credit and Banking* 5 (1): 243–69.

Sherman, M. 2009. "A short history of financial deregulation in the United States". Washington, DC: Center for Economic and Policy Research.

Shin, H. 2009. "Reflections on Northern Rock: the bank run that heralded the global financial crisis". *Journal of Economic Perspectives* 23 (1): 101–19.

Silbur, W. 2009. "Why did FDR's bank holiday succeed?". *Economic Policy Review* 15 (1): 19–30.

Smialek, J. 2021. "Money market funds melted in pandemic panic. Now they're under scrutiny". *New York Times*, 23 April.

Smith, A. 1853 [1759]. *The Theory of Moral Sentiments and on the Origins of Languages*, ed. D. Stewart. London: H. G. Bohn.

Smith, A. 1896 [1763]. *Lectures on Justice, Police, Revenue and Arms*. Oxford: Clarendon Press.

Smith, A. 1904 [1776]. *An Inquiry into the Nature and Causes of the Wealth of Nations*, ed. E. Cannan. London: Methuen.

Solow, R. 1956. "A contribution to the theory of economic growth". *Quarterly Journal of Economics* 70 (1): 65–94.

Stigler, G. 1949. "Monopolistic competition in retrospect". In *Five Lectures on Economic Problems*, 12–34. London: Longmans, Green.

Stigler, G. 1971. "The theory of economic regulation". *Bell Journal of Economics and Management Science* 2 (1): 3–21.

Sutherland, C. 1940. "The historical evidence of Greek and Roman coins". *Greece & Rome* 9 (26): 65–80.

Taylor, J. & P. Van Doren 2003. "Time to lay the 1973 oil embargo to rest". 17 October. Cato Institute. Available at: www.cato.org/commentary/time-lay-1973-oil-embargo-rest.

Tooze, A. 2021. *Shutdown: How Covid Shook the World's Economy*. London: Viking.

Verrastro, F. & G. Caruso 2013. "The Arab oil embargo – 40 years later". Center for Strategic and International Studies, 13 October. Available at: www.csis.org/analysis/arab-oil-embargo%E2%80%9440-years-later.

Vigna, P. 2008. "This day in crisis history: Sept. 15-16, 2008". *Wall Street Journal*, 16 September [updated 16 September 2013].

Visser, W. & A. McIntosh 1998. "A short review of the historical critique of usury". *Accounting, Business and Financial History* 8 (2): 175–89.

Volcker, P. 2018. *Keeping At It: The Quest for Sound Money and Good Government*. Washington, DC: Public Affairs.

Walker, W. 2021. "Nixon taught us how not to fight inflation". *Wall Street Journal*, 13 August.

Wall Street Journal 2021. "The inflation tax rises". 13 October.

Wandschneider, K. 2008. "The stability of the interwar gold exchange standard". *Journal of Economic History* 68 (1): 151–81.

Webel, B. 2013. "Troubled Asset Relief Program (TARP): implementation and status", Paper 7-5700. Washington, DC: Congressional Research Service.

Wheelock, D. 1992. "Monetary policy in the Great Depression: what the Fed did, and why". *Review Federal Reserve Bank of St Louis* 74 (2): 3–28.

Wicksell, K. 1936. *Interest and Prices: A Case Study in the Causes Regulating the Value of Money*. London: Macmillan.

Wiegand, J. 2019. "Destabilizing the global monetary system: Germany's adoption of the gold standard in the early 1870s", Working Paper 19/32. Washington, DC: International Monetary Fund.

Williams, R. 2020. "Why stagflation is back on some traders' radars". *Washington Post*, 14 August.

Wirz, M. 2021. "Ares raises $8 billion fund in private-credit arms race". *Wall Street Journal*, 14 December.

INDEX